Elaborating Professionalism

Innovation and Change in Professional Education

VOLUME 5

SCOPE OF THE SERIES

The primary aim of this book series is to provide a platform for exchanging experiences and knowledge about educational innovation and change in professional education and post-secondary education (engineering, law, medicine, management, health sciences, etc.). The series provides an opportunity to publish reviews, issues of general significance to theory development and research in professional education, and critical analysis of professional practice to the enhancement of educational innovation in the professions.

The series promotes publications that deal with pedagogical issues that arise in the context of innovation and change of professional education. It publishes work from leading practitioners in the field, and cutting edge researchers. Each volume is dedicated to a specific theme in professional education, providing a convenient resource of publications dedicated to further development of professional education.

For further volumes:
http://www.springer.com/series/6087

Clive Kanes
Editor

Elaborating Professionalism

Studies in Practice and Theory

 Springer

Editor
Dr. Clive Kanes
King's College London
Dept. Education & Professional Studies
Waterloo Rd.
SE1 9NH London
Franklin-Wilkins Bldg. (Waterloo Bridge Wing)
B. Wing
United Kingdom
clive.kanes@kcl.ac.uk

ISBN 978-94-007-3360-2   ISBN 978-90-481-2605-7 (eBook)
DOI 10.1007/978-90-481-2605-7
Springer Dordrecht Heidelberg London New York

Springer is part of Springer Science+Business Media (www.springer.com)

Preface

This book comes to publication at a time when many truths relating to professionalism are being severely tested. Whether the issues concern the world's financial system, industrial organisation, methods of government, law, climate change, food and housing, health care, education and security – professionals face challenging tasks, many of which pertain to issues challenging notions of professionalism itself. Among these, public confidence and trust in professionalism, the evolving nature of professionalism, and professional education – referred to as headline challenges in the book – are arguably among the foremost. The aim of this book is to offer practical and theoretical perspectives helpful to practitioners, policy makers, researchers and students in order to better understand professionalism as it is currently practised. It is hoped that this can help address headline issues and envision an increasingly productive future.

I would like to sincerely thank my colleagues, the authors of contributing chapters, for their generosity in entrusting their work to this publication. I would also like to thank them for their promptness and courtesy in advancing this project. I would like to thank Emeritus Professor John Stevenson for his early input to the notion of this publication. I am also very grateful to Ms Astrid Noordermeer and Ms Marianna Pascale of Springer Publications for seeing the work to publication. Thanks are also owed to the anonymous reviewers who have contributed greatly to the quality of the final work. By far my biggest thanks, however, goes to Professor Wim Gijselaers, University of Maastricht, who as the Series Editor has been immensely supportive at every stage in the production of this work.

London, UK   Clive Kanes
February, 2010

Contents

Contributors

Karin Brodie School of Education, University of the Witwatersrand, Johannesburg, South Africa, Karin.Brodie@wits.ac.za

Harry Daniels University of Bath, Bath, UK, h.r.j.daniels@bath.ac.uk

Amy C. Edmondson Harvard University, Cambridge, USA, aedmondson@hbs.edu

Kevin W. Eva McMaster University, Hamilton, ON, Canada, evakw@mcmaster.ca

Clive Kanes King's College London, London, UK, clive.kanes@kcl.ac.uk

Stephen Kemmis Charles Sturt University, Wagga Wagga, NSW, Australia, skemmis@csu.edu.au

Barbara Lovin Western Carolina University, Cullowhee, USA, cblovin@peoplepc.com

Victoria J. Marsick Teachers College, Columbia University, New York, USA, marsick@exchange.tc.columbia.edu

Candia Morgan Institute of Education, University of London, London, UK, C.Morgan@ioe.ac.uk

Ingrid M. Nembhard Yale University, New Haven, USA, ingrid.nembhard@yale.edu

Jean Searle Griffith University, Brisbane, Australia, j.searle@griffith.edu.au

Karen E. Watkins University of Georgia, Athens, USA, kwatkins@uga.edu

About the Authors

Karin Brodie is an associate professor in the School of Education at Witwatersrand University. She obtained her PhD from Stanford University and teaches in the areas of learning, teaching and curriculum and mathematics education. Her research is on interaction in secondary mathematics classrooms and the extent to which it promotes mathematical understanding and equity. She currently co-leads the Data Informed Practice Improvement Project, an in-service mathematics teacher development project where teachers use a range of data sources to understand and engage with learner thinking. She has been a secondary mathematics teacher and joint head of department with particular responsibility for introducing innovative teaching practices; she has also taught in adult education centres and was a consultant to an English literacy project, developing a set of basic numeracy materials for adults. In 2003 she was awarded the Vice Chancellor's Individual Teaching Award for the most distinguished teacher at the University of Witwatersrand. She was president of the Southern African Association for Research in Mathematics, Science and Technology Education in 2006 and 2007.

Harry Daniels is a professor at the University of Bath where he is also director of The Centre for Sociocultural and Activity Theory Research. Previously he was a professor of Educational Psychology and Special Educational Needs at the University of Birmingham for 9 years. He has just completed a 4-year ESRC-funded study of professional learning in and for multiagency working in different LA cultures. He has extensive experience of studies in the SEN and disability field including those which have deployed sociocultural theory in the investigation of the effects of different cultural formations (e.g., nation states, LAs, schools and families). Recent publications include *Vygotsky and Research* (London: Routledge, 2008), (with M. Cole, M. and J. Wertsch, Eds) *Cambridge Companion to Vygotsky* (New York: Cambridge University Press, 2007), (with R. Moore, R., M. Arnot and J. Beck) *Knowledge, Power and Educational Reform: Applying the Sociology of Basil Bernstein* (London: Routledge, 2006), (Ed.) *An Introduction to Vygotsky* (second edition) (London: Routledge, 2005) and *Vygotsky and Pedagogy* (London: Routledge, 2001).

Amy C. Edmondson is the Novartis Professor of Leadership and Management at Harvard Business School. The Novartis Chair was established to enable the study of human interactions that lead to the creation of successful business enterprises for the betterment of society. Edmondson joined the Harvard faculty in 1996, and he studies leadership influences on learning, collaboration and innovation. Before her academic career, Edmondson was director of research at Pecos River Learning Centers and chief engineer for architect/inventor Buckminster Fuller. Edmondson received her PhD in organisational behaviour, AM in psychology and AB in engineering and design, all from Harvard University.

Kevin Eva is editor-in-chief for the journal *Medical Education* and an associate professor in the Program for Educational Research and Development at McMaster University. He received his PhD in Cognitive Psychology in 2001. Since then he has published over 100 scholarly works on, among other things, the development, maintenance and assessment of competence in health professionals; the selection of students; clinical reasoning strategies; and the role of self-regulation in professional practice. Recent awards for his work include the Canadian Association for Medical Education's Junior Award for Distinguished Contributions to Medical Education.

Clive Kanes teaches in the Department of Education and Professional Studies, King's College London. His academic background is in mathematics, economics and philosophy and he has taught mathematics at secondary and tertiary levels and been an economist within the Department of the Treasury, Canberra, Australia. His research interests relate to the social production of expertise, assessment, adult numeracy and mathematics education. He is the author of numerous scholarly works in the fields of mathematics education, activity theory, adult numeracy and educational assessment. He is currently a European Partner in two EU-funded projects: FAMA (Family Maths for Adult Learners) coordinated by Javier Diez-Palomar of the Universitat Autonoma de Barcelona, Spain; and InBalance, developing a European numeracy framework for adult numeracy education, coordinated by Norbert Ruepert, Director of the International Office of ROC Midden, Utrecht, The Netherlands.

Stephen Kemmis is a professor in the School of Education at Charles Sturt University, Australia. His research interests include the study of professional practice, approaches to educational research and evaluation, curriculum, indigenous education and university development. He is co-author with Wilfred Carr of *Becoming Critical: Education, Knowledge and Action Research* (London: Falmer, 1986) and with R. McTaggart (2005) of *Participatory Action Research: Communicative Action and the Public Sphere*, chapter 23 in N. Denzin and Y. Lincoln (Eds) *The Sage Handbook of Qualitative Research*, 3rd edn. (Thousand Oaks, California: Sage), as well as other publications on action research. His most recent book (co-edited with T. Smith) is *Enabling Praxis: Challenges for Education* (Sense Publishers Rotterdam, 2008). This book is a contribution to an international research program on praxis development involving researchers from the Netherlands, Sweden, Norway, Finland and the United Kingdom.

Barbara Lovin, Ed.D, REMT-P, is a retired associate professor of Health Sciences at Western Carolina University, Cullowhee, NC. She holds a doctorate in Adult

Education from Teachers College, Columbia University, and science degrees from Case Western Reserve University and Northeastern University. A paramedic educator for 25 years, she also has an extensive background in adult medical continuing education with publications in the fields of adult education, human resource management and trauma management.

Victoria Marsick is a professor of Education at Teachers College, Columbia University. She is the co-director of the J.M. Huber Institute for Learning Organizations. The Institute's research focuses on ways in which strategic organisational learning and knowledge creation and sharing enhance performance and change. She is also a leader with The Center for Adult Education which has conducted award-winning research on literacy and has also pioneered the Action Research Professional Development (ARPD) program that leads literacy teachers through reflective practice and experimentation in the classroom. Her scholarly interests include informal workplace learning, team learning, action learning, strategic organisational learning and knowledge management, learning organisations and international models of management. She currently serves on the Conference Committee for an upcoming conference to be held at Teachers College entitled, Democratic Practices as Learning Opportunities: Comparing International Experiences and Understandings.

Candia Morgan is a reader in mathematics education at the Institute of Education, University of London. Having started her career as a teacher of mathematics in London secondary schools, she now works with pre-service and in-service mathematics teachers. Her research focuses on the use of social semiotics, critical discourse analysis and social theory as means of understanding practices in mathematics education at the levels of policy, curriculum, classroom and individual.

Ingrid M. Nembhard is an assistant professor of Public Health and Management at Yale University School of Medicine and Yale School of Management. Her research focuses on how characteristics of health care organisations and their professionals contribute to their ability to implement best practices, engage in continuous organisational learning and ultimately improve clinical outcomes. Nembhard received her PhD in health policy and management, with a concentration in organisational behaviour from Harvard University, her SM in health policy and management from Harvard School of Public Health, and her BA in ethics, politics, and economics and in psychology from Yale University.

Jean Searle is an adjunct senior lecturer in the School of Education and Professional Studies, Faculty of Education, Griffith University, where she taught subjects focusing on adult literacy in both under-graduate and post-graduate degrees. She is the vice-president of the Queensland Council for Adult Literacy and a member of the Griffith Institute for Education Research. Her previous projects have included investigating the literacy and numeracy profiles of prisoners on remand in selected correctional centres in South East Queensland.

Karen E. Watkins, PhD, professor, is the associate dean for Research, Technology, and External Affairs and a professor of Adult Education and Human Resource and Organizational Development in the College of Education at The University of Georgia. Previously, Dr. Watkins was an associate professor of Educational Administration at The University of Texas at Austin where she directed the graduate program in Adult and Human Resource Development Leadership. Her research foci have been in the areas of human resource and organisational development. Watkins is the author or co-author of over 70 articles and chapters, and 7 books. Dr. Watkins was voted Scholar of the Year by the Academy of Human Resource Development; served as president of the Academy of Human Resource Development from 1994 to 1996; and she was named a distinguished graduate by The University of Texas at Austin's Community College Leadership Program. In 2003, Dr. Karen E. Watkins was inducted into the International Adult and Continuing Education Hall of Fame.

Chapter 1
Challenging Professionalism

Clive Kanes

Of the world's top 20 financial institutions by market capitalisation, in the 5 years to 2009, the number based in the United States and the United Kingdom had fallen from 15 to just 4 in total.[1] Moreover, of the original 15 top banks, 4 were British based; yet by late 2008, two of these, the Royal Bank of Scotland (RBS) and the Halifax Bank of Scotland (HBOS), faced insolvency.[2] Referring to this debacle, Lord Myners, who was at the time Financial Services Secretary in the British Government, revealed that at one point in October 2008, things had become so difficult that official preparations were being made to entirely close banking operations in the United Kingdom[2]. What contributed to this catastrophy? Myners, somewhat provocatively, referred to banking leaders as self-regarding "masters of the universe", people "who have no sense of the broader society around them"; nor, he continued, are they evidently people who recognised that they have been "grossly over-rewarded". Whether these depictions are fair or not, for him, mismanagement of the sector by banking professionals, is taken to be a major cause of the ensuing financial disaster.

Indeed, just how intensely these issues appears to be felt by the British public, might be gauged by the robust interaction Nick Ainger, Chair of the British House of Commons Treasury Committee, in the opening examination of 4 former leading executives of HBOS and the RBS in its 10 February 2009 cross-examination, who were summoned to give evidence on their roles in this crisis. The transcript of this public episode reads as follows:

> Q779 Nick Ainger: Let us start with you, Sir Tom: what banking qualifications have you got?
>
> Sir Tom McKillop (former Chairman, RBS): I do not have any formal banking qualifications. I was five years in (?) [Nick Ainger cuts to Sir Fred Goodwin]

C. Kanes (✉)
King's College London, London, UK
e-mail: clive.kanes@kcl.ac.uk

[1] Financial Times, http://www.ft.com/cms/s/0/ea450788-1573-11de-b9a9-0000779fd2ac.html?nclick_check=1, accessed 31 August 2009. Published with permission.

[2] http://www.bloomberg.com/apps/news?pid=20601102&sid=a71Sbc4bvDmk&refer=uk

C. Kanes (ed.), *Elaborating Professionalism*, Innovation and Change in Professional
Education 5, DOI 10.1007/978-90-481-2605-7_1,
© Springer Science+Business Media B.V. 2010

<u>Sir Fred Goodwin (former CEO, RBS)</u>: Whether you would call them banking qualifications or not, but I have a degree in law; I qualified as a chartered accountant; I was in public practice, including auditing banks for a number of years; I was involved in winding-up banks and then looking at providing advice for banks; I was Chief Executive of Clydesdale Bank; and I was a Chief Executive of Yorkshire Bank before I joined the Royal Bank of Scotland group in 1998 as Deputy Chief Executive.

<u>Mr Hornby (former CEO, HBOS)</u>: I do not have any formal banking qualifications. I have an MBA from Harvard where I specialised in all the finance courses, including financial services; and before I took over as Chief Executive two years ago I was a Director of HBOS for seven years.

<u>Lord Stevenson of Coddenham (former Chairman, HBOS)</u>: Like Andy, I have no formal banking qualifications. I have of course been Chairman of the Bank for ten years; and before that I was initially, for about 20 years, an entrepreneurial businessman and I have run large businesses since then.

<u>Nick Ainger</u>: I just wanted to get it on the record because one of the recommendations that we made in the run on [Northern] Rock[3] was that all senior staff of banks, chief executives, chairmen and so on, should have a banking qualification (House of Commons Treasury Committee 144-vii, 10 February, 2009[4]).

Without reflecting in any way on the professionalism of individuals, for me, the pointed content of this encounter usefully summarises a set of headline challenges currently facing professionalism. Firstly, we see uncertainty about what can be legitimately expected of professionals; and this, secondly, is linked to a sense that public trust in banking professionalism has proved misplaced. Interrelated with these, thirdly, the quality, appropriateness and "fitness for purpose" of current arrangements preparing banking professionals for practice is implicitly challenged. Here it is notable that Nick Ainger reaches for a traditional solution: academic training within, presumably, institution's higher education. However, in commenting specifically on this exchange in the *Financial Times*, John Kay, a financial journalist, raises issues that question Ainger's line of reasoning. For Kay, the question is not what would constitute adequate academic training, but whether any professional qualification can, given the rate of change of technical developments in the financial sector, suffice for the challenges the sector faces. Kay, focusing on the recent crisis, develops his argument as follows:

someone who had completed such a [formal banking] qualification would know little about the structured products that brought great banks to the point of collapse. Nor would they be well informed about the structure, strengths and weaknesses of the quantitative risk models that failed to give these banks the security they sought. The skills required to understand the advanced products of the modern financial system are of a different kind, perhaps of a different order. The requirement was for an understanding of the mechanics of structured products combined with the economic knowledge to put them in context and the management skills to run the organisations that marketed them. *It is doubtful whether anyone at all had this range of abilities. Certainly no certificate exists that would attest to such an achievement* (*The Financial Times*, 17 February 2009, emphasis added, reprinted with the publisher's permission).

---

[3] Northern Rock is a British bank that was rescued by the British Government from insolvency in 2008.

[4] See a video of this http://news.bbc.co.uk/1/hi/uk_politics/7894717.stm, accessed 31 August, 2009.

Thus for Kay, as professionalism in banking becomes increasingly dependent on nuanced in situ training and interdisciplinary teamwork – the notion of the academically qualified professional who is both "disinterested" and essentially autonomous, is weakened. (Later in the chapter, I explore the extent that these attributes conventionally define professional work.) Yet, precisely because the banking industry trades in novel instruments of unusual complexity, a fraught no-man's-land of communication between those who make prudential assessments using sophisticated mathematical models of risk and those who are best able to make economically informed decisions that can, or should, drive such models is progressively opening. Thus, from this perspective, the case for "disinterested" academic training, capable of supporting needed intra-sector communication, is strengthened – not weakened. An outline of a series of interlocking dilemmas affecting banking professionalism, therefore, emerges. On the one hand, professionalism seems to growingly assume interested, practical accomplishments; yet, paradoxically, on the other hand, it seems to require exactly the opposite, namely disinterested academic engagement with disciplines, albeit ones which themselves are not yet adequately formed. Michael Young, a sociologist, expresses this dilemma into a pithy question (2006, p. 53): How can there be a growth of close inter- and intra-professional working relationships required for production, yet a singular orientation to particular knowledge and dispositions, characteristic of specific professionalisms, be maintained?

The interrelation of headline challenges can also be seen in the dilemmas professionals face in negotiating the boundaries between care and profit. As Kay (*ibid*) explains

> [t]he bond salesman asks whether a new product will be profitable for him and his bank: the doctor asks whether a new treatment will be beneficial to his patient. In the most trusted profession, medicine, the quality of education is clearly the responsibility of medical schools rather than medical employers.

Thus, whilst there is an acknowledgement of need to effectively balance the often competing ends of profit and care; it is not clear that there are shared beliefs about the nature of these or their provision.

Nor are these challenges confined to banking professionals. Other examples, across a range of professional areas, notably medicine, teaching, dentistry, engineering, and so on, can easily be found. Here McPhail (2006) makes the sadly obvious point: "The new millennium has not started well for accountants. The collapse of Enron, and the ignominious fall of the accounting institution Andersens, followed by WorldCom then Parmalat, has thrown the profession into crisis. . .again!" (p. *vi*). McPhail goes on to point out that

> concepts and categories of conventional accounting practice are now outmoded and struggling to cope with contemporary business practice. However, more significantly, the socio-economic context of the Enron debacle also differs from previous cases. Yes, the scandal occurred in a period when international capital markets were distinctly bearish and had been for some time, but more importantly, it happened in a period of changing social attitudes towards both business and the professions. It occurred within a milieu of increased questioning of the role of business in society and post-modern scepticism regarding the authority and function of the professions (pp. *vii-viii*).

This example again shows the complexity of interrelations among headline challenges facing professionalism. Other similar examples, across a range of professional areas, notably medicine, teaching, dentistry, engineering, and so on, can easily be found.

Thus to summarise, professionalism growingly faces three key headline challenges: to (re)build public trust in professionalism; to provide new educational solutions for the training and preparation of professionals; and to re-envision and articulate a new contextually informed and shared sense of professionalism. Keeping these in mindMindful of these, the aim of this book is to contribute to discussion – especially among professionals themselves, managers employing professionals, policy makers and researchers – addressing these challenges. In the next section of this chapter I briefly outline two theoretical approaches that have contributed crucially to the theoretical understanding of professionalism. This is important for what will follow in the book for two reasons: firstly, because background assumptions and information relating to the field of professional practice studied; and secondly, because it builds connections useful in reading the concluding chapter. In that chapter I attempt to bring together the book by exploring implications of work presented here for headline challenges. The final section of this chapter reiterates the purpose and scope of this book, explains how it was assembled, sets out its structure and introduces the contents of its chapters.

Theoretical Considerations

As a first step, I think it important to address what I mean by professionalism. After all, as Eraut (1994) points out, this difficult word has a variety of obviously different, albeit interrelated, meanings. For instance, he explains, when using the word we sometimes think mainly of the standard or quality of work; when this is good enough, it is referred to as being of a "professional" standard and as an example of "professionalism" (Hargreaves, 2000). However at other times, thinking of its scope, we can refer to any work accomplished within certain occupations as "professional". In these cases, the only kinds of occupations that are deemed relevant are those designated, either by convention or by design, to be a "profession". These, Eraut writes, "constitute a subset of occupations the boundary of which is ill-defined. Features such as length of training, licence to practise, code of ethics, self-regulation and monopoly, feature in most discussion about the nature of professionals, but do not provide a workable definition nor remain stable over time" (Eraut, p. 100). Adding to this, Englund (1996), studying the teaching profession, distinguishes between "professionalisation" and "professionalism". For him, "professionalisation" focuses on the "sociological project, relating to the status and authority of [a] profession", whereas "professionalism" foregrounds the "pedagogical project, concerned with the internal quality of teaching as a profession" (p. 76) and depends on the "acquired capacities" and competences that go to the successful "exercise of an occupation" (p. 76).

Thus, in what follows, by "professionalism" I principally refer to the *qualities* of professional work. This is Eraut's first meaning. In particular, the book does not deliberately aim to explore Eraut's second meaning related to the "status and authority" of professionalism – indeed it avoids meeting the "sociological project" head on. Nevertheless, the book does contribute to discussions relating to this second meaning. In the concluding chapter I hope to make some of this explicit.

In the rest of this section I will consider "professionalism" from two contrasting, but prominent, theoretical perspectives. The attempt here is to offer an informative background helpful to understanding the kinds of ideas working in the background of debates about professional work. This material is also of use as background to further work in Chapter 10 of this volume.

The Structural-Functionalist Approach

Max Weber's analyses of European capitalism in the late 1800s (Weber, 1978) have led to important theoretical understandings relating to the social organisation of work. In his theory, professionalism is a kind of social structure – others being those of government, bureaucracy and legal control, and the market place – that serve the overall functions of coordinating and resolving the many competing interests thrown up by society. Central to his approach is the formation and maintenance of strong boundaries among specialisms: these function to demarcate and accumulate privileged access to specialised knowledge, the rights to practice this knowledge within a market economy, and privileged positional status indicated by a spectrum of measures (income, control over working conditions, access to high culture, and so on). For Weber, these structures work to instantiate a rational ideal, by which they are meant to act according to established rules on the basis of rational evidence and (largely internal) regulation; moreover, their authority is open to challenge by competitive reasoning and argument based on free judgements, and the valuing of rational processes. Thus, according to Ritzer (1975, p. 632), for Weber, professionalism is not only a means to produce and deliver high quality specialist services, but also contributes vitally in shaping our general beliefs in a rationally based, open society. The American sociologist Talcott Parsons (1951, 1954) fleshed these ideas into an elaborate structural-functional system. In his analysis professionalism plays a key role in both serving and making possible a pervasive ethos of rationality. The professions, he argued, "by means of their collegial organisation and shared identity [demonstrate] an alternative approach (to the hierarchy of bureaucratic organisations) towards [a] shared normative approach" (Evetts, 2003, p. 400). Thus, though professionalism can work differently to managerial and market based systems, it overcomes conflicts and tensions that arise within and between the bureaucracy and the market in ways that make for complementarity, and maintain an overriding tendency to social cohesion.

These theoretical analyses have offered professionals, professional associations, managers employing professionals, policy makers and researchers with a positive, if abstract, view of the nature of professionalism. This view also helped in building and justifying the relative status of professionalism within broader society. And yet, in practice, as research from the 1970s to the present shows, the overall need for, and general benefits of, professionalism can be doubted.

For example, "professionalism" has been used to defend conditions of work and enhance occupational status (Clarke & Newman, 1997, cited in Sachs, 2001). Yet, on the other hand, "professionalism" has too often merely benefited private interests at the expense of the public good (Larson, 1977; Abbott, 1988, 1991). Indeed, as I argued at the outset of the chapter, these are among the characteristics of professionalism that have led to its weakening and the prospect of it facing heavy headline challenges. Larson (2003), writing about the medical profession in the USA, illustrates these troubles as follows:

> It would be tedious to repeat the too-frequent indictment of American medicine. Briefly, the richest profession in the world (in terms of physicians' average income, equipment, and expenses) has worried very little, through its official representatives, about the collective value of health, which it purports to serve. Practicing in the only developed country without national health insurance, it has contributed to costs that are, on average, double those of other developed countries, with public health results and indicators equal or inferior to theirs. It has resisted public controls, while abusing the public financing that was provided. Recently, it has had to suffer under managerial controls paradoxically brought about by the pressure of costs on the profits of private insurers; yet even the shift to managed care has failed to curb newly rising costs, suggesting that the profession has been more successful in spreading to the public its bias in favour of advanced technology and expensive drugs than in teaching preventive medicine and a sound conception of health. It would be important to ask systematically how much of this and other distorted professional situations can be traced back to the training systems that professions control (p. 460).

Thus, despite the precepts of Weberian/Parsonian theory, in practice the dominance of private over public interests has considerably dimmed belief that professionalism serves as a source of social cohesion. Given that society needs the powers of specialised production, "What" asks Larson "can a democratic society do to protect specialist knowledge, if those in whom it is vested do not find in their midst the strength to nurture and safeguard their public mandate?" (2003, p. 462). A contemporary response commonly encountered is that managerialism and consumerism, construed as brokers of the public benefit, provide a large part of the answer: the first by mandating accountability, the second by facilitating informed choice, and both by applying the rationalities of transparency and efficiency. However others (e.g., Freidson, 1970, 1983, 2001), including practitioners and the professions themselves, reject this view. These critics point out that managerialism and consumerism inevitably work against specialism, and thus against the highest levels of professional competence; yet along the way they create or exacerbate new constituencies of self-interest that are damaging to the public good. Thus, whether the field is medicine (Havighurst, 2003), teaching (Hargreaves, 2000) or accountancy, the public are no better off. And, in some cases, they are almost certainly dramatically worse off.

Facing this theoretical stalemate, alternative knowledge-based paradigms have also arisen. Perhaps one of its best examples is illustrated by Eraut's (1994) attempt to outline the processes of developing professional knowledge and competence. His idea is to represent professionalism in a "map" of its knowledge bases; the utility of such a map would depend on the accurate delineation of salient structures of professional activities from the macro-level down to the micro-level, and using these representations to plan and operationalise projects as diverse as processes and structures of professional education and training (noting that cognitive psychology also shares a knowledge-paradigm focus); management of professional work and its advocacy and accountability; and planning and coordinating content-based research. Informed by good maps of professional knowledge projects can be conducted with increased rationality and efficiency, and interrelated appropriately. However, a problem with this approach is that formulating professional knowledge bases required for these ends is frustrated by unsolved theoretical and practical problems. On the one hand, as Abbott (1988) points out, a researcher does not have recourse to appropriate theoretical categories, nor is she able to handle very numerous databases; the balance required is, in Abbott's words, an "epistemologist's nightmare" (p. 319). Eraut himself agrees; he states

> My task is complicated by the primitive state of our methodology for describing and prescribing a profession's knowledge base. Many areas of professional knowledge and judgement have not been codified; and it is increasingly recognised that *experts often cannot explain the nature of their own expertise*. A variety of methods and approaches have been developed by philosophers, psychologist, sociologists and government agencies, each with its own limitations. However, one central difficulty has been the lack of attention given to different kinds of knowledge. The field is underconceptualised (pp. 102–103, emphasis added).

That said, Eraut's attempt to distinguish among different kinds of knowledge (e.g., propositional, personal and process knowledge) corrects over simplified views about professional work, and has illuminated curriculum debates in workplace learning and competency-based learning, and helped to represent the relationships among theory and practice in the professions. Also, as Boshuizen, Bromme and Gruber (2004) have argued, focus on knowledge-base acquisition has "[changed] how people argue about knowledge, at least in modern industrial societies" (p. 3). As they show, "the fact that a certain piece of knowledge or skill was once accepted and taught, no longer insures its validity" (p. 3). The paradigm also has deep links with assumptions about practice shared with learning theories such as are offered by cognitive psychology; theories of skill acquisition and generic problem-solving processes have all contributed greatly to how we understand professionalism from an operational point of view. What is less clear, of course, are the important questions for professionalism of how knowledge-base paradigms intersect with societies, social spaces and cultural transformation. How does a theory of knowledge bases intersect with sociologies that attempt to illuminate problems concerning competing interests in knowledge, access to knowledge and valorisation of knowledge across different demographic and cultural variables to knowledge? How does it deal with the transformation of knowledge and the production of new kinds of knowledge?

Clearly other important theoretical frameworks for professionalism have also been developed. In Chapter 10, I will briefly refer up the impact of Emile Durkheim,

Michel Foucault (Fournier, 1999; Evetts, 2003, 2005, 2006) and the so-called "new professionalism"/"postprofessionalism" (Hargreaves, 2000).

Elaborating Professionalism

Against this background I now want to turn to the contents of the book. Firstly, I want to emphasise that authors were given the task to respond to issues relating to professional practice with a diverse audience of professional practitioners, policy makers and managerial people, researchers, students and social scientists in mind. However, they were not asked to specifically address the headline challenges I have set out here. My task as editor was limited to gathering the offered works and presenting them as thematically. It also needs to be acknowledged that authors in this collection write within an international, yet predominantly Anglophone community, and also largely draw on data belonging to such a community (Karin Brodie's chapter is an important exception). Sciulli (2005a, 2005b), for instance, has written powerfully on the limitations implied by this approach.

Excluding this chapter, nine chapters are included in the volume. Within this set, two kinds of contributions. The first includes investigations into topics such as problem solving (Eva), workplace literacy (Searle), informal and incidental learning (Marsick, Watson & Lovin), and working in teams (Nembhard & Edmondson). These concerns occupations whether specifically professional or not. Other investigations in this set concern choices professionals make in externally constrained settings relating to their professional identities (Morgan) and the kinds of knowledge content within their purview (Brodie). Though to varying degrees, each of these is empirically focussed, all tease out theoretical and practical implications for a range of issues facing professional practitioners, researchers and policy makers. The second kinds of contributions are mainly theoretical in focus: here the focus lies with questions concerning the nature of professional practice as such (Kemmis) and exploration of the collaborative aspect of practice (Daniels). In the concluding chapter of the volume, I step back from these various contributions in order to identify and comment on some of the ways they address headline challenges. Given that the book started by referencing recent calamities in the world's financial system, these final comments allow me to conclude the book on a more optimistic, if speculative, note.

Before moving to the contents of the book, a word on its title is in order. Working from a modern English-language dictionary (*Oxford English Dictionary*), "elaborating professionalism" could simply mean something like enlarging on the accomplishment of professional work in order to show the manner in which it is accomplished; studies of this kind tend towards unpacking the micro-practices of work settings. As I have already argued, and research of this kind is important as the rationale for this book. However, *elaborating professionalism* is an ambiguous term. It could also mean enlarging on how occupational work becomes the object of professionalism, taking on professional characteristics as it does so. This is a useful observation because a complete understanding of professionalism certainly requires that we understand how micro-practices relate to their designations at macro-levels. Nevertheless, this interrelationship is not the focus of this book. That said, various chapters, especially from Morgan's onwards, track between these alternative interpretations, in the background at least, and thus create a space in which both the micro- and macro-scales of professionalism come into conversation. Information about the contents of the book follows.

Contents of the Contributing Chapters

Eva's study on problem-solving skills and professional practice (Chapter 2), puts domain-specific knowledge into the foreground. For him the place of generic reasoning and problem-solving skills is moot. Offering an historical account, Eva situates the main part of his chapter in exploring aspects of medical diagnostic practice and implications for medical training. Concerning the latter, expert-novice studies aimed at directly comparing practitioner reasoning and problem-solving practices (e.g., generating helpful hypotheses and forward reasoning) are, contrary to earlier beliefs, taken to be "epiphenomenal, the differences observed being better explained by differences in the ability of experts and novices to solve (and subsequently explain) the problem, rather than differences in the reasoning processes that led to the solution". For Eva, context-specific knowledge is decisive; the acquisition of problems skills however has a place, most particularly around analogical transfer. However, the extent to which this processual knowledge can be or needs to be abstracted is problematic. Moreover, in terms of diagnostic practice, he finds that multiple reasoning processes contribute to the final decisions reached for most problems (regardless of experience level). From this he concludes that medical education should emphasise a "flexible interaction between many problem-solving strategies ... and memory-based solutions that do not require problem solving at all". In other words, though general and higher level abstracted skills may be the hallmarks of professional practice, they are not the basis of problem-solving expertise typical of professionalism.

Specificity is also the key theme in Searle's study of workplace literacy in motel and airline industries (Chapter 3). Her analyses of data, focusing on customer service operations, demonstrate that the very concept of "general skills" should be treated cautiously. She shows that even though skills such as "scanning for specific information", "use as synonyms", "use a numeric codes", etc, could be regarded as specific "this classification [would] still be problematic because these skills do not exist in isolation from a range of other skills and practices, and secondly, because the literacies involved are highly situated". Thus, her empirical and theoretical analyses of occupational practices, provide detailed evidence consistent with Eva's central contention relating to the criticality of the specific, the detailed and the elaborated in understanding professional practice. Searle, in advancing doing this, takes her analyses beyond what goes on in the mind of the individual workers. Like Kemmis (Chapter 8), she emphasises that workplace literacy, far from being constructed as a general skill, requires the specific and detailed understanding of how social spaces operate and of the systems of value, repertoire of rules, and highly textualised artefacts that populate them. In her concluding paragraphs, Searle takes these analyses to the topic of professional education. Here she draws attention to the need to supplement knowledge of "technical competencies" with those that refer to the "maintenance of the social order". The latter, she suggests, are not usually addressed, though they are essential to effective workplaces. Searle also makes the important point that "critical literacy" needs to feature in professional education. Noting that the increase in "textualisation" of the workplace is in part driven by a newly enlivened culture of accountability, she argues that practitioners need "not only to be able to complete the forms [of accountability] correctly, but also to use their interpretive procedures to understand the significance of compliance or non-compliance with institutional social orders". Morgan (Chapter 6) illustrates just how significant the development of such literacy practices can be, if professional identities are not to be absorbed into a role of dependency that would, in the view of many, be inconsistent with professionalism.

Marsick, Watkins and Lovin (Chapter 4) offer an update of their well-known informal and incidental learning model, first developed in 1990 by Marsick and Watkins, and previously updated in collaboration with Cseh in 1999 (Cseh, Watkins, & Marsick, 1999). They define "incidental and informal learning" as "learning outside of formally structured, institutionally sponsored, classroom-based activities". In the light of recent research on learning and their own evolving thinking, the authors note four key problems with the model as they previously had it. Specifically, they mention misleading appearances of linearity; undue "cognitive" bias; too great a focus on individual learning and insufficient focus on social interaction, construction, and action; and lack of explanation of the role of context in learning. They use Lovin's (1991) doctoral study on informal learning among paramedics to motivate and illustrate their concerns within a concrete setting. In theoretical terms they consciously move away from thinking about learning that assumes a "disjunction between anticipated and actual experience". Incidental learning, for them, proceeds holistically in "simultaneously drawing on experience, imagination, admission, and practical applications". That process, however, is less stepwise than already integrated; following Heron (1992) they subscribe to a "critical subjectivity" in which many ways of knowing are constantly called on, renewed and "balanced". Further, they emphasise that reflection is needed for learning to take place, and to prompt this organisations could purposefully build reflective episodes into work related protocols. The authors also argued that shifting control of the learning experience to the learner is helpful; yet they acknowledge the complication whereby "there is often a gap between a stated desire that employees (professional or non-professionals) be self-directed in their learning and the reality of the way the workplace is structured". If hierarchical organisational structures are justified by the productive results they produce, then importantly, such structures can also tend to impede workplace learning and thus, over time, result in the de-skilling of their revised model. Their chapter concludes with some implications of their work for providers of professional learning and development. Among these is the important point that continuing education for paramedics could be more valuable when built around "storytelling with appropriate resources brought in to help [practitioners] go more deeply into their learning and role play situations for which they need knowledge".

Previously I noted that interdisciplinary teamwork is emerging as an important feature of professional work. Increasing knowledge, specialisation and interdependence seem set to ensure that team approaches to managing professional obligations will become increasingly crucial. Nevertheless, in addressing specifically the case of medical teams, Nembhard and Edmondson (Chapter 5) point to a number of factors that typically work against effective teamwork. These include the perception that collaborative work is difficult to manage and therefore presents unacceptably high risks to patient care; that expert knowledge is traditionally unshared in medical contexts; that good communication across disciplinary boundaries is not routine and makes sharing difficult; and that differences in status among team members can lead to senior team members crowding out other members with less effective medical, and poor quality improvement outcomes, sometimes resulting. Focussing on the latter, Nembhard and Edmondson offer a detailed empirical investigation of the correspondence of interdisciplinary team leadership and the perception or "psychological safety" of team members. Here "psychological safety" (Edmondson, 1999) refers to the sense of safety from negative repercussions – expressed in terms of employment appraisal, assessment, social standing and sense of self-worth. In a sample of over 40 teams of U.S. Neonatal Intensive Care Units (NICU) involving 1440 health care professionals (e.g., physician, nurses and therapists), their study draws on questionnaire data. The principal findings were that higher professional status correlates positively with higher psychological safety; however, higher leader inclusive behaviours in NICU teams moderated these differences. Their study predicts that teams with higher overall psychological safety are more engaged in "quality improvement". In practical terms, the chapter points to the training of team leaders in NICU to be inclusive of team members, and this "maybe a critical antecedent to more effective quality improvement". The authors believe that their findings may also have general validity – especially across industries where teams are highly internally variable with regard to the status of members.

Morgan (Chapter 6) explores ways professionals define and maintain themselves and the zones of their professional expertise. Her study focuses on the professional identity of mathematics teachers working in England under the mandate of the *National Curriculum* (DES/WO, 1988; DfEE, 1999). This topic is important because, as Beck & Young (2005) argue, "ethical responsibility" in professional practice can only occur if practitioners themselves are responsible for the quality of the service they provide, yet identities of dependence could arise in the context of excessively directive curriculum frameworks. Thus, like the Nembhard and Edmondson, Morgan's study also has important ethical overtones. As touched on again in Chapter 10, the deprofessionalisation of an occupation, whether intended or not, might well be accomplished by driving the identities of practitioners to a dependent status; certainly, aspects of the *National Curriculum* (for instance pedagogic constraints regarding lesson components and timing) are construed by many to be excessively directive. Morgan's analysis, however, provides us with a more highly nuanced understanding of how the professionalism of mathematics teachers is elaborated in practice. Her data show that experienced mathematics teachers are able to "position themselves as compliant with the officially prescribed approach to teaching while simultaneously maintaining a positive identity as expert professionals". Morgan shows that experienced teachers in her study were able to draw on the discursive resources of both the formative curriculum and "teachers' existing principles on ways of accounting for their teaching practices" in the performance of their "identity work", and this enabled them to present as complainant, yet retain an autonomous identity. However, Morgan found in her study that this was not the experience of new teachers, and this, she suggests, problematises the future prospects of professionalism in mathematics teaching. In terms of the broader issues of this book, Morgan's study highlights the elaboration professionalism at work; her study opens the theoretical issue of discursive resources around producing and reconstituting this professionalism, and introduces practical questions about how professionalism can be maintained even in strongly managerialist settings.

If Morgan's study goes to the topic of "identity work", then Brodie's South African study (Chapter 7), contributes to a more nuanced elaboration of (what we might call) the "knowledge work" of professionalism. Her study focuses on two mathematics teachers: Mr Peter, who works in a government school consisting of black learners drawn from very poor home backgrounds, and Ms King, who works in a private school whose learners are predominantly white and come "mostly from extremely wealthy homes". Brodie's aim is to elaborate the professional practice of these teachers, as they engage in the same nominal mathematics topic with their classes, especially as they "attempt to hear and take seriously learners' mathematical meanings and respond to these in appropriate ways"; both teachers thereby aim to help learners build on, and transform their knowledge. Brodie's approach demonstrates how the teachers' mathematics knowledge, pedagogical content knowledge (Shulman, 1987), and knowledge of learners' mathematical thinking, are mobilised with positive effect in their different teaching contexts. In analysing the data, Brodie classified the kinds of learner contributions elicited in the classroom teachers, using two salient categories of contributions. The first she called Appropriate Errors (errors students "normally" present at their nominal level of mathematical attainment), and the second Basic Errors (errors students made that are basic to the concepts being developed at the nominal learning objective). Concerning the distribution of these errors, both classes had a similar number of the Appropriate Errors, yet Ms King's class exhibited a vastly larger number of Basic Errors. Brodie argues that these differences also correspond with key differences in the pedagogy she observed. Mr Peter spent more time searching for learners' understanding Appropriate Errors, whereas Ms King reflected less on the underlying mathematics relating to these errors. Although Brodie found this could have been because Mr Peter's class exhibited more errors over all, it was also because in Ms King's class Appropriate Errors were not widely shared and she could therefore rely on fellow students to help learners who needed it without her plenary intervention. Brodie's chapter thus demonstrates how professionalism works out differently in two contrasting settings in which the nominal objectives are identical. Her elaboration of professional "knowledge work" provides both theoretical and methodological suggestions as to how, in Kemmis's terms, professional practice is "reconstituted by human agency and social actions". Brodie concludes the chapter by suggesting that teachers, purposefully applying the schema identifying learner contributions she constructed in this study, may help professional development experiences of mathematics teachers.

Kemmis (Chapter 8) offers a view of professional practice that is richly elaborated in theoretical terms. His view is that professional practice is and must be understood from a broad range of perspectives. Certainly the knowledge perspective of Eraut (1994) and Higgs, Titchen & Neville (2001), which focuses principally on the individual, is one of these. Yet drawing on "theorists of practice" such as MacIntye, Bourdieu, Foucault and Habermas, Kemmis explains that we could elaborate understanding of professional practice in terms of at least two additional perspectives. The first of these is the social perspective. Here, when our goals are educative, the key is to understand how professional knowledge (including the technical, craft and personal) is constructed in the social domain. The second additional perspective required is the understanding of the reflexivity between the individual and the social. For Kemmis, the decisive point here is that subjective–objective relations are reflexive–dialectical in character. According to this view the task of "critical social science" is to understand professional practice as both socially constituted and "reconstituted by human agency and social action". Kemmis's analyses offer a valuable systematic account of numerous sites from which reflexivities emerge. In elaborating professional practice, he identifies seven dimensions that he shows cut across the binary divide. These are listed as follows: meaning and purpose, structure, situation, temporal location, system, reflexivity and transformation, and forms of reasoning about practice. True to the interdisciplinary character of Kemmis's work, his references are from philosophy (Aristotle, Wittgenstein, Schatzki), sociology (Bourdieu), historical studies (Toulmin, Foucault), psychology (Vygotsky, Leontiev), and activity theory (Engeström). Kemmis concludes his chapter with powerful remarks concerning prospects for professional practice in a world nearly dominated by technical rationality.

Daniels (Chapter 9) picks up the issues of status and teamwork raised by Nembhard Edmondson, taking these to the problem of how to mirror these in a theoretical space. In focusing on inter-agency professional teamwork he starts with the work of Pirkalainen, Kaatrakoski & Engeström (2005) concerning the formation of hybrid activity systems (those, for example, corresponding to the substantive expertise of inter-agency team members; e.g., nursing, social work and psychology professionals). To this he brings an array of sociological and socio-linguistic resources in order to analyse and account for the process of hybridisation and formation of positional changes among agents. Holland's concept of "figured world" provides Daniels with a tool to discuss inter-subjective relationships that he sees as crucial to better understanding this hybridity. He argues that there is a need to develop understanding of hybridity "in such a way that we can theorise, analyse and describe the processes by which [such a hybrid] world is 'figured'". Interestingly, he argues that this might be achieved within the context of activity theory around the study of communication. In order to further advance theoretical understanding of teamwork of professional practice he makes two useful kinds of suggestions. The first is that further theoretical and methodological work leading to better understanding of the "ways in which objects of activity are transformed within the networks of activity systems" is needed. The second concerns how, related to these networks, discourses are produced and subjects positioned. Whilst these conclusions are of particular interest to researchers, they also provide a basis for practitioners and policy makers to consider further the value of hybrid relationships.

In Chapter 10, the final chapter, Kanes aims to discuss how studies presented in the book could be useful to professional practitioners, scholars, policy makers and others interested in professionalism. This is done in two ways. In the first, a summary of how each of headline challenges (this chapter above) are addressed by the book is set out; and a thematic analysis of these contributions is made. Four key themes emerge: specificity; holism; plasticity and illimitability; boundary crossing and hybridity. In the second approach, building on the work of this chapter, some recent scholarly work relating to boundary crossing, specificity and ethics is picked up and discussed. Here the discussion centres on a recent report commissioned by the Royal College of Physicians of London on the future of professionalism with medical practice.

References

Abbott, A. (1988). *The system of professions: An essay on the division of expert labour*. Chicago: University of Chicago Press.

Abbott, A. (1991). The future of occupations: Occupations and expertise in the age of organisation. *Research in the Sociology of Organisations, 8*, 17–42.

Beck, J., & Young, M.F.D. (2005). The assault on the professions and the restructuring of academic and professional identities: A Bernsteinian analysis, *British Journal of Sociology of Education, 26*(2), 183–197.

Boshuizen, H., Bromme, R., & Gruber, H. (2004). *Professional learning: Gaps and transitions and the way from novice to expert*. Dordrecht: Kluwer.

Cseh, M., Watkins, K.E., & Marsick, V.J. (1999). Re-conceptualizing marsick and watkins' model of informal and incidental learning in the workplace. In K. P. Kuchinke (Ed.), *Proceedings of the Academy of HRD* (pp. 349–355). Baton Rouge: Academy of Human Resource Development.

Edmondson, A.C. (1999). Psychological safety and learning behaviour in work teams. *Administrative Science Quarterly, 44*, 350–383.

Engeström, Y. (2005). *Developmental work research: Expanding activity theory in practice*. Berlin: Lehmanns Media.

Englund, T. (1996). Are professional teachers a good thing? In I. Goodson & A. Hargreaves (Eds.), *Teachers' professional lives*. London: The Falmer Press.

Eraut, M. (1994). *Developing professional knowledge and competence*. London: The Falmer Press.

Evetts, J (2006). Short note: The sociology of professional groups: New directions. *Current Sociology, 54*(1), 133–143.

Evetts, J. (2003). The sociological analysis of professionalism: Occupational change in the modern world. *International Sociology, 18*(2), 395–415.

Evetts, J. (2005). *Management of professionalism: A contemporary paradox. In changing teacher roles, identities and professionalism*. Paper presented at Changing Teacher Roles, Identities and Professionalism Seminar Series, King's College London, October 19th, 2005.

Fournier, V. (1999). The appeal to 'professionalism' as a disciplinary mechanism. *Social Review, 47*(2), 280–307.

Freidson, E. (2001). *Professionalism: The third logic*. Oxford: Polity.

Freidson, E. (1970). *Professional dominance: The structure of medical care*. Chicago: Aldine-Atherton.

Freidson, E. (1983). The theory of professions: The state of the art. In R. Dingwall & P. Lewis (Eds.), *The sociology of the professions*. London: Macmillan Press.

Havighurst, C. (2003). An apology for professionalist regimes. *Journal of Health Politics, Policy and Law, 28*(1), 159–163.

Hargreaves, A. (2000). Four ages of professionalism and professional learning. *Teachers and Teaching: Theory and Practice, 6*(2), 151–182.

Heron, J. (1992). *Feeling and personhood: Psychology in another key*. London: Sage.

Higgs, J., Titchen, A., & Neville, V. (2001). Professional practice and knowledge. In J. Higgs & A. Titchen (Eds.), *Practice knowledge and expertise in the health professions* (Chapter 1). Oxford: Butterworth-Heinemann.

House of Commons Treasury Committee, United Kingdom. (2009). *Uncorrected transcript of oral evidence: Banking crisis – former bank executives, Tuesday 10 February 2009*. To be published as HC 144-vii. Retrived 28 February, 2009, from http://www.publications.parliament.uk/pa/cm200809/cmselect/cmtreasy/uc144_vii/uc14402.htm

Larson, M. (1977). *The rise of professionalism: A sociological analysis*. London: University of California Press.

Larson, M. (2003). Professionalism: The third logic. *Perspectives in Biology and Medicine, 46*(3), 458–462 (review).

Lovin (previously Larson), B. K. (1991). Informal workplace learning and partner relationships among paramedics in the prehospital setting. (Doctoral dissertation, Teachers College, Columbia University, 1991). *Dissertation Abstracts International 52/02B*, 0732.

McPhail, K. (2006). *Ethics and the individual professional accountant: A literature review*. Edinburgh: Institute of Chartered Accountants of Scotland.

Parsons, T. (1951). *The social system*. New York: Free Press.

Parsons, T., (1954). The professions in the social structure. In Parsons, T. (Ed.), *Essays in social structure*. Glencoe: Free Press.

Ritzer, G. (1975). Professionalisation, bureaucratisation and rationalisation: The views of Max Weber. *Social Forces, 53*(4), 627–634.

Sachs, J. (2001). Teacher professional identity: Competing discourses, competing outcomes. *Journal of Education Policy, 16*(2), 149–161.

Sciulli, D. (2005a). Continental sociology of professions today: Conceptual contributions. *Current Sociology, 53*(6), 915–942.

Sciulli, D. (2005b). Escaping without eliding an Atlantic divide, etymological and conceptual. *Current Sociology, 53*(6), 952–958.

Shulman, L. (1987) Those who understand: Knowledge growth in teaching. *Educational Researcher, 15*(2), 4–14.

Weber, M. (1978). In Roth, G., & Wittich, C. (Eds.), *Economy and society*. Berkeley: University of California Press.

Young, M. (2006). *Bringing knowledge back in: From social constructivisim to social realism in the sociology of education*. London: Routledge.

Chapter 2
On the Relationship Between Problem-Solving Skills and Professional Practice

Kevin W. Eva

How did you do that? It is the first question out of everyone's mouth when they witness a problem being solved that they are not sure they could have solved for themselves. No wonder then that it is the question at the core of both research and rhetoric regarding how professionals are able to solve problems that seem bewildering to lay people or novices. No wonder also that many pedagogical efforts have been aimed towards nurturing problem-solving skills among trainees. Teach novices how experts reason their way through problems and the novices themselves will become experts. While seemingly straightforward and laudable in goal, this model of expert practice as highly developed problem-solving skills has proven to be erroneous. In fact, one could argue that expertise and problem solving are not correlated with one another at all. In this chapter the relationship between problem solving and professional practice will be explored in four parts. First, I will provide an historical overview of basic research into human problem solving, defining the concept and tracing the evolution of the field. Second, this chapter will outline the search for problem-solving skills within the professional domain of medical practice, focusing on how such skills relate to the hallmarking of expertise. Third, I will outline a current model of professional decision making within which it must be said that problem-solving skill plays only a minor role. Finally, the chapter will conclude by providing explicit strategies for the development of expertise that use problem solving as a means to an end rather than treating skill in problem solving as an end unto itself.

A Brief History of Problems and Their Solutions

For over a century psychologists have studied problem solving as a way of better understanding how humans think and in an effort to enable better problem solving in the future. In the 1920s Karl Duncker created many of the tasks still in use for

K.W. Eva (✉)
McMaster University, Hamilton, ON, Canada
e-mail: evakw@mcmaster.ca

C. Kanes (ed.), *Elaborating Professionalism*, Innovation and Change in Professional Education 5, DOI 10.1007/978-90-481-2605-7_2,
© Springer Science+Business Media B.V. 2010

the study of problem solving (Schnall, 1999), his radiation problem being one of the most famous:

> Suppose a patient has an inoperable stomach tumour. Unless the tumour is destroyed, the patient will die. There is a kind of ray that, at a sufficiently high intensity, can destroy the tumour. Unfortunately, at this intensity the healthy tissue that the ray passes through on the way to the tumour will also be destroyed. At lower intensities the rays are harmless to healthy tissue, but will not affect the tumour. How can one destroy the tumour without injuring the surrounding healthy tissue?

Other classic examples include (a) Luchins' three-container problem: You have three containers that hold 21, 127, and 3 L of water, respectively – use these three containers to extract exactly 100 L of water from a well (Luchins, 1942), (b) Glucksberg's (1962) candle problem: Mount two candles on the wall given only a box of matches and thumb tacks, and (c) Scheerer's matchstick problem: With only six matchsticks of equal length, create four equilateral triangles, each side of each triangle being equal to the length of a match (Scheerer, 1963). Common to each example is that a current state is defined (i.e., conditions are laid out), there is a known goal to be achieved, and the way to move from the current state to the goal state is not clear.[1] These three features have been identified as the defining features of problems (Mayer, 1977), but it must be recognised that the precision with which the current and goal states are specified is variable (Reitman, 1965).

In the early days of research into problem solving, participants would be presented with a problem and asked to think aloud while the investigator tried to determine how solutions were achieved. In Duncker's case it was noted that people typically began by re-formulating the problem in a more general way that would enable specific solutions to be mentally tested. As one example, questioning whether or not there was a path to the stomach that would not require passing through tissue would lead some participants to consider passing the rays through the esophagus. Recognising that rays travel in straight lines, thus making this approach impossible, invalidated the hypothesis, but freed the participants to explore other possibilities. Some would inevitably stumble upon the possibility of splitting the ray such that a series of rays of low enough intensity as to do no harm could be aimed at the tumour from multiple directions. The rays would then converge on the tumour and sum to a high enough intensity to accomplish the goal of destroying it (Duncker, 1945).

As more stimuli were created and studied in the first half of the twentieth century, it became clear that there were some fundamental challenges that made problems problematic. Perkins summarised the challenges by drawing an analogy to searching for gold in the Klondike (Perkins, 2000). First, there is a wilderness of possibilities with little gold being spread over a lot of space, thereby making persistence despite lack of reward necessary for success. Second, there are few clues regarding whether or not one is on the right track and lots of potential for plateau traps (i.e., searching nearby rather than exploring other places). Third, people may not

---

[1] To fully appreciate the problems, the reader is encouraged to pause to try solving each in turn. The answers will be provided later in the text.

be aware of the assumptions they have made in approaching a problem; thereby making it difficult to notice that one is focused upon a "narrow canyon of exploration." Finally, Perkins notes that there are many oases of false promise (i.e., having received enough promising signs, the prospector gains hope that the mother lode will be struck with the next shovelful of gravel). Like plateauing traps, oases of false promise make it difficult to explore other, potentially more fruitful, avenues.

These four metaphorical traps illustrate that difficulty in problem solving arises, in part, when one gets locked into thinking about a problem in a particular way. Indeed, while the phrase "think outside the box" has become a cliché, it still nicely summarises how problem solving can go awry. We have likely all had the experience of getting locked into a particular way of thinking about a problem and then, once the answer is revealed, having to resist the urge (sometimes unsuccessfully) to slap ourselves in the forehead while groaning "How could I have missed that?" Luchins' three-container problem provides a wonderful demonstration of this sort of fixation. The answer, for those who haven't encountered the problem before, is to fill the large (127 L) container and then pour out enough to fill the medium (21 L) container and enough to fill the small (3 L) container twice (i.e., $127 - 21 - 3 - 3 = 100$). Now if you were asked to solve a similar problem in which you had containers of 23, 49, and 3 L and the goal was to come up with exactly 20 L you could likely do so. Luchins found, however, that most people, after having seen a series of similar problems, solved this one by subtracting 23 L from 49 L and then twice subtracting 3 L from the 49 L container without ever recognising that it would be easier to simply subtract 3 L from the 23 L container. More dramatically, presenting a problem in which three containers of 28, 76, and 3 L must be used to create 25 L often led to an inability to solve the problem because $76 - 28 - 3 - 3$ no longer led to the desired amount (Mayer, 1977).

Similarly, we often create problems for ourselves by failing to recognise that we routinely make implicit assumptions about how the information available to us should be interpreted. The key to Glucksberg's candle problem is to recognise that the matchbox can be used as a shelf rather than as a container. Simply emptying the box, tacking it to the wall, and placing the candles on top solves the problem of hanging the candles on the wall. Perhaps more importantly, in terms of practical application, is that Glucksberg's studies revealed a negative relationship between intensity of motivation and cognitive flexibility. When participants were told they might win a $20 reward for the correct solution it took them longer to come up with the answer than it took a group of control subjects who were not offered a reward (Stuyt, de Vries Robbe, & van der Meer, 2003).

As one might easily imagine, findings like these proliferated a search for general problem-solving heuristics; lowering the intensity of one's search for a solution and considering other interpretations of the provided information are two examples of heuristics that have become the basis of many workshops on creativity. Two further examples include working backwards from the solution and making the problem more concrete by using pictures or diagrams. To apply both to Scheerer's matchstick problem, take out a pencil and draw four equal-size equilateral triangles. Now envision how they might be combined by overlaying one side of a particular triangle with one side of another triangle. Doing so reduces the number of lines required to draw two triangles from 6 to 5. Adding a third triangle to the mix and trying to overlay two of its sides with sides of the two joined triangles might lead to the realisation that a third dimension can be used. Joining the triangles in a pyramid rather than a plane restructures the problem so that an "aha" moment becomes more likely – one can easily use 6 matchsticks to create four equilateral triangles by creating one triangle and then attaching one end of the other three matchsticks to each corner of the triangle and bringing the loose end of those matchsticks together at a point above the centre of the base triangle.

At this point in history (the late 1960s and early 1970s), observations like these supported the view of Gestalt psychologists, a school of psychology in which it was believed that organisation was the root of all mental activity, that mental restructuring (i.e., re-organising) was at the heart of most problem solving (Gleitman, 1991). That is, it was thought that "breakthrough thinking" was enabled by simply encouraging people to "look at the world with fresh eyes" (i.e., to approach problems from different directions). Incubation (i.e., walking away from the problem for a period of time) was considered to provide another general problem-solving heuristic, as it would encourage mental restructuring by reducing both mental fixation and the pressure one felt to solve the problem (Wickelgren, 1974). Still, two seemingly opposite views of this research led the field in a brand new direction.

First, the belief that the problems being studied captured the fundamental characteristics of "real-world" problems led educators to strive to incorporate problem-solving heuristics training into their educational programs. If people can learn to solve problem, the logic went, teachers should worry less about teaching students specific material and focus more upon teaching them to become good problem solvers; no amount of training would prepare students for every situation they might encounter, so they must be empowered to solve novel problems when they arise. At the same time, the opposite view of the research performed on problem solving to this point led researchers in the same direction. Many became increasingly convinced that these "eureka" problems that were being studied were too tightly constrained to allow generalisation to the complex problems that are encountered in "real life". Of what use is the three-container problem when the goal is to help engineers solve the less constrained problem of determining how to improve fuel efficiency in a new car? Again, however, this concern led researchers to more real-world environments including the classrooms of professional trainees in an effort to continue the search for a key to unlocking our full problem-solving capacity.

Using Problem Solving to Solve the Problem of Professional Training

As researchers became increasingly interested in exploring the intricacies of problem-solving processes in more complex domains, the field quickly diversified. Some began using computerised labouratory tasks in an effort to model the complexity and semantic richness of real-life problems (Berry & Broadbent, 1995).

More commonly, others moved their research base to naturalistic domains, studying specific content areas and abandoning attempts to create a unified theory of problem solving as it appeared as though different knowledge domains utilised fundamentally different problem-solving processes (Sternberg, 1995). de Groot (1965), and Chase and Simon (1973) performed some of the earliest and best-known work in the field of chess mastery. At the same time, however, research into the education of professionals, physicians in particular, began to expand, the early days being dominated by an exploration of clinical problem solving (Norman, 2005).

Unlike chess, medicine is a domain in which the knowledge-base professional practitioners are expected to maintain is constantly evolving. As a result, innovative curricula like the problem-based learning approach were developed in the late 1960s with the premise of inculcating problem-solving (i.e., clinical reasoning) skills (Barrows & Tamblyn, 1980). Knowledge mastery was reduced to a secondary agenda and research efforts again returned to the think aloud approach as utilised by Duncker (1945). This time, however, clinicians of varying levels of experience were asked to verbalise their reasoning process either before or after working through clinical problems (typically presented by simulated patients) in attempts to identify differences between novices and experts in a manner that might facilitate the transfer of expertise from practitioners to trainees. While there is evidence that verbal reports of mental processes are susceptible to error (Ericsson & Simon, 1980), a consistent picture emerged from this early research that has yet to be refuted adequately. Elstein, Shulman, and Sprafka (1978) reported evidence in favour of a "hypothetico-deductive model" of clinical reasoning in which the features presented early in a new case (i.e., a new "problem") lead rapidly to the generation of tentative diagnostic hypotheses that then serve as an orienting framework for further exploration of the case. While this model provided a general summary of the clinical problem-solving process, the supporting data failed to isolate process differences between novices and experts. For example, both students and experts were seen to generate 5–7 hypotheses over the course of a clinical encounter and to do so equally rapidly (Neufeld, Norman, Barrows, & Feightner, 1981). The difference between novice and experienced physician was simply that experts' hypotheses were more likely to be correct than were those generated by novices. Patel and Groen (1986) did use think aloud protocols to support the claim that "forward reasoning," a systematic search of a diagnostic problem that proceeded from data (i.e., clinical features) to diagnosis, provided a hallmark of expertise in comparison to a novice-like "backward reasoning" approach in which diagnoses were generated and used to test the fit of the data that were available (Patel, Groen, & Arocha, 1990). However, more recent work has shown that this difference is probably epiphenomenal, the differences observed being better explained by differences in ability of experts and novices to solve (and subsequently explain) the problem rather than differences in the reasoning processes that led to the solution (Eva, Brooks, & Norman, 2002).

Furthermore, data have accumulated over the last three decades that strongly suggest success with one clinical problem is poorly correlated with success on the next clinical problem regardless of what outcome measures are used (data gathering, diagnostic accuracy, management strategy, etc.) – a phenomenon known as context specificity (Eva, Norman, & Neville, 1998). The phenomenon is very robust, both inside and outside of medical practice (Eva, 2003), but within the medical profession specifically it has been observed so frequently that it has led John Norcini (personal communication, 2006) to state "context specificity is the one truth in medical education." Success at solving a problem simply does not predict success on the next problem, even within a specialty area (Norman, Tugwell, Feightner, Muzzin, & Jacoby, 1985). More recently it has been shown that the "context" that yields specificity is more narrow than had previously been assumed – one's success in terms of diagnostic accuracy when faced with a particular clinical problem does not even predict one's success in data gathering or patient management, for example, within the very same problem (Norman, Bordage, Page & Keane, 2006).

Taken together, these findings cast doubt on the value of "problem-solving skill" as a construct that should be deemed important to the development of professional practice (Norman, 1988). If novices and experts reason in the same way, and if ability to correctly solve problems is not generalisable across problem, then problem solving is not very skill-like and, therefore, there is little point in attempting to train students to develop problem-solving "skill." In fact, as the next section will clarify, the more experience one has in a given domain, the fewer problems one has to solve.

When One Knows the Answers There Are No Problems

In the late 1980s and early 1990s a transition occurred in which medical education researchers began to focus more directly on the centrality of knowledge, largely abandoning the previously held notion that a successful problem-solving process could be harnessed and engineered. While the hypothetico-deductive model of clinical reasoning provided a useful description of the diagnostic process and helped to re-focus the literature, it was unable to answer a number of important questions. For example, from where did the generated hypotheses arise? What made experts more likely to generate accurate hypotheses relative to novices? As a result, a number of frameworks were developed to describe expert–novice differences in how knowledge is organised within the minds of medical professionals and trainees. Bordage and Lemieux (1990) proposed a model that relied on semantic axes, mentally crafted continua along which clinical features could be assigned in a diagnostically helpful way; Barrows and Feltovich (1987) proposed that experts became expert through the development of "illness scripts", records of typical cases associated with each condition; Mandin and colleagues (1997) proposed that experts utilise scheme induction through *elaborate* decision trees that allow algorithmic tracing of features towards particular disorders; Elieson and Papa (1994), among many others, promoted a more Bayesian approach within which it was argued that expertise arises from better internalisation of the probabilistic relationships between features and diagnoses.

While unique in application, characteristic of all these models are the fundamental beliefs that (a) rules corresponding to reality can be created to link features (e.g., signs and symptoms) to diagnoses, and that (b) improved clinical reasoning is derived from greater appreciation and *elaboration*of such rules. That is, each model described to this point is very "analytic" in nature in that each relies on the clinician to explicitly link pieces of information in order to solve diagnostic problems (Eva, 2005). There remains, however, another class of reasoning that has gained increasing attention in the past two decades – that of non-analytic strategies. To illustrate, try to solve the following problem: With only six matchsticks of equal length, create four equilateral triangles, each side of each triangle being equal to the length of a match. Presumably, most readers quickly recognised this problem as Scheerer's matchstick problem (presented earlier in the chapter). Also, most readers were presumably able to quickly recall that organising the six matchsticks in a three-dimensional pyramid provides an adequate solution. As a general rule, the more experience one has with these types of problems, the easier they become, because the more likely one is to have encountered a similar problem before. In fact, however, by definition, this "problem" is not a problem at all – the current state, goal state, and method for getting from one to the other were all known.

Medical professionals are in a similar position in that they quite often have no need to "reason" at all. There is no problem to be solved if the current case is so similar to a previously seen case that one simply knows the correct diagnosis and treatment. The term *non-analytic* was used to emphasise that this form of "reasoning" is believed to take place automatically, without intent, and often without awareness. A great deal of empirical evidence has accumulated, in fact, that suggests that more human behaviour and decision making is driven by non-conscious processes than most of us would intuit (Wilson, 2002; Bargh & Chartrand, 1999). Despite our tendencies to confabulate explanations for our behaviour, we appear to remain blissfully unaware of the real reasons for many of our actions and, in fact, can sometimes reduce our effectiveness if we try to verbalise reasons for our decisions (Wilson et al., 1993; Wilson, Hodges, & LaFleur, 1995). Within the medical domain, Norman and Brooks (1997) have been the predominant champions of non-analytic models of clinical reasoning. Brooks, Allen, and Norman (1991) revealed that diagnostic accuracy is higher for dermatological cases similar to those that have been seen before relative to perceptually distinct cases. Hatala, Norman, and Brooks (1999) further illustrated that this influence of similarity is likely unintentional as they were the first to show that diagnostically irrelevant similarities such as patient occupation also influence the diagnoses assigned to subsequent patients.

While sufficient evidence has accumulated to make the notion that non-analytic processing influences clinical decision making irrefutable, it would be inappropriate to imply that non-analytic processes or any one of the more analytic models of clinical reasoning is independently sufficient to capture the clinical reasoning process of experts (Custers, Regehr, & Norman, 1996). Consider the following: With only twelve matchsticks of equal length, create six squares, each side of each square being equal to the length of a match. While you are unlikely to have seen this particular problem before, I suspect you very quickly recognised its similarity to Scheerer's matchstick problem. Furthermore, I suspect that the same pattern recognition likely also led you to quickly recall the solution principle – using three dimensions – and attempt to apply it to this new problem. Still, reasoning through the problem likely required some conscious trial and error to arrive at a satisfactory conclusion as the solution details for this problem do not perfectly replicate those of the earlier example used.[2] In other words, the problem was solved by way of a coordination of analytic and non-analytic processes.

Schmidt, Norman, & Boshuizen. (1990) presented a developmental model of medical expertise in the early 1990s in which they suggested that novice clinicians rely predominantly on an understanding of basic science mechanisms and only later, through experience, come to rely heavily upon past exemplars when considering new cases. Again, however, it should be noted that more recent research has shown that (a) even the first few cases absolute novices encounter will influence subsequent diagnostic problem solving (Ark, Brooks, & Eva, 2006), and (b) when considering the influence on diagnostic accuracy, there is no interaction between level of expertise and type of reasoning used as a diagnostic strategy (i.e., experts perform better than novices, but the degree of difference is independent of the reasoning strategy used) (Coderre, Mandin, Harasym, & Fick, 2003; Norman & Eva, 2003). In other words, while the relative contributions of each form of reasoning may shift with experience, multiple processes appear to be active at all levels of expertise. Evidence is also accumulating that shows a strong relationship between performance on knowledge-based multiple choice exams and subsequent clinical success (Norcini, Lipner, & Kimpball, 2002), thereby further suggesting that knowledge is a more important determinant of ability than problem-solving "skill" and that differences in problem-solving approach across levels of expertise may be a matter of degree rather than a matter of strategy.

It is unlikely that a newly presenting patient will present exactly like a previously seen case and rarely will a real patient present exactly as the textbook rules suggest a patient with a particular disorder will present. As a result, Eva has argued that flexibility in approach is paramount to expertise in clinical decision making. In fact, various lines of research being carried out currently appear to suggest that excessive reliance on any one diagnostic strategy can be a source of diagnostic error much like becoming fixated on one set of assumptions was shown earlier to mislead problem solvers participating in early research on this topic.

First, at the level of trainee, we have been able to show that novice diagnosticians who are empowered to utilise multiple problem-solving strategies through simple instruction tend to outperform colleagues who are instructed to utilise a more focused approach (Ark, Borrks, & Eva, 2007). In a series of studies, psychology students were taught to diagnose electrocardiograms (ECGs). After receiving 1 hour of training in ECG interpretation, during which participants learned the 12-lead structure of ECGs and the features associated with up to 11 diagnostic categories, participants were randomly assigned to different practice conditions. Some were

---

[2]Create a cube by using eight matchsticks to form two squares and joining the corners of each square with the 4 remaining matchsticks. The top, bottom, and four sides of the cube form six squares.

told to be very analytic (i.e., to carefully consider the features presenting on each ECG and use the features to generate a diagnostic conclusion). Others were told to trust non-analytic processes (i.e., to diagnose based on any sense of familiarity they were experiencing as the familiarity might be due to the current ECG being similar to previously seen ECGs). Other participants still were given no instruction regarding how to proceed (i.e., they were left to adopt whatever reasoning strategy they thought seemed most appropriate). None of the participants in these groups performed as well on subsequent testing as groups of participants who were instructed to use a combined approach to clinical reasoning (i.e., to trust any sense of familiarity they felt, but to avoid "jumping the gun" by explicitly considering the features that were present). The advantage of the more flexible combined approach appears to be particularly pronounced with ECGs that are made difficult by biasing participants towards an incorrect diagnosis, either through clearly suggesting an incorrect diagnosis as a possibility or through directing attention to a feature consistent with the incorrect diagnosis (Eva, Hatala, LeBlanc & Brooks, 2007).

Second, research into the role of basic science in medical problem solving has revealed an interesting picture supportive of the claim that diagnostic expertise is heightened through the availability of multiple reasoning strategies. It is nearly ubiquitous, at least since the time of Flexner (1910), that medical training programmes devote a substantial amount of time to training students in basic sciences like biology, chemistry, and physics. However, when researchers first looked into the use of basic science, as it pertains to solving clinical problems, think aloud protocols suggested that the principles of basic science rarely constitute even part of experienced clinicians' reasoning processes (Boshuizen & Schmidt, 1992). Still, when difficult or ambiguous cases are encountered, there is some evidence that experts will revert to basic science explanations, reasoning from first principles as it were, and increase their levels of success as a result (Norman, Trott, Brooks, & Smith, 1994). Schmidt and Boshuizen (1993) have used tests of clinician memory to argue that basic biomedical knowledge becomes encapsulated within clinical knowledge and hence, is available, even if it is not often used in one's description of their thought processes (Eva, Norman, Neville, Wood, & Brooks, 2002). More directly, Woods, Brooks, & Norman (2005) have recently shown that, despite findings that suggest it is rare for basic science information to be explicitly required, training in the basic sciences does yield pedagogical benefit. Students given a basic science explanation of disease processes revealed increasing diagnostic accuracy over time whereas those trained simply with the probabilistic relationship between features and diagnoses suffered a decline in performance over the same 1-week period. Again, these findings indicate that basic science information may be used more often than clinicians are likely to express as it provides a mnemonic benefit that raw probabilities do not convey.

Finally, one can also look to the practice of more experienced medical professionals to observe the dangers of relying too heavily on any one diagnostic problem-solving process. It is logical to believe that the more experience one has, the more prior cases one can draw upon (unconsciously or otherwise) to help solve new problems. Again, most of the new problems experienced practitioners encounter will not be problems for them at all (as few as 1 in 100 cases according to an informal study performed by Norman (1988)). As such, one would not be surprised if, as suggested by Schmidt, et al., experienced clinicians came to rely more heavily on non-analytic processes like pattern recognition when making diagnostic decisions (Schmidt et al., 1990). It would appear, however, that this could cause problems when the pendulum swings too far in that direction (Eva, 2003). The Physician Review and Enhancement Program, operated by the College of Physicians and Surgeons of Ontario (Canada), has reported that age (years of experience) is the single best predictor of lessened clinical competence (Norman et al., 1993). That is not to say that all older physicians fail to maintain their abilities, but rather that the proportion of physicians who struggle rises with years since graduation. Caulford, et al. (1994) have further shown that the nature of the problems encountered tend to be errors that one would expect to arise as a result of premature closure (i.e., relying too heavily on one's first impressions): They include conducting abrupt interviews with many interruptions, and incomplete history taking. We have recently tested the hypothesis that more experienced physicians rely more heavily on their first impressions by experimentally varying the order in which clinical features were presented to physicians. When features consistent with pneumonia, for example, are presented in a case history before those consistent with pulmonary embolus, physicians with greater years of experience tend to be more confident that pneumonia is the correct diagnosis than do physicians with less experience. The same is true of pulmonary embolus when the order of features is reversed (Eva & Cunnington, 2006).

In summary, this section of the chapter has presented evidence that suggests multiple ways of solving clinical problems are available to diagnosticians and that these strategies are not mutually exclusive of one another. In fact, it is highly probable that multiple reasoning processes contribute to the final decisions reached for most problems (regardless of experience level). As a result, the optimal form of clinical reasoning should be considered to be a flexible interaction between many problem-solving strategies (the relative contribution of each being heavily dependent on context) and memory-based solutions that do not require problem solving at all. When professionals (and lay people alike) are most likely to meet with trouble is when they fall into the trap of the limited contractor who, having nothing but a hammer, treated the whole world like a nail. Clinical teachers should, therefore, strive to promote multiple forms of reasoning in combination, thereby leaving us with the problem of how to do so.

Using Problems to Solve the Problem of How to Teach Problem Solving

Despite the admonitions in the last section to be flexible in one's approach to new problems, it is still true that the most straightforward way to solve a problem is to remember how the problem was solved the last time it was encountered. That, in and of itself, however, does not ensure that analogies will be used even when they are available nor that the analogies that are available will necessarily provide the optimal solution. Consider two final problems: (1) Gick and Holyoak's (1983) fortress problem: A small country is ruled by a dictator who has built a strong fortress surrounded by farms and villages. A rebel general knew that his army was strong enough to capture the fortress, but he soon discovered that the dictator had planted weight-sensitive mines on each of the roads leading to the fortress. An explosion would destroy the road and many neighbouring villages. Small groups of troops were able to travel the road to the fortress, but not in great enough number to overthrow the dictator. How should the general proceed? (2) With twelve unbroken matchsticks of equal length, create exactly five squares.[3]

Particularly savvy readers will have recognised that Gick and Holyoak's problem is very similar to Duncker's radiation problem, as presented earlier in this chapter. The solution requires spreading the militant forces across multiple roads and then having each approach the fortress at the same time, thus avoiding having too much weight on any one road while also ensuring that enough force converges at the fortress to result in a successful operation. In other words, the principle of convergence, used to destroy the tumour in Duncker's problem by aiming sub-threshold rays at the target from multiple directions, can also be used to overthrow Gick and Holyoak's dictator. The reader who did not recognise the analogy, however, should take solace in the fact that (s)he is in the vast majority. Gick and Holyoak observed that only 10% of their participants were able to solve the radiation problem. When participants were presented with the fortress problem and its solution before presentation of the radiation problem (as was done here in the reverse order), the proportion of participants who were successful increased, but only to 30%. That is, over two-thirds of participants did not spontaneously recognise that the principle learned in the context of one problem could be applied to solve the other. The problem is clearly not one of the solution principles being too dissimilar, because 75% of participants were able to solve the tumour problem after being given the hint that the fortress problem was related.[4] Many other researchers have reported further evidence that participants do use analogies to solve problems, but that spontaneous, uninstructed use of analogies is quite rare.

That statement is surprising until one reflects carefully on all of the factors that must align to enable a potential problem solver to use spontaneous analogical transfer. Needham and Begg (1991) might have put it best when they said that, to use analogy to solve a target problem, one must "(1) encode the target problem in a way that (2) retrieves the encoded analogue and (3) selects the analogue rather than other information brought to mind during retrieval, and then (4) adapt the solution procedure from the analogue to the needs of the target problem". In other words, we encounter a lot of problems in our day-to-day lives and, unless a new problem

---

[3] Again, the reader is encouraged to pause and try to solve these problems before the answers are revealed later in the chapter.

[4] In fact the "hint" condition may be the most analogous to the way in which the problems were utilised in this chapter given that the context in which this section is presented may provide a sufficient hint.

is similar enough to a relevant old problem as to prompt both its recollection and awareness of how the solution can be adapted, that previous experience is unlikely to be of much help.

The basis on which we judge similarity may, therefore, create a challenge for us as problem solvers. Outside of medicine there is some evidence that suggests individuals with less experience in a particular content area are more likely to focus their attention on the superficial characteristics of a problem (e.g., the fact that radiation or military strategy is being considered) relative to those with experience who are more apt to categorise problems based on deeper principles (e.g., convergence) (Chi, Feltovitch, & Glaser, 1981; Novick & Holyack, 1991). The matchstick problem presented in this section (i.e., use 12 matchsticks to create exactly 5 squares) provides a further illustration of this phenomenon. To this point the reader has been presented with multiple matchstick problems in which the solution required working in three-dimensional space. The similarity of superficial features of the current problem with those prior examples likely led some readers in search of a way to adapt the same solution principle. In reality, however, a different strategy is required in this case. The solution is to create a "+" sign with four matchsticks and then to enclose the "+" sign with the remaining eight matchsticks to form what looks like a window (i.e., one large square with four smaller squares within it). Novice "eureka" problem solvers are likely to have spent more time trying to use the three-dimensional solution principle than are more experienced "eureka" problem solvers who are less likely to be swayed by the context created by "matchsticks". This also provides another example of the "fixation" problem discussed in the context of Luchins' work (presented earlier in this chapter).

Returning to the world of the professional, the million-dollar question is how can medical practitioners best take advantage of the lessons that experience provides? The simple answer remains that one becomes a better problem solver by experiencing a lot of problems. The more problems one has seen, the more likely it is that one of the problems will be remembered in a manner that facilitates solving the current problem. More interesting, however, is that it matters how one approaches the problems one has encountered. Needham and Begg presented research participants with training problems along with instruction either to study the problems with the purpose of (a) remembering the material, or (b) understanding the problem's solution (Needham & Begg, 1991). Those who worked towards understanding the solution were 20% more likely to accurately solve analogous test problems encountered later in the experimental session than were participants who simply tried to memorise the material. That was true regardless of whether the training problems were presented with solutions or as unsolved problems. Nor did it matter whether or not participants were successful in their problem-solving efforts. In other words, what matters is experience thinking about the problems in terms of their structure (as opposed to their surface characteristics), not having generated an accurate solution.

Clearly the deep structure that will be most useful in the future is not always readily discernible when new problems present, as illustrated with the various matchstick problems. For this reason, exposure to multiple problems can be said to be useful for more than just increasing the number of examples to which one can compare a new problem. A strategy known as contrastive learning is arguably the most successful strategy for enhancing transfer rates in problem solvers and is almost certainly one of the most extensively studied strategies (Catrambone & Holyoak, 1985 ; McKenzie, 1998; Gentner, Loewenstein, & Thompson, 2003). Contrastive learning involves prompting the learner to explicitly search for similarities and differences between problems. Doing so, it is thought, enables individuals to better avoid being distracted by the superficial elements of problems (e.g., the specific clinical presentation) by helping them understand the underlying deep structure (e.g., the pathophysiology of the disease) that enables the solution principle to be applied across variable problems. While some would argue that true analogical transfer can only succeed by virtue of making a comparison across the deep structural level of problems, we have recently shown that promotion of a contrastive learning style also helps students on tasks like ECG diagnosis by assisting them to learn which features discriminate most accurately between categories.

After learning the basics of ECG interpretation, participants were provided with a series of example cases from each of eight diagnostic categories. Participants in the contrastive learning condition were asked to explicitly compare diagnostic categories that were (a) similar by virtue of their having features in common and (b) known to be easily confusable based on the results of previous studies. For example, participants were asked to compare and contrast the features of ischemia with those of left ventricular hypertrophy with strain as both share ST depression and T wave inversions in many of the leads on an ECG. This instructional manipulation was contrasted with a non-contrastive condition in which normal practices were applied – participants were asked to learn (and identify) the features of each diagnostic category in sequence, as they would when working through most courses and textbooks (Stuyt, de Vries Robbe, & van der Meer, 2003). Prompting participants to highlight the similarities and differences between disorders in terms of the features present on an ECG appears to have promoted understanding of the diagnosticity of each symptom as participants in the contrastive learning condition revealed greater diagnostic accuracy at test than those in the non-contrastive learning condition, even after a 1-week delay.

In summary, this section has laid out an argument for why working diligently to understand the underlying principles that enable problems to be solved can facilitate future problem solving despite the inappropriateness of applying the word "skill" in terms of creating good generic problem solvers. Further strategies have been summarised by Eva, Neville, and Norman (1998), and an example of how this literature has been used to inform medical curriculum development is provided by the final report of McMaster University's task force on the MD program curriculum. Before concluding, however, it is important to reinforce two final points that were only implied in the preceding text. The first is that whereas analogical transfer is less likely to spontaneously lead to improved problem solving than one might intuit, simply accepting that one should explicitly consider analogies is also likely to be ineffective. Rather, many of the strategies outlined here require a deliberate effort on the part of the professional to learn what the underlying concepts are that make superficially distinct problems relevant to one another. Ericsson and colleagues (Ericsson, 2004) have demonstrated on repeated occasions, in variable contexts, the importance of *effortful*, individualised training on specific tasks, selected by qualified teachers, for the generation of expertise. Despite the recommendations provided by the literature with respect to general heuristics that might assist in solving problems, there are no magic bullets, and true ability to solve problems in a particular domain will only come from a conscious and concerted effort to better understand the underlying causal nature of the problems one has encountered to date.

Finally, it should be noted that "self-directed learning" has become a common value in the health professions despite widespread debate over whether or not adults are capable of self-directing their own learning (Regehr & Eva, 2006). At the root of the problem is an accumulation of evidence that we, as humans, are unable to accurately assess our abilities and, therefore, are unable to judge the extent of our learning needs or how successful our learning efforts have been (Eva & Regehr, 2005). As professionals we must strive to become better at solving the problems we face while recognising that we are often poorly positioned to judge whether or not our solution is indeed optimal. As such, it is essential to seek external guidance (be it from self-administered exams or collegial feedback) even when we are successful at generating seemingly satisfactory solutions. The first step towards becoming a "good problem solver" then may be to recognise that evaluating the quality of one's solutions is in and of itself a problem.

Summary and Discussion

Murray Gell-Mann, the American-born Nobel Prize winner in physics, is believed to have once described the problem-solving algorithm used by Richard Feynman, another American Nobel laureate, by suggesting that there are three steps involved: "(1) Write down the problem; (2) Think very hard; (3) Write down the answer." Were it only so easy for the rest of us there would be no need to talk of problem-solving skills and their relationship with professional practice. Fortunately, however, at least for those of us who are intrigued by the topic, problem solving is not that straightforward and, indeed, we still have much to learn.

This chapter has been written in an attempt to trace the evolution of the study of problem solving from its roots (laid down in the first 60 years or so of the twentieth century) as a pure method of inquiry into human thinking to the branch of professional pedagogy that it has sprouted. While problem-solving tendencies now appear to be somewhat domain specific, some general conclusions can be drawn.

First, problem solving is not a skill that one can possess: The overwhelming robustness of context specificity suggests that the problem-solving strategies we possess are not uniformly effective (or ineffective). Also, pure knowledge of a domain has been shown to be a better predictor of ability than any problem-solving variable. Taken together, these findings suggest that the professional community should focus more on the sorts of experiences its practitioners engage (and the learning that is derived) rather than trying to nurture a gaggle of good problem solvers.

Second, in many respects, the most experienced professionals should not be deemed to be problem solvers at all. The best predictor of success with a given problem is having seen the problem (or a similar one) before. Yes, there will be problems to solve even for the most experienced of professionals, but their quantity will be inversely related to experience.

Third, no professional, regardless of degree of experience, should get locked into any one particular way of problem solving. The feeling of "having seen it all before" can be deceptive in a manner that causes practitioners to fixate on one particular solution (i.e., diagnostic hypothesis) without collecting the data that would enable one to notice that more accurate solutions are available. Similarly, trainees should be empowered to "reason like professionals" by making them aware that many possible problem-solving strategies could be particularly useful for solving particular problems and that no one method, therefore, will be sufficient. Finally, despite the preceding conclusions, it is still appropriate as a professional community to pay specific attention to the construct of problem solving. There are deliberate educational strategies that one can adopt to raise the likelihood of successfully solving problems by the analogical transfer of previously seen solutions. In that context, however, the problems should be deemed as a means to the end of finding solutions rather than as a means to the end of creating good problem solvers.

References

Ark, T. K., Brooks, L. R., & Eva, K. W. (2006). Giving learners the best of both worlds: Do clinical teachers need to guard against teaching pattern recognition to novices? *Academic Medicine, 81*, 405–409.

Ark, T. K., Brooks, L. R., Eva, K. W. (2007). The benefits of flexibility: The pedagogical value of instructions to adopt multifaceted diagnostic reasoning strategies. *Medical Education, 41*(3), 281–287.

Bargh, J. A, & Chartrand, T. L. (1999). The unbearable automaticity of being. *American Psychologist, 54*, 462–479.

Barrows, H. S., & Feltovich, P. J. (1987). The clinical reasoning process. *Medical Education, 21*, 86–91.

Barrows, H. S, & Tamblyn, R. M. (1980). *Problem-based learning: An approach to medical education*. New York: Springer.

Berry, D. C., Broadbent, D. E. (1995). Implicit learning in the control of complex systems: A reconsideration of some earlier claims. In P. A. Frensch & J. Funke (Eds.), *Complex problem solving: The European perspective* (pp. 131–150). Hillsdale: Lawrence Erlbaum Associates.

Bordage, G., & Lemieux, M. (1990). Semantic structures and diagnostic thinking of experts and novices. *Academic Medicine, 66*, 70–72.

Boshuizen, H. P. A., Schmidt, H. G. (1992). Biomedical knowledge and clinical expertise. *Cognitive Science, 16*, 153–184.

Brooks, L. R., Allen S. W., & Norman, G. R. (1991). Role of specific similarity in a medical diagnostic task. *Journal of Experimental Psychology: General, 120*, 278–287.

Catrambone, R., & Holyoak, K. J. (1985). Overcoming contextual limitations in problem-solving transfer. *Journal of Experimental Psychology: Learning, Memory, and Cognition, 15*, 1147–1156.

Caulford, P. G., Lamb S. B., Kaigas, T. B., Hanna, E., Norman, G. R., & Davis, D. A. (1994). Physician incompetence: Specific problems and predictors. *Academic Medicine, 60*, 16–18.

Chase, W. G., Simon, H. A. (1973). Perception in chess. *Cognitive psychology, 4*, 55–81.

Chi, M. T. H., Feltovich, P. J., & Glaser, R. (1981). Categorisation and representation of physics problems by experts and novices. *Cognitive Science, 5*, 121–152.

Coderre, S., Mandin H., Harasym P. H, Fick G. H. (2003). Diagnostic reasoning strategies and diagnostic success. *Medical Education, 37*, 695–703.

Custers, E. J. F. M., Regehr, G., & Norman, G. R. (1996). Mental representations of medical diagnostic knowledge: A review. *Academic Medicine, 71*, 24–26.

de Groot, A. D. (1965). *Thought and choice in chess*. The Netherlands: Mouton.

Duncker, K. (1945) *On problem-solving*. Washington, DC: American Psychological Association.

Elieson, S. W., & Papa, F. J. (1994). The effects of various knowledge formats on diagnostic performance. *Academic Medicine, 69*, S81–S83.

Elstein, A. S., Shulman, L. S., & Sprafka, S. A. (1978). *Medical problem-solving: An analysis of clinical reasoning*. Cambridge: Harvard University Press.

Ericsson, K. A., & Simon, H. A. (1980). Verbal reports as data. *Psychological review, 87*, 215–252.

Ericsson, K. A. (2004). Deliberate practice and the acquisition and maintenance of expert performance in medicine and related domains. *Academic Medicine, 79*, 70–81.

Eva, K. W., Brooks, L. R., & Norman, G. R. (2002). Forward reasoning as a hallmark of expertise in medicine: Logical, psychological, and phenomenological inconsistencies. In S. P. Shohov (Ed.), *Advances in Psychological Research* (Vol. 8, pp. 41–69). New York: Nova Science Publishers.

Eva, K. W., Cunnington, J. P. W. (2006). The difficulty with experience: Does practice increase susceptibility to premature closure? *Journal of Continuing Education in the Health Professions, 26*(3), 192–198.

Eva, K. W., Hatala, R. M., LeBlanc, V. R., Brooks, L. R. (2007). Teaching from the clinical reasoning literature: Combined reasoning strategies help novice diagnosticians overcome misleading information. *Medical Education, 41*(12), 1152–1158.

Eva, K. W., Neville, A. J., & Norman, G. R. (1998). Exploring the etiology of content specificity: Factors influencing analogical transfer in problem solving. *Academic Medicine, 73*, 1–5.

Eva, K. W., Norman, G. R., Neville, A. J., Wood, T. J., & Brooks, L. R. (2002). Expert/Novice differences in memory: A reformulation. *Teaching and Learning in Medicine, 14*, 257–263.

Eva, K. W., & Regehr G. (2005). Self-assessment in the health professions: A reformulation and research agenda. *Academic Medicine*, 80, 46–54.

Eva, K. W. (2003). On the generality of specificity. *Medical Education, 37*, 587–588.

Eva, K. W. (2003). Stemming the tide: Implications of cognitive aging theories for continuing education in the health professions. *Journal for Continuing Education in the Health Professions, 23*, 133–140.

Eva, K. W. (2005). What every teacher should know about clinical reasoning. *Medical Education, 39*, 98–106.

Flexner, A. (1910). *Medical education in the United States and Canada*. New York: Carnegie Foundation.

Gentner, D., Loewenstein, J., Thompson, L. (2003). Learning and transfer: A general role for analogical encoding. *Journal of Educational Psychology, 95*, 393–408.

Gick, M. L., & Holyoak, K. J. (1983). Schema induction and analogical transfer. *Cognitive Psychology, 15*, 1–38.

Gleitman, H. (1991). *Psychology* (3rd Ed.), New York: W.W. Norton and Company.

Glucksberg, S. (1962). The influence of strength of drive on functional fixedness and perceptual recognition. *Journal of Experimental Psychology, 63*, 36–41.

Hatala, R. M., Norman, G. R., Brooks, L. R. (1999). Influence of a single example on subsequent electrocardiogram interpretation. *Teaching and Learning in Medicine, 11*, 110–117.

Luchins, A. (1942). Mechanisation in problem solving: The effect of Einstellung. *Psychological monographs, 54*(248).

Mandin, H., Jones, A., Woloschuk, W., Harasym P. (1997). Helping students learn to think like experts when solving clinical problems. *Academic Medicine*, *72*, 173–179.

Mayer, R. E. (1977). *Thinking and problem solving: An introduction to human cognition and learning*. Glenview, IL: Scott, Foresman, and Company.

McKenzie, C. R. M. (1998). Taking into account the strength of an alternative hypothesis. *Journal of Experimental Psychology: Learning, Memory, and Cognition*, *24*, 771–792.

Needham, D. R., & Begg, I. M. (1991). Problem-oriented training promotes spontaneous analogical transfer: Memory-oriented training promotes memory for training. *Memory and Cogntion*, *19*, 543–557.

Neufeld, V. R., Norman, G. R., Barrows, H. S., & Feightner, J. W. (1981). Clinical problem-solving of medical students: A longitudinal and cross-sectional analysis. *Medical Education*, *15*, 26–32.

Norcini, J. J., Lipner, R. S., & Kimball, H. R. (2002). Certifying examination performance and patient outcomes following acute myocardial infarction. *Medical Education*, *36*, 853–859.

Norman, G. R., Bordage, G., Page, G., & Keane, D. (2006). How specific is case specificity? *Medical Education*, *40*, 618–623.

Norman, G. R., & Brooks, L. R. (1997). The non-analytical basis of clinical reasoning. *Advances in Health Sciences Education*, *2*, 173–184.

Norman, G. R., Davis, D. A., Lamb, S., Hanna, E., Caulford, P., & Kaigas, T. (1993). Competency assessment of primary care physicians as part of a peer-review program. *JAMA*, *270*, 1046–1051.

Norman, G. R., & Eva, K. W. (2003). Doggie diagnosis, diagnostic success, and diagnostic reasoning strategies: An alternative view. *Medical Education*, *37*, 676–677.

Norman G. R., Trott, A. L., Brooks, L., & Smith, E. K. M. (1994). Cognitive differences in clinical reasoning related to postgraduate training. *Teaching and Learning in Medicine*, *6*, 114–120.

Norman, G. R., Tugwell, P., Feightner, J. W., Muzzin, L. J., & Jacoby, L. L. (1985). Knowledge and clinical problem-solving. *Medical Education*, *19*, 344–356.

Norman, G. R. (1988). Problem-solving skills, solving problems and problem-based learning. *Medical Education*, *22*, 279–286.

Norman, G. R. (2005). Research in clinical reasoning: Past history and current trends. *Medical Education*, *39*, 418–427.

Novick, L. R, & Holyoak, K. J. (1991). Mathematical problem solving by analogy. *Journal of Experimental Psychology: Learning, Memory, and Cognition*, *17*, 398–415.

Patel, V. L, Groen, G. J., & Arocha, J. F. (1990). Medical expertise as a function of task difficulty. *Memory and Cognition*, *18*, 394–406.

Patel, V. L., & Groen, G. J. (1986). Knowledge-based solution strategies in medical reasoning. *Cognitive Science*, *10*, 91–116.

Perkins, D. (2000). *The Eureka Effect: The art and logic of breakthrough thinking* . New York: W.W. Norton and Company.

Regehr, G., & Eva, K. (2006). Self-assessment, self-direction, and the self-regulating professional. *Clinical Orthopaedics and Related Research*, *449*, 34–38.

Reitman, W. R. (1965). *Cognition and thought: An information processing approach*. New York: Wiley.

Scheerer, M. (1963). Problem solving. *Scientific American*, *208*, 118–128.

Schmidt, H. G., & Boshuizen, H. P. A. (1993). On the origin of intermediate effects in clinical case recall. *Memory and Cognition*, *21*, 338–351.

Schmidt, H. G., Norman, G. R., & Boshuizen, H. P. A. (1990). A cognitive perspective on expertise: Theory and implications. *Academic Medicine*, *65*, 611–621.

Schnall, S. (1999). Life as the problem: Karl Duncker's Context. In *From Past to Future* (Vol. I). Worscester, MA: Frances L. Hiatt School of Psychology, Clark University.

Sternberg, R. J. (1995). Conceptions of expertise in complex problem solving: A comparison of alternative conceptions. In P.A. Frensch and J. Funke (Eds.), *Complex problem solving: The European perspective* (pp. 295–321). Hillsdale, NJ: Lawrence Erlbaum Associates.

Stuyt, P. M. J., de Vries Robbe, P. F., & van der Meer, J. W. M. (2003). Why don't medical textbooks teach? The lack of logic in the differential diagnosis. *The Netherlands Journal of Medicine, 61*, 383–387.

Wickelgren, W. A. (1974). *How to solve problems*. San Francisco, CA: Freeman.

Wilson, T. D., Hodges, S. D., & LaFleur, S. J. (1995). Effects of introspecting about reasons: Inferring attitudes from accessible thoughts. *Journal of Personality and Social Psychology, 69*, 16–28.

Wilson, T. D., Lisle D., Schooler J., Hodges S. D., Klaaren K. J., & LaFleur, S. J. (1993). Introspecting about reasons can reduce post-choice satisfaction. *Personality and Social Psychology Bulletin, 25*, 379–400.

Wilson, T. D. (2002). *Strangers to ourselves: Discovering the adaptive unconscious*. Cambridge, MA: The Belknap Press of Harvard University Press.

Woods, N. N., Brooks, L. R., Norman, G. R. (2005). The value of basic science. *Medical Education, 39*, 107–112.

Chapter 3
A Lens on Literacy: Workplace Competence and Professional Practice

Jean Searle

In this chapter, the focus will be on workplace literacies – that is, the use of spoken, written and viewed language as systems of meaning making in the workplace. In discussing the relevance for professional practice first the notion of competence will be problematised in terms of individual skill versus social practices, then the focus will turn to examples drawn from a number of workplace studies in which the literacies involved are examined. For the purposes of this chapter, the discussion will revolve around how individual workers make sense of workplace texts as well as considering language and literacies as workplace practices which are imbued with ideological significance. Examples are drawn from a number of workplace studies involving customer service operations, in the front offices in motels and at airline customer inquiry counters, as well as research concerning literacy and learning in the construction industry. Data from these studies then inform a discussion regarding learning and professional practice.

Conceptualising Literacy Competence

In this section, I will argue that the section title "conceptualising literacy competence" refers to a discourse[1] that locates all discussion of language and literacy in terms of an individual's knowledge or ability. However, this is only part of the story, one dominant in current vocational education and training systems that focus on productivity, competition and the reduction of knowledge to performative skill. This "autonomous" model of literacy (Street, 1996) privileges a unitary view of literacy as a decontextualised basic skill or "general competence". As a result, literacy is seen to be a technical method of achieving a practical purpose. In later sections, we shall see that this view underpins the introduction of competency-based training and associated literacy assessments to determine who needs what literacy training

J. Searle (✉)
Griffith University, Brisbane, Australia
e-mail: j.searle@griffith.edu.au

[1] Discourse: way of speaking/writing which reflects a particular view of the world.

C. Kanes (ed.), *Elaborating Professionalism*, Innovation and Change in Professional Education 5, DOI 10.1007/978-90-481-2605-7_3,
© Springer Science+Business Media B.V. 2010

either prior to training (bolted-on) or "built-in" to on-the-job training. An alternative "ideological" perspective (Street, 1996) would be one which is drawn from socio-cultural theories of language in use, with a focus on how people make meaning within particular social situations. In order to understand how these models of literacy were derived and what this might mean for language, literacy and learning, I shall start by outlining some reading and writing theories before exemplifying how these play out in particular work situations.

Autonomous Model – Reading Theories

A number of reading theories start from the premise that an individual has to learn how to process information systematically. Thus, a bottom-up model (Gough, 1972) proposes a movement from literally de-coding text features (letters or phonemes), through searching for pre-learnt structures which fit the incoming information, to an output of sound or meaning gained from recognition. Such a model underpins a basic skills or phonics approach to literacy learning. However, the focus of this model is on the neurological processing of information, which while important, does not acknowledge the role of experience or the tacit knowledge of language (grammar/syntax, semantics and so on) brought to the task by individuals. An alternative, top-down model, "analysis by synthesis" as proposed by Goodman (1967, 1985) and Smith (1971), suggests that readers begin by reviewing what is already known and in the process of analysis, individuals set up expectations, predict and make inferences about the meaning of the written text. They then use a range of semantic, syntactic or grapho-phonic "cues" within the text, to confirm or reject the predictions.

Building on this, the interactive model of reading (Ruddell & Speaker, 1985) acknowledges that reading performance is influenced not only by information processing by the reader but also by the nature of the text, the purpose for reading and the environment. Thus, this early model provided a link between reading as a skill and reading as a practice. Rather than reading being literally de-coding text, it began to be seen as being strategic, that readers would use different approaches to meaning making depending, for example, on whether the text was procedural or declarative. Further, it was recognised that authors usually organise their texts through use of a particular structure. One example would be the use of top-level-structure (Meyer, 1981) which suggests that all non-literary (expository or procedural) information may be en-coded, and subsequently de-coded, utilising one of four structures: list, comparison, problem–solution or cause–effect. Thus, one strategy for meaning making would be to recognise the particular structure in use in the text as it relates to the purpose for reading. Moreover, it was contended that effective readers also monitor their meaning making as they read. Not only are such individuals able to identify the purpose of the task, but they also have the ability to sift through a repertoire of resources to select the most appropriate strategy, while at the same time monitoring their performance – as we shall see in some workplace examples in a later section.

Another advance on the autonomous view of reading is found in the work of Mikulecky (1982, 1984) who argued that literacy is a variable construct. For example, Diehl and Mikulecky (1980) found that the level of reading ability required for successful performance in the workplace varied according to the job and, moreover, that the actual reading practices also varied with context. Mikulecky demonstrated that transference of literacy practices from school (mainly "reading-to-learn") to out-of-school and work contexts in which reading is used as an aid to performance (reading-to-do), "is severely limited by differences in format, social support networks and required background information" (Mikulecky, 1990, p. 25).

Nevertheless, in recent times, many governments, concerned with the management of the economy and associated skills development, have returned to a recycled autonomous model of learning: this time, in the form of auditing individuals' competencies and competency-based training. This view of learning constructs education as an assembly line producing human skills and capacities. It also allows for the codification of knowledge, so that educational outcomes can be stated in advance and individual performance assessed, in relation to these objectives, reported and audited. From this perspective, literacy is perceived to be a tool or conduit for performance, a means of en-coding and de-coding information, a general skill or key competency. It is this view which is held by those who espouse a "bolted-on" approach to literacy skills development prior to vocational education and training. That is, that the purpose of education is to ensure that students or trainees have general literacy skills first, then training can be undertaken. The assumptions are firstly, that there are "general" literacy skills and secondly, that these skills will transfer to different situations but, as we will see, literacy in the workplace is not that simple.

Ideological Model

In contrast to the autonomous model of literacy, the "New Literacy Studies" movement takes an ideological approach that is grounded in the seminal ethnographies of communication of Scribner and Cole (1981) in Liberia and Street (1984) in Iran, and in the detailed studies of everyday literacies of Brice Heath (1983) and Taylor and Dorsey-Gaines (1988). Rather than concentrating on the cognitive aspects of how individuals learn to read or write, these studies focused on how literacy was used in the home or community. As a result, new theories of language and literacy, and new research methodologies emerged which have informed the more recent work of Barton and Hamilton (1998) in relation to community literacies, Prinsloo and Breier (1996) and colleagues in South African communities, and Gowen (1995), Hull (1995, 1997), Gee and Lankshear (1997) and Jackson (2000) in the workplace. These researchers argue that "literacy" cannot be treated either as "neutral" or as "technical", neither can literacy be generalised across contexts. Rather, uses of literacy are meaningful; they are embedded within social situations and have implications for power relations. In other words, *how* literacy is used depends on the context and the relationships among participants. In fact, given that the meanings derived from literacy depend upon the social context in which they are embedded, and that the particular speaking, reading and writing practices involved depend upon social structures within that context, then there cannot be a single, autonomous "literacy". It would be more appropriate to refer to multiple "literacies".

However, some would argue that the very notion of context as somehow circum-scribing spoken or written language is also problematic (Edwards & Fowler, 2005). Often a narrow view of context leads to a reified view of literacy such that those literacies and practices which are associated with formal learning, in school or other educational institutions are valued, while those which are practised in the commu-nity or some workplaces have lesser worth. Barton and Hamilton (1998) first raised this issue when they explored the nexus between what they refer to as public lit-eracies (institutional literacies) and vernacular literacies (personal local literacies) and what this meant for members of a community in England, while Castleton and McDonald (2002) conducted a similar but smaller study in Australia. What emerged was evidence to suggest that ability with certain literacies gave individuals access to more power or status, or in Gee's (1996) terms, access to social "goods", good jobs, good income and social status.

The New London Group (Cope & Kalantzis 1995, 2000) take this a step further in recognising the different domains in which individuals operate (working lives, public lives, private lives and, increasingly, virtual lives) as well as the pluralistic nature of Western societies. They reconceptualised literacy in terms of available designs, the process of designing, and the outcome or "redesigned", all of which require multiple literacies. Members of this group of researchers use the term *mul-tiliteracies* in attempting to capture how individuals operate within the different, often multimodal, domains. For example, Kress and Van Leeuwen (2001, 2003) are interested in the processes of designing and redesigning images in print and online, while Gee (2003) is reconceptualising learning and identity as they occur in the virtual domains of computer video games.

The New London Group are also concerned about the implications of workplace reforms and the emergence of *fast capitalism* (Gee & Lankshear, 1997), a term taken from business management, based on the design and production of high quality, often customised, goods and services, produced by smart workers in "enchanted workplaces" (p. 83). In these workplaces, the roles and responsibilities once held by middle management are now passed on to frontline workers, who transform them-selves into committed partners in the enterprise. As we shall see in examples from the construction industry, this has had an enormous impact on the world of work and workplace literacies. The importance of such research is that it goes beyond the economic imperative to produce knowledge workers, to investigate what this means for marginalised workers. More recent research (Falk, 2001) also explores the links between literacy and lifelong learning and the development of civic responsibility or social capital within communities.

The Four Resources Model

In a move to bridge the divide between cognitive and socio-linguistic approaches to reading, Freebody and Luke (1990) and Luke, Freebody, and Land (2000) focused their research on the resources required by the individual when engaging in a range of literacy practices. So, rather than advocating the primacy of a particular theory or strategy in understanding how people read or at which point an individual might be considered to be "literate", they argue that people select from a "repertoire" of resources and literate practices used for different purposes. So, for example, to be a successful reader, a person would need to be able to use each of the following four related resources. The first resource is the ability to literally de-code text, drawing on cognitive skills as well as knowledge of word meanings. Even good readers use this ability at times when words or texts are unfamiliar, or in the case of airline staff, when they are constructing or deconstructing fare codes. The second resource is having a repertoire of reading strategies on which to draw in order to make sense of text. Thirdly, the individual requires the ability to use language appropriately to participate in the social practices of the workplace or community. Finally, it is important that individuals possess knowledge of how to analyse texts. That is, readers need to become aware of the ideological nature of texts, how texts are often used to position the reader in certain ways or are constructed in the interests of others. For example, the implementation of quality assurance measures in many workplaces requires that workers understand and comply with documentation relating to compliance with standard operating procedures, government and industry regulations, as well as texts related to safety, risk and performance monitoring (Jackson, 2000). In order to comply, readers bring a combination of the above four resources and their "interpretive procedures" (Fairclough, 2001) to meaning making. Interpretive procedures include knowledge of the institutional social order (the specific workplace), the situational context (the front office, or work site) and the intertextual context (knowledge of work practices and spoken, written or viewed texts). That is, workers will predict the meaning of a workplace text by drawing on the four resources as well as associating the overall structure of the text with those known to be integral to a social practice, within the particular context. For example, computer programs and databases are used in many industries. Because they are often multi-user, the design or structure of the program/database is given, so there are few opportunities for workers to redesign these texts. However, workers do bring critical literacy skills to the interpretation and processing of online data. In order to further understand how they do this it is useful to briefly outline genre theory.

Genre Theory

A socio-cultural approach to understanding how language is used was also taken by Halliday (1985) who, influenced in part by the work of anthropologists such as Malinowski, argued that language use is an integral part of social interactions. That is, language and literacy should be seen as social practices which cannot be separated from their contexts of use. As such, language is functional; it has a purpose, that of making, conveying and interpreting meaning. But language is also systemic; that is, language as a resource for meaning making is also a system of choices. Further, through the concept of "register", it is possible to account for the overall structure of resulting texts, as these are determined by a combination of variables within a specific social situation. These variables, or metafunctions, include firstly, the words used to name the topic being written or spoken about (ideational meta-function), for example at the front office in motels "Checking-out a guest"; secondly, the words used to communicate the mood (statement, question or directive) "Have you used anything from the mini-bar?" and modality – the relationship among the participants in an exchange (interpersonal metafunction), for example the decision to refer to the guest by name or use the more formal "Sir/Madam"; and thirdly, the structure of the text (genre), which will vary depending on whether it is spoken, written or viewed (textual metafunction). As a result, the external context and social practice will affect the internal text structure or genre. In practice this means that motel staff, for instance, would expect certain types of text to be in use in the front office. They would also have an expectation about the overall structure of each type of text (the genre) as each would reflect the purpose for which it is used. This means that experienced motel staff would have no difficulty in distinguishing between a guest registration form and a housemaid's instruction form. It will be shown later that experienced office staff, regularly bring this tacit knowledge of workplace texts to bear on the task. In other words, drawing on the work of Bakhtin (1953, 1986) the principle of "intertextuality" is used to demonstrate that in order for any text, utter-ance or action to be interpreted meaningfully, it must be read against the background of other texts and operations within the specific context or social situation. Thus the social theory of genres recognises that language and literacy use is a purpose-ful, staged, goal-orientated action which cannot be separated from its socio-cultural context.

Ideological Nature of Workplace Texts

In workplaces, it must be recognised that the generic (from genre) structure of texts can, and often does have, a normalising effect. For example, in some workplaces the use of such texts may become routinised to such an extent that they perform an ide-ological role, for example, in determining what information is deemed important (or omitted) for a range of purposes (for auditing, accountability, standardisation, etc) and agendas (responsibility being passed down to individual workers, to comply with government, industry or corporate agendas). In the construction industry, liter-acy is seen as an enabling skill, useful to maintain the social order of the workplace (Kelly & Searle, 2000; Searle & Kelly, 2002). This was articulated by the train-ing coordinator of one construction company in terms of signing off on "Pre-Start Checks for equipment".

> "A bloke gets on a dozer in the morning, he does his pre-start bla bla bla and away he goes. Now again if he has literacy problems, is he actually understanding what is supposed to be in there or is he ticking the box so it keeps him out of trouble?" (Searle & Kelly, 2002, p. 50)

But it is not just a question of de-coding or "understanding what it says on paper". In the "high performance" workplace the bottom line is getting the job done, right the first time, safely, thus reducing costs and providing an audit trail of account-ability. As a result, workplace texts (e.g., forms, standards and procedures) are pre-designed by government, industry groups or enterprise management, for com-pliance by staff. The penalty for non-compliance is separation. For example, one construction worker "didn't follow the [company] philosophy and wanted to do his own thing ... so they decided that perhaps he wasn't the man for them".

In Freebody and Luke's (1990, 2003) terms, construction workers are required to go beyond being "code breakers"; they must be proficient users of text, that is, knowing how to read a range of texts for different purposes, while at the same time knowing how to use language and literacy appropriately in order to contribute to "Work Activity Briefings" with the engineer, project manager and other team members. The Systems Manager commented on this when he argued that

> "... good communication skills remain a core basic requirement for a good outcome, [because] we've got things like Work Activity Briefings and Job Safety Analyses that we do. We record or document those, and more and more we're trying to thrust that respon-sibility back down the workforce, to the people that carry out the work." (Searle & Kelly, 2002, p. 71)

So, from an ideological perspective, literacy is also about being able to participate successfully in what is considered by the company to be "workplace communica-tion", that is, engaging in the social practices of the workplace. While from the company perspective this is seen as being transformative for workers, the above example suggests that it is also constraining.

In the next section, data from studies of language and literacy in the hospitality and airline industries will be used to demonstrate how workers draw upon a reper-toire of resources and interpretive procedures to make meaning from workplace texts and utilise them in a range of workplace practices.

Identifying General and Site-Specific Knowledge in Workplaces

Method

In order to conceptualise the nature of meaning making in the workplace a num-ber of workplace studies were conducted. Data were collected from observations in the front offices of a number of motels (Searle, 1996) and airline customer inquiry counters (Searle, 1997) as well as on site and in training rooms in the construction industry (Kelly & Searle, 2000; Searle & Kelly, 2002). Data were obtained through a combination of prolonged observations of activities at each site; the collection of artefacts and documents; and informal interviews with key informants.

Data from the hospitality and airline industries were classified firstly into actions, for example those related to transactional office procedures. Secondly, each action was analysed in terms of the component operations which related to site-specific contexts. For example an action such as "checking-in a guest" might include a number of operations such as "greeting the guest", "checking the reservation", "requesting guest information", "requesting a credit card imprint", "issuing a key", "offering directions to the room/use of a porter", and "closing the action". In addition, for each operation, the language and literacy skills used were grouped into those which might be considered "general" skills and those which were site specific. Data from the construction industry were analysed in relation to company training policies, the implementation of competency-based training and, for one company, the movement towards becoming a learning organisation. Emerging from all the data was a tension between what might be referred to as general or basic skills and site-specific literacy competences.[2]

General Skills and Site-Specific Literacy Competences

The following example (Table 3.1) is an extract from a transcript of interview with a service officer (SO) at an airline customer inquiry counter. This example concerns an action "Dealing with a telex". The SO outlines the task first and then works on one telex (a hard copy relating to a computer record) dealing with a Frequent Flyer Redemption ticket. The different text types or genres being referred to in the transcript below are the telex about a Frequent Flyer Redemption ticket (hard copy), a "bring up file: today's actions" (computer record), a Personal Name Record which should have the same information as the telex (computer record), and reference made to a valid ticket. Each of these texts or genres has its own "generic" structure and one of the issues outlined below relates to what the SO refers to as an incorrect "format" (or generic structure).

The picture that emerges from this example, in which a valid ticket is generated, is one of highly complex interactions among the social order (in this case the airline industry), the particular social setting (the customer inquiry counter), the service officer as agent and the texts (telex and computer record). What should not be overlooked is the ability of the service officer to move from printed text (hard copy) to the visualised form on screen, while at the same time giving a spoken commentary. This interaction, which takes place among different semiotic modes, could make high cognitive demands on the individual in order to process the multiple representations of data. In the above example, the service officer was inputting data, manipulating data, and trying to develop complex relationships among data on the basis of limited information and within fairly rigid database structures in order to achieve the end result – the construction of a transactional text.

If we now examine this event from the perspective of which resources would be required by the service officer during this event, a number of tensions are apparent. For example, it is clear that the service officer requires the resources associated with the general skills of de-coding and re-coding information, such as those used

---

[2]Literacy teachers and researchers deliberately use the term *competence* which connects knowledge and performance with social goals in a particular context instead of *competency* which often connotes decontextualised skills.

Table 3.1 Extract "Dealing with a telex" from transcript of a commentary in the airline industry

Transcript	General skill	Comment
I'm just sorting through some of the telexes we had in the what we call the "bring up file" which is "today"s actions' ... and seeing what status they have; whether they have been completely repaired or whether we still need to do anything with it. Just checking where they're up to basically ...	Sorting Checking status	A routine task which requires prior knowledge of a) the task b) the site-specific texts c) what features to check.
These telexes are delivered to our printer and they're put away. Mostly we try to action them as soon as they come up or on the same day at the very least ... and then they're put into the day that's relevant to the day that they'll actually be like the ticket issued or the person'll turn up ...	Filing by date of future use	While the principles of filing might be considered a general skill, in this case the goal and operation are site specific and come at the end of an action.
This is ... a Personal Name Record (PNR) – a computer record and this (telex) is just a hard copy of exactly the same thing. So what I am doing now is just checking to make sure that that hasn't changed. It's what is reflected here. This is actually a Frequent Flyer Redemption ticket which is frequent flyer points so they don't actually pay for the ticket. Taxes and things still apply so we'll still need to get some money ... for that. I better correct details. Sometimes these are set up for us by Frequent Flyer and sometimes not. At the moment I'm going to have to correct some of the details because they're not quite right ...	Identify PNR Checking for changes Identifying incorrect details	The PNR (computer record) and the telex are general texts; however, the specific language features change. As such the SO needs prior knowledge of the genre in order to predict what text should be present, as well as the ability to check specific details, which are combinations of words and codes.
I haven't actually changed anything yet ... what they haven't done is put this into the normal format ... so I'm just correcting the format so we're ready to go. It will still print this way ... but the autoticket readers that we have in our revenue department ... won't work on what they've put in ... it's got to be in the standard format ...	Recognises incorrect genre	This is an example of the "normalising" effect of genres – in this case for the standardisation of processing. However the SO needs knowledge of "intertextuality" to critically evaluate the present text against the normal genre.

Table 3.1 (continued)

Transcript	General skill	Comment
[So, that's saying] Brisbane, Sydney to Canberra no charge and then back to Brisbane no charge. Actually I should have (( )). So that's Brisbane to Canberra and then Sydney to Brisbane . . .	Reading as literally de-coding airline codes, then re-coding data	The basic skills of de-coding and re-coding are only operationalised as a result of critical analysis of a specific text.
These NUCs are what we call "Neutral Units of Construction" which are basically the techniques that is used. So no matter what country you're working from . . . you still end up with . . . I've run out of line space . . . you will always end up with the same numbers, theoretically . . .	Numeracy (NUCs used instead of calculating exchange rates)	While individually the skills being demonstrated might be considered general or even basic skills they are very seldom used in isolation: a) the SO is monitoring several things at once: PNR, telex, NUCs.
. . . This is all coded in formats which bear no relation at all to how it will appear on the ticket format. . .	Knowledge of genres	b) the SO is working in a multimodal semiotic: hard copy print, computer displays.
. . . there are four lines available now. It was just making sure that there wasn't already something on line two because you can't put something there . . . you can't make an "original entry" if is something already there. You can't make a "change entry" if there isn't something there . . .	Prior knowledge of rules of data entry	A text user will arrive at an interpretation partly on the basis of the situational context. In this case the institutional social order has prescribed certain rules and therefore only certain operations are possible.
This code here is for the taxes that are the same here [telex]. There you go . . . that's the response you get when you try to put in something with a change if it's not already there. These keyboards are quite different to the other ones so it does take a bit of getting used to. Also the logic by which they operate is a little different . . . . You can't do it like Word Perfect or Lotus and just go straight to the end. . . I shouldn't have that in there. What I'm looking to do is just make sure that everything's there so that the ticket can just be printed straight off the itinerary . . . I'll check the itinerary once more. So now we can just save that . . .	De-coding

Problems with transfer of general knowledge | The SO refers to the intertextual context and then operates on the basis of assumptions about previous discourses and experiences. In making her interpretation, the SO observes that she could have drawn on interpretations from other domains as part of her "resources". However she recognises that there is a problem with transfer. |

Table 3.1 (continued)

Transcript	General skill	Comment
If the passenger turns up here now, we will just retrieve the PNR and say "Is this what you want to do?" and then tell them that they've got to pay the taxes, tell them how much it will be, enter the form of payment for the taxes and print the ticket . . .	Generic structure of spoken language transaction	As a text user, the SO can quickly summarise the stages of a spoken language transaction, based on an interpretation of the context and an interpretation of the text.

in constructing Neutral Units of Construction. But in practice, because these skills are not used in isolation, they are in effect interpretive procedures used by the service officer to relate them to a specific text ("This is all coded in formats which bear no relation at all to how it will appear on the ticket format") and a particular task (in this case knowing the rules in relation to data entry). In addition, she needs the ability to sift through her available resources and interpretive procedures and decide which should be applied. However, it is apparent that certain resources developed to operate in one context do not neatly transfer to another ("These keyboards are quite different to the other ones so it does take a bit of getting used to. Also the logic by which they operate is a little different"). In this example, the texts are pre-designed by the company to ensure the efficient operation of airline ticketing. Staff are aware that the texts are constructed for particular purposes, usually by management, and as such represent one or more value systems, such as, efficiency, accuracy or accountability; for example, the SO commented "You have to have standard formats or you'd have people putting anything in these computers. . . . [It's] not just us that read them either." So, not only does the service officer require knowledge of those resources related to organisational or systemic genres, she also needs an awareness of company values.

The second example (Table 3.2) is taken from the hospitality industry. The following is an extract from a transcript from a front office in a motel. The staff member, Steven, is discussing the problem of whether a motel guest has paid for accommodation and checked out as the information does not appear to have been entered into the database.

Again, what is important here is that similar to the airline service officer, in the motel the staff member sifts through his own resources and interpretive procedures to decide which reading strategies might be useful to make sense of the available data, and to work his way through the problem, in this case without resolution. Thus, we have an example of an employee who is aware of company values, in this case accuracy and efficiency (has a guest payment been made?) but is having difficulty with the pre-designed nature of workplace texts, as these do not provide an immediate way forward. In short, a tension, as illustrated in the above example, revolves around the problem of what to do when the strategies fail. It was observed that the staff used a range of interpretive procedures to enhance their

Table 3.2 Extract "Check-out problem" from transcript in the hospitality industry

Transcript	General skill	Comment
So we have a problem where this one hasn't been City Ledger [a motel: editor] Researcher: How do you know it should be? Because that was part of the group relating to . . . It was relating to this group here, . . . Room 29.	Problem-solving	The staff member, realises there is a problem (using site specific knowledge)
Researcher: And how do you know that? Just because I had it all attached together and also from the rooming list, so I will check the rooming list . . . that's his name there okay. So I will have to follow that through and find out why it hasn't appeared. It has got me intrigued because everybody has checked out, we've already done a "Due-outs" and everybody's checked out – there is no payment received for that, at least I don't think so. There is no payment on there. At the moment though all of these check out with my report so I will just put that on there. I am going to be doing another one of those anyway so.	Scanning for specific information Flipping through screens looking for specific alpha-numeric coded data	Databases are "designed" to store vast amounts of information that can be accessed in multiple visual displays. While the database may be considered as generic in overall structure, the operator needs knowledge of the site-specific codings and applications to search for meaningful data.
Researcher: So what will you do with that, just leave that there? I will just have a look at these – these up in Lisa's office. What I am going to do is I am just going to reproduce the folio just to find out what he is doing. I might just go in first and check on the update which is where the reservation, where we updated it before – just see what the status is.	Reproducing the folio Checking codes	Prior knowledge of the database utilised to confirm "given" information in order to scope the problem. Reference to intertextuality.
Now with this here it has got a status. I am going in here, this is actually an activity status, meaning, where it is in our system, if it was "I" it would mean that it is in-house, if it is "R" it's Reservation, if it's "O" it is checked out ( ) cancellation, so he's actually been checked out, so it is out of the system. The dates correspond, 10 and 12 so I am intrigued to find out where it's gone. So I will get out of it and I will just reproduce the file and see if actually payment has been made on it. This is the time when I came . . .	Checking the activity status. Confirming guest has checked out. Reproducing file to check for payment.	Reference to an understanding of "systems of genres" (see below). By working through known text structures it may be possible to locate specific features that should be present. In terms of situated practice, this problem-solving activity takes place seamlessly, despite the phone interruption.

Table 3.2   (continued)

Transcript	General skill	Comment
[Phone ringing] "Reception this is Steven. Yes, Steven, I just had a call from ( ) Yes I am on my way back I will be there in 10 min."		
I will put in the synonyms, I will just check – I can't remember what code it's under – this is an instance where I can't remember – just have a look.	Use of synonyms (e.g., RGF).	In this instance, the member of staff is aware that the database is governed by a set of rules. When he can't remember the specific rule he is forced to rely on other strategies. This produces some information but not what he is searching for. The final strategy is to ask the supervisor.
Researcher: So you're going through synonym choices?	Use of numeric codes.	
That's right. "Reproduce Guest Folio" – so it's simply RGF. Put in the folio number and I will just try and find out whether or not payment has been made on them. O.K. – well we've got the balance ( ) which relates to what I've got there, but it hasn't appeared anywhere. So this is a job for the supervisor I think – unless I've overlooked something.	Checking the balance & matching with other data.	

performance on the job. The staff were required to update their knowledge regularly but rather than relying on access to their resources or general strategies such as referring to procedural manuals, many had developed their own ways of organising information through the use of heuristics, personalised files or personal organisers. Another example of organising a task occurred when an airline SO dealing with a particular problem had not completed the task before the end of the shift, and another officer had to take over. This was possible because of the given design or overall generic structure of the texts with which they have to work. However, as the specific details vary with each airline ticket or guest payment, it was found to be more efficient and less stressful for the person taking over, if a brief explanation of the problem and what had been done so far, was presented as a written text.

As each element within this complex system is unpacked in the next section, it will become evident that indeed the concept of general skills is over-simplistic.

Mal-Alignments of General Labels and Actual Practices

From the previous examples it is possible to label certain of the skills observed in the workplace as being "general" (see centre column of tables). However, this classification is still problematic firstly, because these skills do not exist in isolation from a range of other skills and practices, and secondly, because the literacies involved are highly situated. So, for example, front office motel staff require an understanding of what Bazerman (1994, p. 97) refers to as "systems of genres", that is knowledge of how genres interrelate. In any given action "only a limited range of genres may appropriately follow upon another in particular settings, because the success conditions of the actions [operations] of each require various states of affairs to exist" (p. 98). Thus in the above example, issuing a valid ticket required an investigation of several interrelated genres starting with the arrival of the telex which generated an operation (looking up "Today"s actions') followed by another operation, accessing the Personal Name Record (PNR) computer record, in order to check and re-format the information to enable a valid ticket to be issued. Further, the operations associated with these print or electronic genres would require the use of the appropriate spoken language genre associated with a transaction: that is, a greeting, a request for a ticket, a request for identification and so on. So, not only does the service officer require a knowledge of the texts and practices of the airline industry, she also requires a range of spoken language genres, reading and interpreting resources for print and electronic texts, as well as the necessary interpretive procedures to sift among the available resources and select one or more which appear to be the most appropriate for a particular purpose.

In both the front offices of motels and at the airline customer inquiry counter, staff regularly have to operate in a multimodal environment and were observed to be using the basic skill of de-coding. For routine tasks, reading as a skill involved the cross-referencing of names and codes between hard (print) copy and screen; scanning for names and codes; scrolling computer screens and flipping between screens in search of codes. However, as the example of "Dealing with a telex" demonstrates there is much more to reading and interpreting than just de-coding and re-coding. For example, the information presented on an airline ticket appears as a series of abbreviations and codes: QF = QANTAS Flight, DOM = domestic and AUD = Australian dollars. There is also a range of "class of travel" codes and fare calculation codes to be de-coded and en-coded. So, in order to complete the task of "repairing" a Personal Name Record (PNR) the service officer also needs to take on the role of text participant and text user. That is, bringing her prior knowledge of the text (PRN genre) to bear on the task, recognising the data were incorrect and incomplete, and then drawing on other resources to resolve the task. Thus the process becomes iterative and intertextual – from a predication based on prior knowledge of the particular genre, to checking of specific language features, back to a modified structure which is acceptable to external processes. Similarly, in attempting to resolve the problem of a guest check-out and payment, the front office staff member went beyond de-coding to draw on other resources to activating prior knowledge (in this case, knowledge of front office systems as applied to this particular site).

However, if the above actions are analysed as examples of socially situated practices, not only is it insufficient to focus purely on the general skills or competencies which an individual may, or may not, possess, the practice itself needs to be set against the institutional social order, the particular workplace discourses and the implied social relations. As with the earlier example of the construction industry, the discourses of both the hospitality and airline industries reflect the values of profitability, safety, reliability, efficiency, customer service and so on (Stevenson, 2002). As a result, systems are implemented to audit, systematise or standardise operations. Thus, in the social situation of the customer inquiry counter, systems such as the rules governing fare structures, print genres and computerised databases are all prescribed with little room for modification by the SO. In this sense such discourses are ideological as they become normalised within the workplace and do not allow for alternative interpretations. As Franklin (cited in Bigum & Green, 1993, p. 7) argued

> The ordering that prescriptive technologies has caused has now moved from ordering at work and the ordering of work, to the prescriptive ordering of people in a wide variety of situations.

This then affects how the SO is positioned in relation both to the company and the discourses. It also explains why new staff that may come with differing interpretative frameworks may have difficulty in adjusting to the new context. Although users are aware of links in hypertext (that whether they "click on" or "highlight" a word or an icon it will still result in the same new screen), not every user is aware that such links are not the same and do not imply the same semic relationship. The associations involved can be quite idiosyncratic and in many cases (particularly in workplaces) the relationships reflect the tacit assumptions and values of the software designer (Burbules, 1997). One informant in the airliner industry explained the problem as follows:

> "These key boards are quite different to the other ones, so it does take a bit of getting used to . . . Also the logic by which they operate is a little different. See, the other one will ignore everything to the right of where your cursor is when you make an entry but this one won't. You have to go over to the end manually. You can't do it like Word or Lotus and just go straight to the end." (Searle, 1997, p. 35)

What emerged from the research in the airline, hospitality and construction industries was that there is some recognition within these industries of literacy as being a "general" or "enabling" skill, as a key competency in reproducing codified knowledge. However, the individual literacies which underpin organisational communication, and the staff attitudes and dispositions in relation to company or industry values, are not as recognised and yet are crucial to successful communicative performance. These issues will be taken up in the next section.

Explaining Professional Literacy

What Is Learning?

If we accept that to engage in any literate practice an individual must adopt one or more roles (Freebody & Luke, 1990, 2003) then learning must have something to do with knowing: how language is constructed (the mechanics of de-coding and en-coding); how language works (spoken, written and viewed genres); how language is used purposefully (to convey meaning) and how language is ideological (value laden). Learning then becomes developing a knowledge of a range of possible discourse patterns and generic structures which may be produced or interpreted within specific contexts, while acknowledging that discourses and genres are not static but are products of continually changing social institutions. In addition, learning incorporates the development of, firstly, a repertoire of resources or strategic approaches to reading, writing, speaking and viewing across a range of texts, and secondly, the development of interpretive procedures such as, a knowledge of purpose (for reading, writing and viewing) and the ability to be strategic – to choose appropriate strategies for the task. Of crucial importance is the ability to relate the text to the context – to say or write the right thing at the right time and to interpret data appropriately.

> "... knowing how to handle someone when they're coming up and yelling and screaming at you because they're desperate - they missed their flight - you've just got to know how to deal with them and try and reassure them that they will get there" (Searle, 1997, p. 41).

It is in the interests of employers if their employees are able to master those competencies required on-the-job through online or pre-packaged modules in their own time. However, the move to commodify learning as sets of competencies reifies certain "given" types of knowledge. As a result "self-directed learning" often becomes compliance with externally valued or top-down sanctioned sets of skills directly related to corporate goals and mission statements. Further, while such packaging of skills is convenient for auditing and accountability purposes, for this type of learning to succeed, workers must be convinced that it is their interests to comply with the "visionary" leaders, that is, buying into the rhetoric. The concept of the learning organisation where the leaders become "champions" and the workers form project teams which are "empowered" to make decisions, thus arises.

> "One of the things that came out of the training summit was a brief that we will ensure that we can do everything we can to make people the best they can be in their roles. ... It's continuous improvement. Within this company it's from the very top down to the very bottom. Our Managing Director; he probably drives the culture...but again that culture permeates down through the company – our supervisors, foremen and superintendents. They're pushing because it's their crews."(Searle & Kelly, 2002: 22)

In examining what this means in terms of literate practices and workplace discourses, what was noticeable across all sites was just how many different documents were constantly in use. As one training officer stated, "when you delve deeper into it, more and more we ask people to fill out more forms because of safety and environmental legislation etc, etc and probably insurance as well". This increased "textualisation" of the workplace is a direct response to the implementation of continuous improvement and accountability measures, and auditing processes such that individual workers must accept responsibility for meeting company goals. So, any account of learning in the workplace must consider both the knowledge required to perform the task as well as knowledge of workplace discourses.

How Is New Behaviour Related to Experience?

The knowledge required to perform a task may be "acquired" on-the-job or learnt through formal training that may be conducted on or off the site. In workplaces, on-the-job acquisition of knowledge is socially constructed and mediated through engagement in a range of tasks and with the relevant texts "and then we were "buddied" – John trained me – and I think I was extremely lucky. John's knowledge was great and he was able to give me a lot of information" (Searle, 1997, p. 44). That is, through the repetition of tasks, through observation, engagement with others, demonstration and participation, the individual builds up experience and the intertextual knowledge required for later recall.

> "What they haven't done is put this into the normal format . . . so I'm just correcting the format so we're ready to go. It will still print this way . . . but the autoticket readers that we have in our revenue department . . . won't work on what they've put in . . . it's got to be in the standard format . . ."

As this extract from the transcript suggests, the SO would have used a range of interpretive procedures both to consign previous experiences and knowledge to memory, then used the procedures both as an aid to stimulate recall and to access intertextual knowledge. In order to engage in other literate practices in the workplace, as we have seen, an individual would have to develop a repertoire of these resources and interpretive procedures as well as a thorough knowledge of site-specific genres and discourses. Further, as we have seen, in some workplaces staff are mentored or buddied up with experienced staff and then develop their own ways of organising information: for example, "I use. . .an index book. I find that's easier for me because I know where everything is in my book" or "If people can just get used to writing a quick explanation it makes life so much easier – and putting their initials on it". It is through such processes of socialisation (Gee, 1996) that individuals become aware of and gradually engage in workplace discourses.

Can Knowledge That Has Been Learned in One Situation Be Transferred to Another?

One view is that there is a body of structured, discipline-based knowledge that once acquired can be transferred to a range of situations. However, as the earlier examples have indicated, the nature of workplaces, the tasks and texts are changing so rapidly that this view is over-simplistic. Further, the impact of new technologies on today's society and workplaces means that individuals are subject to an overload of information; what is required are the strategic resources to search for specific information for site-specific tasks.

From the analysis of texts and tasks in the studies cited earlier, it was evident that there were some actions which occurred across sites and which required the use of general office skills – for example, records handling, filing and so on. Also, some texts could be said to be generic in structure as they exist in genre sets such as those usually found in front offices of motels (guest registration forms, housemaid instruction forms, credit-card imprints etc) which are different from those found at airline counters (Personal Name Records, airline tickets, boarding passes and so on). However, the language features of these texts (print or electronic) and the environment in which those texts were used varied with the sites. Further, as demonstrated in the extracts above, those skills which in isolation may be deemed to be "general", are in practice embedded within complex interactions or are enacted at the closure of an action. It was also evident that there were limitations on the transfer of skills from one situation to another as indicated in the following extract. "You can learn computer inputs from training courses but really you learn everything on the job. . . . we usually buddy up." (Searle 1997, p. 43)

While the knowledge gained from formal learning may present the learner with some resources and a knowledge of basic texts and tasks, it may not include practice in the use of interpretive procedures such as those related to prioritising, problem solving or the ability to conceptualise based on experiences of discourse patterns, such as those described in the following extract.

> "You've got to be able to listen to the passenger who's right in front of you, first of all as your first priority, then any messages from the stenophone, staff that come behind the counter or who need some assistance, and then that might be going as well and the phones, you know, there's three phones here that are going. Obviously if there is one of you here, sometimes you've really got to be, you know, prioritise and you have got to say step one, step two and then . . . " (Searle, 1997, p. 40)

So, if the learner is engaged in one task, in a situation which is familiar and the texts, the participants and social relations are clear and according to type, then there may be no problem with the transfer of knowledge, although the actual language of the workplace might be job or site specific. However, knowledge gained from formal learning may not allow for the fact that in many workplaces "there will be too much information for any given task, just the opposite of what has been true in the past. Workers will need to cope with an abundance of information, to select critically, considering the source and the relation to what is known" (Bruce, 1995, p. 4). Secondly, workers need to understand the intertextual components of how the patterns, rules or discourse types relate to other discourses and the more general social order.

New ways of working, involving work teams, use of new technologies and multi-skilling require new ways of learning and communicating on the job. For example, labouring jobs in the construction industry have now given way to the use of laser levelling and computerised bulldozers. Also, work is increasingly collaborative, with less individual specialisation and more co-ordination through information networks and through informal communication, thus allowing another member of the team to complete a task. Further, work is often characterised by the imposition of top-down bureaucratic rules requiring institutionalised interpretations of texts and discourses. Therefore, learning on-the-job "normalises" certain ways of producing and interpreting texts. In such situations there is likely to be a mismatch between the prior knowledge brought by the learner and the situational properties of the context, thus transfer will collapse. As a result, the worker as learner must make a choice between becoming socialised into the specific ways of learning, interacting, valuing and being in the workplace, or resisting, or withdrawing.

Implications for Professional Education

How Can Teaching and Learning Be Made More Effective?

It is imperative that there is an understanding of the discourses that operate within the specific sites in which teachers and trainers are operating. As social practices vary across domains (schooling, vocational institutions and individual workplaces), so teachers and trainers need to understand the site-specific organisational systems, work practices, underpinning values and literacies. This is partly for pragmatic reasons, so that training is organised to suit staff needs or climatic or economic conditions (e.g., training in one construction company only took place in down time, when it rained) and partly in order to contextualise learning and build a rapport or positive learning environment.

As workplace literacies are highly contextualised, the teacher or trainer requires an in-depth knowledge of the site-specific texts and tasks. As we have seen in the previous sections the literacies required to participate in workplace activities are quite site specific. If the hospitality or airline industries are considered as particular industry cultures, then it is possible to ascribe certain attributes which distinguish one from the other. For example, although each culture is marked by practices generally associated with customer service, the actual actions, language used and literate practices vary according to the culture, whether "checking in" or "checking out" guests in motels, or dealing with flight arrivals and departures, baggage handling, and fares and ticketing at airports. In order to understand how workplace literacies are related to a particular cultural context and to individual social situations, it would be useful for teachers and trainers to have some knowledge of genre theory (Halliday & Hasan, 1986). As indicated above, this theory adopts a social view of language as meaning making and therefore, given a particular context, it should be possible to account for the function or purpose of communication and the appropriate form of the text using actual workplace texts and practices. Any study of workplace literacies should therefore start with an examination of the actual workplace practices and texts in relation to the overall cultures in which they are embedded. The next step might be to address the literacy resources required to operate successfully in the workplace – for example, the ability to de-code text, use text, participate in activities with text, and analyse texts. In addition, learners require a range of interpretive procedures in order to adopt appropriate strategies for both routine tasks and more complex situations involving multiple tasks, multiple modes and problem solving.

With the recent moves towards workplaces becoming earning organisations, there is a necessity for all workers not only to be proficient users of workplace texts but also to engage in a range of communicative activities and learn new literacy practices. In the construction industry, for example, each employee from project manager to leading hand, is encouraged to contribute to workplace activities and must "sign-off" as accepting individual responsibility as indicated in the following extract from interview.

> "[G]ood communication skills still remains a core basic requirement for a good outcome, and we've got things like Work Activity Briefings, Job Safety Analyses that we do. We record or document those, and more and more we're trying to thrust that responsibility back down the workforce, to the people that carry out the work." (Searle & Kelly, 2002, p. 71)

In terms of workplace literacies, this is not only about being able to participate successfully in what is considered a learning organisation but there are also socio-legal implications. Previously responsibility for workplace health and safety and environmental damage was taken by middle management but with the introduction of work teams this responsibility has been pushed on to the workers. While the company see this as empowering the workers to make decisions, it is apparent that there is a slippage between literacy as a social practice (engaging in these meetings) and the necessity for workers to have the basic skills of literacy and numeracy in order to comply with audit requirements and to progress with training. There is also a tension between the stated objectives of becoming a learning organisation and the "accepted evil" of having to "teach these people how to read and write". As a result, some trainers espouse a view of literacy as an autonomous skill which a worker learns prior to training – the "bolted-on" approach referred to earlier in the chapter. But literacy in the workplace is not just a question of de-coding or "understanding what it says on paper". In the so-called high performance workplace, the bottom line is getting the job done, right the first time, safely, thus reducing costs. So, along with focus on developing a training culture, there is also a strong emphasis on workplace communication as a means of ensuring that everyone working on a project is fully informed about the project by participating in the meetings referred to above. Thus, from an ideological perspective, literacy is also about being able to participate successfully in what is considered "workplace communication". This leads to a second tension for industry trainers.

While in some workplaces the literacies which underpin technical competencies are addressed in association with the technical competencies, those literacies which are critical to the maintenance of the social order within the workplace are not usually addressed. These essential literacies play a crucial role in the socialisation of workers into the workplace culture and the distributed literacy knowledges valued by staff in the organisation. Further, as we have seen, they are generally acquired through "buddying" or mentoring employees into the discourses of the workplace. Therefore in developing a curriculum, those literacies which are required to achieve the stated competence should be embedded in the training and consideration should be given to other social literacies and the use of workplace mentors.

There is also a need to include critical literacy within the curriculum. We have seen how the move for increased employee accountability has led to increased textualisation in the workplace. As a result, there is a need for appropriate training so that all workers can become text analysts, not only to be able to complete the forms correctly but also to use their interpretive procedures to understand the significance of compliance or non-compliance with institutional social orders.

Conclusion

By viewing the language and literacy environment of the workplace as "language in context", as discussed earlier, it is possible to account for the effects of social and cultural factors on communication. Increased use of technology means that front-line employees are dealing with more multimodal information than ever before, and that staff are required to take on increased responsibility for dealing with data (input, manipulation and output). As a result they are constantly checking their work. Work is becoming increasingly collaborative, with less individual specialisation and more co-ordination through information networks, thus allowing other members of the team to complete a task. At the same time, employees are being required to keep up-to-date on new systems and new programs, often learning on-the-job. Therefore, individuals require a repertoire of literacy skills (text de-coding, text using, text participating and text analysing) and a range of interpretive procedures to apply appropriate knowledge and strategies in new situations. Further, as workplaces are sites of changing work practices, employees need an understanding of the institutional order, that is, the social organisation of work and the discourses that support it. It has been argued therefore that to focus only on general skills and observable competencies loses sight of the complexity and highly contextualised nature of work. Learners need to be equipped with a repertoire of resources including knowledge of how texts are constructed and interpreted in a range of contexts, as well as the interpretive procedures to apply strategies appropriately. However, it must be recognised that it is only through socialisation on-the-job that learners become members of particular communities of practice in which essential social meanings and the distributed knowledge of workplace literacies are known and valued.

References

Bakhtin, M. (1953/1986). *Speech genres and other late essays*. Texas: University of Texas Press.

Barton, D., & Hamilton, M. (1998). *Local literacies*. London: Routledge.

Bazerman, C. (1994). Systems of genres and the enactment of social intentions. In A. Freedmand & P. Medway (Eds.), *Genre and the new rhetoric* (pp. 79–101). London: Taylor & Francis.

Bigum, C., & Green, B. (1993). Technologizing literacy: or interrupting the dream of reason. In A. Luke & P.Gilbert. *Literacy in contexts*. Sydney: Allen & Unwin.

Bruce, B.C. (1995). *Twenty-first century literacy. Technical Report No. 624*. Centre for the Study of Reading, College of Education, University of Illinois at Urbana-Champaign. Illinois: University of Illinois at Urbana-Champaign.

Burbules, N.C. (1997). Rhetorics of the web: hyperreading and critical literacy. In I. Snyder (Ed.), *Page to screen* (pp. 102–122). Sydney: Allen & Unwin.

Castleton, G., & McDonald, M. (2002). *Multiple Literacies and Social Transformation*. Melbourne: Language Australia.

Cope, B., & Kalantzis, M. (1995). Designing social futures. *Education Australia, 30*, 5–7.

Cope, B., & Kalantzis, M. (Eds) (2000). *Multiliteracies: Literacy learning and the design of social futures*. South Yarra: Macmillan.

Diehl, W., & Mikulecky, L. (1980). The nature of reading at work. *Journal of Reading, 24*(3), 221–227.

Edwards, R., & Fowler, Z. (2005). Mobility and context in literacy practices: between work and college. *Proceedings 4th International Conference on Researching Learning and Work*, CD. Sydney: University of Technology.

Fairclough, N. (2001). *Language and power* (2nd ed.). Harlow Essex: Pearson Education Ltd.

Falk, I. (2001). Sleight of hand: Job myths, literacy and social capital. In J. Lo Bianco & R Wickert (Eds). *Australian policy activism in language and literacy* (203–220). Melbourne: Language Australia.

Freebody, P., & Luke, A. (1990). 'Literacies' programs: Debates and demands in cultural context. *Prospect, 5*(3), 7–16.

Freebody, P., & Luke, A. (2003). Literacy as engaging with new forms of life: The 'four roles' model. In G. Bull & M. Anstey (Eds.), *The literacy lexicon* (pp. 54–61). Frenchs Forest: Prentice Hall.

Gee, J. P. (1996). *Social linguistics and literacies: Ideologies in discourses* (2nd ed.). London: Taylor & Francis.

Gee, J. P., & Lankshear, C. (1997). Language, literacy and the new work order. In C. Lankshear, J. Gee, M. Nobel, & C. Searle (Eds.), *Changing literacies* (pp. 83–102). Buckingham: Open University Press.

Gee, J. P. (2003). *What video games have to teach us about literacy and learning*. England: Palgrave Macmillan.

Goodman, K. (1967, 1985). A linguistic study of cues and miscues in reading. In H. Singer & R. Ruddell, (Eds.), *Theoretical models and processes in reading* (pp. 129–134). Newark: International Reading Association.

Gough, P. (1972). One second of reading. In J. Kavanagh & I. Mattingly, (Eds.), *Language by ear and by eye* (pp. 331–358). Cambridge: Massachusetts Institute of Technology Press.

Gowen, S. (1995). "I'm no fool": Reconsidering American workers and their literacies. *Critical Forum, 3, 2, & 3*, 27–41.

Halliday, M. A. K. (1985). *Spoken and written language*. Geelong: Deakin University Press.

Halliday, M. A. K., & Hasan, R. (1986). *Language, context and text: Aspects of language in a social semiotic perspective*. Victoria: Deakin University Press.

Heath, S. B. (1983). *Ways with words*. Cambridge: Cambridge University Press.

Hull, G. (1995). Controlling literacy: The place of skills in 'high performance' work. *Critical Forum. 3, 2, & 3*, 3–26.

Hull, G. (1997). Preface and Introduction. In G. Hull (Ed.), *Changing work, changing workers: Critical perspectives on language, literacy and skills*. New York: State University of New York.

Jackson, N. (2000). Writing-up people at work: Investigations of workplace literacy. *Working knowledge conference proceedings* (pp. 263–272). Sydney: University of Technology Sydney.

Kelly A., & Searle J. (2000). *Literacy on the motorway: An examination of the effects of the inclusion of literacy and numeracy in industry standards in training packages on the quality of learning and work outcomes*. Melbourne: Language Australia.

Kress, G., & van Leeuwen, T. (2001). *Multimodal discourse: The modes and media of contemporary communication*. London: Arnold.

Kress, G., & van Leeuwen, T. (2003). *Reading images: The grammar of visual design*. London: Routledge.

Luke, A., Freebody, P. & Land, R. (2000) *Literate Futures: The Queensland State Literacy Strategy*. Brisbane: Education Queensland.

Meyer, B. J. F. (1981). Organisational aspects of text: effects on reading comprehension and applications for the classroom. In J. Flood (Ed.), *Reading comprehension*. Newark: International Reading Association.

Mikulecky, L. (1982). Job literacy – the relationship between school preparation and workplace actuality. *Reading Research Quarterly*, *17*(3), 400–419.

Mikulecky, L. (1984). Preparing students for workplace literacy demands'. *Journal of Reading*, *28*(3), 253–257.

Mikulecky, L. (1990). Basic skills impediments to communication between management and hourly employees. *Management Communication Quarterly*, *3*, *4*, 452–473.

Prinsloo, M., & Breier, M. (1996). *The social uses of literacy*. Cape Town, SA: Sached Books and John Benjamins Publishing Company.

Ruddell, R. B., & Speaker, R. B. (1985). The interactive reading process: A model. In H. Singer & R. B. Ruddell (Eds.), *Theoretical models and processes of reading* (pp. 751–793). Newark, DE: International Reading Association.

Scribner, S., & Cole, M. (1981). *The psychology of literacy*. Cambridge, MA: Harvard University Press.

Searle, J., & Kelly, A. (2002). *Acting Smart: An Investigation of Assumptions and Principles which Underpin Training and Assessment within One Civil Construction Company*. Melbourne: Language Australia.

Searle, J. (1996). Language and literacy competencies. In J. Stevenson (Ed.), *Learning in the Workplace: Tourism and Hospitality* (pp. 22–50).Brisbane: Centre for Learning and Work Research, Griffith University.

Searle, J. (1997). Workplace language and literacy competencies. In F. Beven (Ed.), *Skill Formation in the Airline Sector of the Transport Industry* (pp. 19–57).Brisbane: Centre for Learning and Work Research, Griffith University.

Smith, F. (1971). *Understanding reading*. Toronto: Holt.

Stevenson, J. (2002). Normative nature of workplace action and knowledge. *International Journal for Educational Research*, *37*(1), 85–106.

Street, B. V. (1984). *Literacy in theory and practice*. Cambridge: Cambridge University Press.

Street, B. V. (1996). Preface. In M. Prinsloo & M. Breier (Eds.), *The social uses of literacy* (pp. 2–9). Cape Town, SA: Sached Books and John Benjamins.

Taylor, D., & Dorsey-Gaines, C. (1988). *Growing up literate*. Portsmouth: Heinemann.

Chapter 4
Revisiting Informal and Incidental Learning as a Vehicle for Professional Learning and Development

Victoria J. Marsick, Karen E. Watkins, and Barbara Lovin

Introduction

Marsick and Watkins' (1990) theory of informal and incidental learning grows out of scholarship and practice centred in learning from experience, self-directed learning, action science and transformative learning. The theory starts with a focus on the learning process of an individual and adds stages of reflective learning that usually occur incidentally but that, with coaching, can deepen informal learning. Over the years, Marsick and Watkins increasingly placed the learning of individuals in larger social contexts (e.g., groups, communities of practices, organisations, and society more generally conceived). Research using this model (e.g., Cseh, 1998) showed that context was perhaps more influential in the way people learned than other factors, such as learning habits, preferences, or even resources (Cseh, Watkins, and Marsick, 1999). Recently, a review of research and reflection on the experience of informal and incidental learning led Marsick and Watkins on a quest to re-conceptualise the model – due, in part, to limitations not only in our earlier thinking, but also to a broader reading of trends in theory and practice that influenced our understanding of the learning process (Marsick, Watkins, Callahan, & Volpe, 2008). In this chapter, we revisit informal and incidental learning theory as a vehicle for professional learning and development, addressing the following questions.

1. What is our model? How does an example taken from a study of paramedics by Lovin illustrate the learning process and challenges to the model as we have recently re-conceptualised it?
2. What tensions emerge when building informal and incidental learning more intentionally into the support of the learning of professionals (and managers

V.J. Marsick (✉)
Teachers College, Columbia University, New York, USA
e-mail: marsick@exchange.tc.columbia.edu

C. Kanes (ed.), *Elaborating Professionalism*, Innovation and Change in Professional Education 5, DOI 10.1007/978-90-481-2605-7_4,
© Springer Science+Business Media B.V. 2010

and other employees)? Given these tensions, what can organisations and individuals do to support and enhance informal and incidental learning without over-regulating it?

Introducing the Study of Paramedics

In order to make the model and the thinking in this article come alive, we draw on a study of informal learning and partner relationships among paramedics in the pre-hospital setting conducted by Barbara (Larson) Lovin (1991), a doctoral student of Victoria's at Teachers College. Barbara observed that paramedics did not seem to learn from the many mandated hours of continuing education in which they participated and was curious about whether and how they learn from their experience. Her observation was confirmed by the study, although the reason, in part, is that continuing education was not designed in engaging ways and seldom introduced new compelling information. In contrast, paramedics described their own work in the following way: "[N]o matter how many calls you run ... [it's] never boring" (p. 154).

Barbara found some evidence for self-directed learning projects, but she also learned that many of her participants did not complete or follow through on this mode of learning because of

- A bureaucratic culture (with a para-military structure) that emphasised conformity to rules and regulations
- Mixed messages in the organisation (do what I say, not what I will support; and learn on your own, but mostly through mandated continuing education)
- A culture of negative feedback, or lack of positive feedback: "How do you know when you've done a good job? ... I guess basically you don't get any negative feedback is the way you find out around here." (p. 90)
- A respected, but over-burdened training director who could not give paramedics needed time to design and carry out their learning projects.

Lovin found that the overriding means of learning in this setting was from experience, especially the "calls" or "runs" themselves – and especially when a call was non-routine in some way and thus presented an opportunity to learn something new. Many studies have been done about health care teams in various settings that make it clear that learning is a collaborative, collective event. In this study, the partnership becomes the key context for learning.

Paramedics in this study were paired in partnerships for a 24 h shift beginning each day at 8 am, with 48 h off duty before beginning another shift. When they are called, they "have 2 min to reach the ambulance and report back to the dispatcher by radio that the ambulance is en route to the designated destination." (p. 74) "A system of standing orders and treatment protocols approved by the system's medical director allows the paramedics to perform a variety of advanced medical procedures including cardiac defibrillation, intravenous fluid administration, and the administration of some drugs based on the findings of the patient assessment and without direct contact with the hospital or physician" (p. 75). One paramedic drives to the hospital while the other continues treatment. The driver cleans and prepares the ambulance while the "lead paramedic documents the call on a standardised run report and the crew usually returns to service within 45 min" (p. 75). This 45 minute "hospital time frame" becomes a key performance indicator. "As part of a yearly performance evaluation, the shift supervisor reviews with each paramedic the monthly reports of hospital times and … a hospital time objective below the 45 min allotted" is negotiated as a hospital-wide objective/target (p. 80). "Most paramedic teams rotate responsibility on patient care calls." That is, on the first call, "one paramedic will assume the role of primary decision maker and then, on subsequent calls, alternate that role with the other paramedic member of the team." While done to "equalise the workload", it also "imposes some limits on the member who is not 'in charge.'" But both members feel they share responsibility for patient success (pp. 97–98).

While much learning can and does happen individually, the context for learning is clearly the pair, fed by the intensive 24 h duty pattern: "after spending 24 h with somebody every third day you get to know them real well and you either become good friends with them or you don't get along at all" (p. 96). Paramedics are typically "hired to work for a specific shift" and "appear to associate more closely with their shift than the organisation as a whole" (p. 77). Regular partners are sometimes compared to marriages, and new partner relationships to getting to know a new girlfriend or boyfriend (p. 78). Partners often work with one another for a long duration, although at times, paramedics could "swap out" shifts so that paramedics could find themselves working with someone new periodically, and sometimes with many different people for extended time periods (p. 114).

Lovin identified four kinds of partner interactions that she labelled "synergistic, potentiated, additive, and antagonistic, … terms … used commonly in the science of pharmacy to indicate the interactions that may occur when two drugs are taken together" (p. 100). Lovin came upon this metaphor when mulling over her data on her own and through conversations with colleagues: "one plus one can be greater than, equal to, or less than two."

"Synergistic drugs taken in combination increase each other's effectiveness. In a synergistic interaction between paramedic partners, the partners, not just the state, consider themselves equals. … When this happens the opportunity exists for a relationship to develop which ultimately results in each partner increasing the effectiveness of the other to where the team response to patient care may result, in mathematical terms, in the whole being greater than the sum of its parts." This type often occurred in long-term partner relationships. Several of Barbara's participants "report having no difficulty moving back into this relationship on short notice." "They believe that to achieve this working relationship they needed to learn more than skills, they also needed to learn about each other." Trust develops. They know how one another thinks so that they can complement one another's strengths and weaknesses. "'What do you think?' is a very common question between synergistic partners'" (pp. 101–102).

"When one drug is able to increase the effectiveness of another the interaction is potentiated. So too, does the effectiveness of one paramedic seem to be increased by the presence of another in certain situations. ... one plus one has the potential to be greater than two. ... These potentiated interactions occur in this system when paramedics are deliberately paired by the organisation in a mentoring type relationship. They may also occur in long-term partnerships where, for various reasons, an informal mentoring arrangement is accepted by partners" (p. 106). The relationship, however, is not one of "equals. Paramedics being mentored trust their mentors .... Mentors, however, do not trust their partners .... This is different from the synergistic interaction where partners do not feel the need to be present to be assured that this situation is being handled appropriately" (p. 108). Learning is potentiated for one person but not the other. A mentor, for example, describes how he puts the mentee "in a situation where he has to make the decisions – he has no choice. Leave him with the third rider. Be in ear contact so that if something goes wrong I can be in there real quick. Otherwise I stand back and I supervise what he does. If I happen to see a question that he has not asked, I throw it in there real quick" (p. 107). Lovin points out that "only under certain circumstances can this mentoring relationship be deemed potentiated. When the patient condition is such that the mentor feels comfortable relinquishing control, the interaction is probably potentiated" (p. 109).

"Just as the effectiveness of additive drugs equals only the sum of their individual effectivenesses, so too, with additive paramedic partners .... Effectiveness is not enhanced by their working together. This occurs most frequently when experienced paramedics who have occasionally worked together before are paired for only one shift but it may also be the interaction that develops between two partners in a longer term relationship" when, after trying many things, there is not a good fit (p. 109). When the time involved is brief, a paramedic makes decisions about how much benefit will result from pushing for doing something differently, making their reasoning explicit in hopes of influencing the other, or otherwise dong more than getting the task done in the best possible way with little additional effort expended in light of what is best for the patient. Sometimes tacit knowing is involved, for example, when a long-time partner would pick up on a cue that someone new does not: "it's not that they should have known it's just that you expected your partner by certain actions you did to pick up on them and do things without your telling them" (p. 110). Most of the time, even though glitches occur, "routine imposed by standing orders and treatment protocols prevents patient harm" (p. 111). So "task performance will be satisfactory provided the situation does not deviate from the expected" (p. 112), but one is left to conclude that problems could arise in non-routine situations when partnerships are merely additive.

In antagonistic partnerships, "the whole is less than the sum of the parts ... in a pharmacological sense where antagonistic partners, like antagonistic drugs, interfere with one another" (pp. 112–113). Lovin identifies "three different sets of circumstances" where this may occur:

- "at the beginning of a long term partner relationship which both members want to develop into an effective working relationship" but where it takes time to learn one another's preferences and thinking (p. 113);
- in "short term pairings where a regular member … is teamed with an individual who is not well known … [e.g.] a full-time employee from a different shift who has 'swapped' time or a part-time employee" (p. 114) because each has different routines that they don't communicate well enough or quickly enough; and
- in cases where a paramedic has an "open slot" rather than a regularly assigned partner in which case, paramedics often choose to act as individuals and "make the decision, depending on who you work with, how competent you feel they are, how comfortable you feel with them" and how "critical" the decision (p. 114).

In these kinds of partnership interactions, it may be that partners "have a difficult time accepting each other as equals" or lack trust in one another or the situation (p. 115). "However, it appears that the individual may require the experience of a synergistic partner relationship to understand the difference and effects that an antagonistic relationship may produce" (p. 116).

Having painted a picture of these partnerships, we now turn to our model and how we have re-conceptualised it over time because of what we came to discover as inherent limitations of our theorising about informal and incidental learning.

Our Model

Marsick and Watkins (1990) developed a model of informal and incidental learning that they later re-conceptualised with Cseh (Cseh, Watkins, & Marsick, 1999). (See Fig. 4.1) We defined informal and incidental learning as "learning outside of formally structured, institutionally sponsored, classroom-based activities" and asserted that such learning "often takes place under non-routine circumstances, that is, when the procedures and responses that people normally use fail" leading to greater attention to, and awareness, of "tacit, hidden, taken-for-granted assumptions" that may help learners rethink situations in which they find themselves and re-frame their understanding of the kind of learning they might need to undertake. We further distinguished incidental from informal learning by defining it "as a by-product of some other activity, such as task accomplishment, interpersonal interactions, sensing the organisational culture, or trial-and-error experimentation." We contrasted the sometimes intentional and more possibly planned nature of informal learning with the accidental and often semi-conscious nature of incidental learning.

Informal and incidental learning outcomes depend, in part, on the degree of conscious awareness with which one attends learning and the environment that brings learning opportunities. Formal learning opportunities heighten awareness, but such learning is divorced from real life action. Informal learning benefits from being linked to meaningful job activities, but it requires greater attention to making the most of the learning opportunity, something that might involve planning and almost

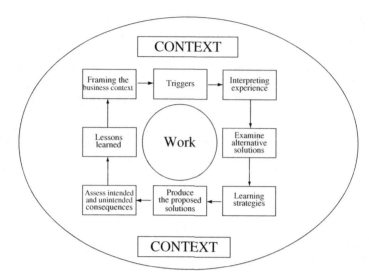

Fig. 4.1 Re-Conceptualised Informal and Incidental Learning Model (1999). (Source: Cseh, Watkins, & Marsick, 1999)

certainly involves some conscious attention, reflection, and direction. Incidental learning, while occurring by chance, can be highly beneficial when one moves the accidental learning opportunity closer into the informal learning realm through conscious attention, reflection, and direction.

What the Model Looks Like in Action

In this model, people use reflection to become aware of the problematic aspects of the experience, to probe these features, and to learn new ways to understand and address the challenges they encounter. Context is pervasive and influences every step. The following example from the paramedic study will be used to walk through the cycle, narrated by a paramedic with 3 years' experience who "described a process of decision making undertaken with a regular partner in an unusual situation" (Lovin, 1991, p. 133):

> "As [we] pulled up that day, we knew that we were in for a mess because there was a truck halfway on a car and the car was hanging over the bridge. We were sort of stumped when we first got out of the truck. 'Where do we go from here?' We went to try to see what the extent of the patients' injuries were. We couldn't even get to one. You could see her arm, and you could hear her, but that was about it ... We knew we had to get to her without hurting one of us or hurting her more, not knowing what was against her, if anything. We would talk about a way to get her out and then spend a minute thinking what would happen if we did that. It was so easy to rule out a way not to do it because we'd say, "Well, if we did that, this could happen. Then we'd really be in a mess." That probably went on during

the whole call, but each step we would talk about it, and think, "Well, if we did it this way, what would happen? Should we take that particular risk or not? One in a million chance it could happen." Luckily, all the decisions we made ended up being the right ones, I feel like. She wasn't injured anymore when we got her out, and she didn't die. ... I guess through the whole call, we weren't really sure of anything we were doing. If we could think of a reason not to do it, we would do it...I never really encountered a call like that one before.... Nobody ever taught us to get a truck off a car hanging off a bridge...We were totally blind going in. It was like being blindfolded, I guess, feeling around with our hands. We made decisions one at a time." (Lovin, 1991, pp.133–134)

Looking at the model (see Fig. 4.1) and using this example, we see problem-solving steps located on vertical and horizontal axes (centred on the Work component in the figure) that can be located (clockwise) at Top, Right, Bottom and Left. Learning steps are located in between problem-solving steps, and are located (beginning clockwise just before Top) as Top Left, Top Right, Bottom Right and Bottom Left.

We start at the Top. Problem solving and learning are triggered when people encounter a new experience. They frame the new experience based on what they learned from past experience (Top Left). They assess similarities or differences, and use interpretation to make sense of the new situation. Often, people make these judgements quickly, without much conscious reflection. Reflection slows down the diagnosis, but it also helps a person to become aware of the complexity of the situation and the assumptions used to judge the new challenge.

In the above example, the paramedics arrived on the scene assessed the challenge in light of their experience with prior calls. They assessed the patient's injuries and decided they had never encountered a problem like this one before, but they may have encountered other situations on which they could build their thinking as they figured out how to solve the problem.

After examining alternative solutions, a decision is made about a course of action (Right); a person develops or gathers resources and decides on learning strategies to implement the decision (Bottom Right). Reflection might be anticipatory, and lead to the development of new capabilities in order to implement the solution. Often, reflection occurs while the action is being implemented over time. When people reflect in action (Schön, 1987), they typically do so when they are taken by some surprise in the course of action. Because they are learning as they implement, people may make quick judgements based on partial information. They may also seek further information during action.

In the emergency example above, the paramedics did decide on a course of action after ruling out what they knew they could not do, and as they took action, they tested their strategy at each step, pausing to ask questions the whole way through about the pros and cons of taking certain risks. Lovin (1991) found that this pattern was repeated in example after example of handling something that was not routine and learning through action in the experience. Many of these stories were described in the "we" of a partnership, but some were stories of individual learning and not all of them afforded quite as much time for rational consideration of alternatives, such as the time a paramedic was "really having a hard time intubating the kid. Blood was just coming from everywhere and the classical part about the learning was that I knew how to find where the trachea was. I was relying on that. Going through the steps of the anatomy, doing all the procedures right and it wasn't working. Had on a previous experience with a drowning victim noticed that the water would flow out of the esophagus and back into the airway. You could tell by how the fluid was moving where the two different holes were and that's how I found it. Just watched where the blood was going and placed the tube." (Lovin, 1991, p. 135)

Once an action is taken (Bottom), people assess consequences and decide whether or not outcomes match their goals (Bottom Left). Reflection after the fact allows for a full learning review. It is relatively easy to assess intended consequences when goals are reasonably explicit and data are available to make sound judgements. It is harder to recognise unintended consequences, although reflection can lead one to ask questions of a wide range of people and explore sources of information that might otherwise be ignored. A learning review leads to conclusions about results (Left) and lessons learned that can be of help in planning future actions. Reflection at this point brings a person full circle to the new understandings (Top Left) that are drawn in a new iteration of the cycle.

We aren't privy to the conversation that these paramedics had after extracting the woman from the truck–car accident, but we do know from Lovin's (1991) account that the requirement for preparing a "standardised run report" (p. 139) directly after the call provides a mechanism for learning from experience after the fact and carrying lessons learned forward to future activities. Report writing does not always result in learning, but many paramedics talked about how writing things down, step by step, helped them see things they should not have done or should have done differently:

"When I finally write it, I'll say, 'You dummy, you should have done the opposite direction' or I'll write it and get to the cause and effect and I say, 'I don't know. I forgot to go back and check what the change was'. It makes a lot of difference to finally see all the progressions, the vital signs written. You know, maybe you should start looking at something else. Or how the patient did really had no bearing on being a diabetic. Probably very appropriate not to even worry about the D[dextrose] stick. But now that I'm writing the report I'm thinking about what the liabilities might be if this had kicked back. Then maybe next time I'll be sure to do that just for this one reason (Lovin 1991, p. 140).

Reflection is central to every phase of learning from experience although everyone does not always consciously use reflection to its fullest potential. Reflection sensitises people to surprises and mismatches that signal the inadequacy of their prior stock of knowledge. Through reflection-in-action (Schön, 1987), people adjust their course of action and learn while they are carrying out the solution. Reflection after the fact helps to draw out lessons learned that are useful for the next problem-solving cycle.

Lovin (1991, p. 142) reports that many paramedics in her study did not stop reflecting with the run report. They "run a call once, physically . . . . Mentally you run the call dozens of times after that. Over and over and over. Not only just in the telling other people . . .but you may be studying something and it comes back to you and you think about it."

Based on subsequent research using the model, Cseh, Watkins, and Marsick (1999) re-conceptualised the model to emphasise the pervasive influence of context on all aspects of the model of informal and incidental learning. Cseh (1998) found 143 dissertations between 1980 and 1998 that discussed aspects of informal learning, including over twenty built on the informal and incidental learning model that Marsick and Watkins, separately and together, developed and modified over time. Several studies emphasised the role of context in informal and incidental learning research.

Cseh (1998) examined learning experiences that enabled owner-managers of small private companies in Romania to lead successfully in the transition to a free market economy. She was interested in what triggered their learning, what strategies they used, and what lessons they learned. In-depth, face-to-face interviews using a critical incident technique were conducted with 18 managers, between 28 and 62 years of age, representing both genders and the nationalities (Hungarian and Romanian) specific to the two regions selected. Cseh found that the foremost task faced by her participants was to make sense of the rapidly shifting environment and that, in this, interpretation of context dominated: "... context permeates every phase of the learning process – from how the learner will understand the situation, to what is learned, what solutions are available, and how the existing resources will be used" (Cseh, Watkins, & Marsick, 1999, p. 352).

Context in the paramedic example was critical to informal learning patterns in the paramedic study, not only in the learning done in the moment, but also in extracting lessons learned going forward. For example, Lovin (1991) explains that synergistic partners often go one step further than learning through the writing of run reports. They may rehearse the situation together and plan ahead for what they would do on a future run when they encountered such circumstances: "On the way back from a call, we critique it. [For example, we] say, 'Well, next time we'll try something a little bit different' or 'You stay with me instead of separating to the other patients'. That's the big part – critiquing the call afterwards" (p.142). Because synergistic partners did critique and rehearse to prepare for doing things differently, Lovin also found that "fewer of the experiences of the synergistic partners will be perceived by them as unusual events." Lovin also noted that she did not find this pattern of rehearsal among antagonistic or additive interactions "and that it is more directive than consultative in the potentiated interaction." (ibid., p. 142)

Lovin (1991) underscored the many ways that the context of the partnership greatly affects whether, in what ways, and how much learning goes on. Long term partners describe the deep relationship they build that enables them to think together continually, asking questions of one another, acting on tacit cues that they had learned over time, and better able to work and learn quickly together in the many non-routine circumstances that paramedics always face. Their relationship makes this learning possible:

"You laugh so much. You go through so much with every partner and so many different experiences with each partner. You make mistakes together. You get pats on the back together. You're up all night together. You're held over the next day and you're walking zombies. Gone through so much together, especially in a fast paced system . . .. Even though

you may not have the same views morally or any other way, you do develop a way to adapt
to each partner. You take on a little different attitude, personality with each person because
you know that' what it's going to take to get along with this person and be friends with
them." (ibid., p. 127)

When partners are not synergistic "the adaptation which occurs in antagonistic
or additive partnerships is reported as being directed towards accomplishing a task
with the least amount of discord. . . . Whereas . . . in a synergistic relationship, discord surrounding task accomplishment is viewed as necessary and appropriate and
a potential learning opportunity" (ibid., p. 128).

Theory Behind the Model

Our model of informal and incidental learning from and through experience is based
on Dewey's (1938) cycle of problem solving through reflective thought. Reflective
thought begins with a disjuncture between what is expected and what occurs, which
can lead to re-thinking the nature of the problem and the directions in which one
might look for solutions. Solving a problem involves one or more cycles of trial
and error in which learning takes place as one seeks to achieve a desired outcome.
Observation of what occurs leads to course corrections and eventually to conclusions and planning for how one will address similar situations going forward. Dewey
essentially adapted the scientific method to solving problems of everyday life. This
same cycle is at the heart of action research, developed by Kurt Lewin (1947) and
others based on systematic cycles of problem definition, data gathering, reflection
on evidence, learning, and future planning. Lewin added an emphasis on collective
problem solving of socially shared concerns. Lewin thus moved the more individually oriented learning cycle in interaction with one's environment, as advocated by
Dewey, to a group and organisational learning level.

Of the various theorists who built off Lewin's work, Chris Argyris and Donald
Schön (1974, 1978) developed action science, a systematic theory for learning from
experience in groups and organisations. They developed the idea of a theory of
action, comprised of espoused theories, which represent an individual or organisational ideal, and theories in use, which represent how such theories are carried out.
Argyris and Schön sought ways to close the gap between the ideal and the actual.
They adopted Dewey's idea of a disjuncture between what was expected and what
occurred (an error) as a trigger for learning how to correct a course of action or
tactics (single loop learning) to achieve one's goals. When changes in tactics do not
achieve desired ends, they suggest switching to double loop learning in which one
examines values, assumptions, and beliefs that influence how a situation or problem
is framed. Reframing the situation or problem often leads to more effective desired
solutions, which typically one then has to learn how to implement.

Marsick and Watkins (1990) adopted Argyris and Schön's basic framework for
their theory of informal and incidental learning. Depending on the degree of awareness, intention, and direction, one might be engaging in either informal or incidental

learning. But in both kinds of learning, one's attention might be focused on either single or double loop learning. Marsick and Watkins further adopted Simon's (1965) distinction between routine and non-routine work. They noted the shift, fuelled by globalisation and high technology, towards rapidly changing environments and a knowledge era that lent itself more often to what the Army Defense College was calling VUCA environments – volatile, uncertain, complex, and ambiguous. They suggested that increasingly, employees throughout most organisations were likely to find themselves addressing non-routine problems and challenges that call for customised responses that require greater levels of judgement and learning.

They drew on Polanyi's (1967) discussion of tacit knowledge from which Schön (1987) also drew in developing his theory of reflective practice. Now more widely known through the work of Nonaka and Takeuchi (1995) on knowledge creation, Polanyi pointed out that discoveries in chemistry and other scientific disciplines were not at all rational, value free, and objective. In making interpretations of complex situations, as does Dewey, Polanyi noted how our past experience and understanding influences interpretations of present circumstances, and how much of that framing of the situation remains outside of our critical awareness and purview.

Updating Our Model

Recently, a review of research and reflection on our own experience of informal and incidental learning led us on a quest to re-conceptualise the model – due, in part, to limitations not only in our earlier thinking, but also to a broader reading of trends in theory and practice that influenced our understanding of the learning process (Marsick et al., 2008). These problems can be summarised as follows:

- The model "looks" linear even though that was not the intent;
- The model "feels" cognitive;
- The model focuses on individual learning but does not adequately account for social interaction and social construction of meaning or action; and
- The model engages context but does not explain the role of context in learning

The stories of the paramedics in action illustrate these four problems. Learning in the face of non-routine circumstances through experience can involve moving back and forth among steps, but a more apt description is that learning occurs simultaneously at many levels, and that the personal learning of the paramedics that surrounds their partnership intertwines with the performance-oriented learning needed on the call. Their past history together, or lack thereof; the extent to which they understand emotions and cues before they are made explicit; the degree to which they have been able to accommodate one another's task and learning preferences without giving up their own needs; and many more factors operate all at one time. While it may be possible to untangle the pieces of their momentary interaction and learning in a written document, it is not feasible. And what is left out of an excessively rational analysis is the personal signature, preferences, and commitment that these paramedics bring to their work.

One final story from Lovin's (1991) study helps to illustrate the challenges to our model that we have recently identified. This story describes a seven-car wreck that brought together two former synergistic partners who happened to meet and work together in ways that others on the scene recognised as vitally important. As the paramedics learned how to help the people in the accident, they also kept in mind their new "rookie partners" and how they were doing, even as they fell into patterns of learning and interaction that they had developed over a long period of time in working together:

> "[The] driver of one vehicle looked like he should be gravely injured. His passenger, his wife, was horribly trapped ... Two other subjects in one of the vehicles were both trapped but not injured that bad. Just couldn't get the doors open. ... Quickly assessed everybody in the seven cars and realised we needed more ambulances ... My good old buddy finally shows up on the scene with his new partner (in one of these ambulances). And we really dismissed them [the two inexperienced partners] to take care of everybody else and he and I were working on this lady that was dying in front of us. The good old days! Put the blanket over her and he is leaning in through the door that I am cutting on and he's nasally tubing her underneath the blanket while I'm cutting around him. That's the way we worked all the time. So he gets the tube and there was no doubt that he would get it. I finally get the door off of her and then I get the dash off of her and the transmission off of her and we're both saying, 'We got to get her out of here' ... having not worked as closely as we were used to, we were still – I was over-emphasising cause of being with my new guy. He's over-emphasising cause of being with his new partner and we're both saying, 'Yeah, yeah, I know you're doing it' ... We're finally getting everything done that needs to be done and get to the truck and he says, 'Is this tube in?' and it's like, knowing him, it's got to be in" (ibid., pp. 102–103).

Ultimately, the supervisor on the scene, recognising the way they worked together on this one patient, told them to take the woman to the hospital together. They pointed out, "but remember, we've got our two rookie partners out here running around", but the supervisor said the rest of them would take care of that situation so that these two former partners could wrap up the case:

> "And that was wonderful! We'd discussed it while we were getting the lady packaged that that's what we wanted to do. We wanted the opportunity to work together again but we knew we couldn't because we couldn't leave our rookies out there by themselves. So it was really a highlight knowing that, not only to do what I thought was a good job, I got to work with my buddy." (ibid.)

This example illustrates the challenges with the model as it was originally conceived. The learning in action was largely tacit, which our original model accommodates, but the learning in action is not linear, not always cognitive, and it has much to do with the context of the fact that these two key partners had worked together synergistically in the past. They could not have learned and worked together without this prior social interaction that enabled whole person learning; this would not have been feasible had this work been done by either of the paramedics with his/her new rookie partner.

We recognised that although the model was never intended to be used in a linear manner, basing our thinking in Dewey led us to construct a version of the scientific method triggered by a disjuncture between anticipated and actual experience. However, experience, as Yorks and Kasl (2002) suggest, becomes a "noun" rather than a "verb" in the more holistic, phenomenological tradition, which they adopt. Beginning with Heron's (1992) integrated model that proposes we learn in ways that simultaneously draw on experience, imagination, cognition, and practical application and thus by critical subjectivity, balance and in doing so by critical subjectivity, balances different kinds of knowing (experiential, presentational, propositional, and practical) on an ongoing basis. The paramedics do follow a roughly linear set of steps in technical problem solving but the infusion of their relationship with one another brings a non-linear dimension into the learning through problem solving based on prior and current perceptions of what the other person knows, how much they can trust that the other will carry out tasks in certain ways, and whether/how they can communicate with one another in ways that they think are understood and will be acted upon. Heron's framework, and others that explain the non-linear paths of complexity as well as the characteristics of implicit and tacit learning (Cleermans, 1995; Seger, 1994), helped us to look at informal and incidental learning less as problem-solving steps and more as a "messy" process that ultimately helps learners to make sense of their experience in loops and folds rather than straight lines.

We could also see that our model separated cognition from affect even though that, too, was an unintended consequence. Our own learning, as we created the model, was stimulated by delving into the arts and space for frame breaking aesthetic experiences that ultimately allowed us to engage in fresh ways with our experience. But our model seemed to emphasise critical reflection over multiple ways of knowing. In addition to work on emotional intelligence (e.g., Goleman, 1995) and aesthetic expression as a way of knowing (e.g., Allen, 1995), we looked at new brain research that debunks the myth that emotions have no place in rational decision making (e.g., Damasio, 1995; LeDoux, 1996). And we returned again to Heron's emphasis on presentational knowing – through story, art, and other means of visual or sensory expression – for expressing a reality that seems important but has not yet been cognitively processed into an if-then kind of lesson learned.

Lovin (1991), in fact, reports that, "Although they report 'watching and observing others,' … participants most frequently learn from experience of others through storytelling," a mode that enables presentational knowing as a bridge between experiential and propositional knowing that further enables practical knowing. As she engaged in participant observation, she noted that "it's been one story after another all morning" … as people washed down their vehicles, carried out station duties, or engaged in conversation as they left the paramedic station. For example, a question, "have you defibrillated in the rain" began a "litany of stories as the four of us related experiences we had with water and electricity supplied by a defibrillator. Questions followed the stories for using the machine in the presence of water in an unusual and potentially lethal experience." Lovin noted that her "role as participant/observer landed me right in the middle of a learning experience. I heard stories about calls I've never run before." Paramedics recognised these stories as "good learning experiences" (pp. 143–133).

Over time we had come to realise that our model focused on the individual too much to the exclusion of social interaction and the social construction of knowledge. In addition to our own work in this area (e.g., Watkins and Marsick, 1993), we looked particularly to Wenger's (1998) conceptualisation of learning through communities of practice. His discussion, for example, of the interaction of imagination, engagement, and alignment helped us to understand better how to value difference in social learning, appreciate the role played by social context in learning, and respect the challenges involved in aligning viewpoints around the negotiation of meaning and action. Wenger explains many of the dynamics of communities of practice using three core concepts: engagement (to create and maintain the community), imagination (which is central to learning), and alignment (which involves social interaction). Wenger (1998, pp. 217–218) argues that "Engagement, imagination, and alignment are all important ingredients of learning – they anchor it in practice yet make it broad, creative, and effective in the wider world." Wenger adds that reflective practice emerges from the joining of engagement and imagination. Among other things, "Imagination enables us to adopt other perspectives across boundaries and time, to visit 'otherness' and let it speak its own language." When alignment combines with imagination, continues Wenger, people can "align our activities" and "understand why" because it is clear that what we do contributes to a larger vision that is meaningful to the community. "Imagination thus helps us direct our alignment in terms of its broader effects, adapt it under shifting circumstances, and fine tune it intelligently."

Finally, while the 1999 update of our model focused on the pervasiveness of context, we did not draw out implications for learning in the model, particularly with respect to diagnosing and addressing the learning culture that is needed to support learning of individuals, groups, and the organisation. Research helped us to focus more specifically on how context interacts with and influences learning. For example, a study by Watkins and Cervero (2000) of two different organisational settings of CPA practice showed that while opportunities in each firm were equivalent, the organisational culture substantially influenced whether or not CPAs learned informally. This pointed them to assessing organisational culture, support, structures, and incentives as a context for learning of individuals and the firm.

The work of Rob Poell and Ferd Van Der Krogt on learner network theory (e.g., see Poell, Chivers, Van der Krogt, & Wildermeersch, 2000) widened our understanding of different types of learning networks – vertical, horizontal, external, and liberal – as a holding environment for different kinds of informal learning needs and patterns. Their learner network theory looks at orientation, learning and optimising, and continuation phases of learning undertaken within four different ideal types, so classed based on who and how learning is initiated and managed: liberal-contractual, vertical-regulated, horizontal-organic, and external-collegial. Learning within the liberal-contractual ideal type is initiated by proactive, self-directed individuals who facilitate their own learning projects. Learning within the vertical-regulated ideal type is initiated and directed by experts, who often represent the organisation. Learning within the horizontal-organic ideal type is carried out by collaborative work teams. Learning within the external-collegial ideal type is influenced externally by professional standards and knowledge advances brought into the organisation from outside of it. Context – social as well as organisational – helps explain which of these ideal types are likely to predominate in different informal workplace learning projects.

This review of theory and research led us to conclude that while our early model was still relevant, it needed to be modified. It becomes a looser, non-linear framework that contains learners in interaction with self, one another, and the environment as they set, modify, and pursue learning goals. We concluded that a better analogy for thinking about informal and incidental learning would be an amoeba-like process, multi-dimensional in nature. We always thought of such learning as iterative, but more so in phases of reflection in and on action that led to the next learning event.

Our revised thinking, reflected in our model, is that as learners grapple with puzzles, feeling, and ambiguity, learning must be considered as iterative. Typically, learning would be social as well as individual, intertwining and simultaneously engaging both experiencing through acting, emotion and affect as one acts, reflection in action as well as on action. While reflection can aid learning, it can also embed error into the learning process when it is private and when it is guided by strong mental models such as those often held by professionals as experts or managers as holders of power.

Implications for Providers of Professional Learning and Development

Tensions arise when effort is made to provide structure and support that would encourage informal and incidental learning. Providers of informal and incidental learning face the dilemma of how they can provide structure and support without over-formalising the organic, self-directed nature of this kind of learning. Similar observations have been made about mentoring and about communities of practice. It appears that organisations can better exert "pull" – for example, by setting expectations, providing incentives and rewards, increasing access to resources (including thought leadership), and modelling desired behaviour – in these areas than "push" – for example, mandates, prescriptive practices, or even structured training. When people engage in informal or incidental learning, and they seek to learn from that experience, their motivation is likely to be intrinsic. Research on intrinsic motivation suggests that providing extrinsic rewards and direction can extinguish the flame of learning. It may be better to work towards cultivating a culture of learning.

As we discuss in our early work on informal and incidental learning (Marsick & Watkins, 1990, p. 8), "there is no formula that guarantees learning, whether it is formally organised or not. People may or may not learn when they are on the job, in classrooms, observing others, or participating in structured or unstructured conversations." In our early work, we distinguished among degrees of emphasis on action or reflection as a way of thinking about differences in informal, incidental, and formal learning. It is not that either kind of learning is better or worse, but each has its advantages or disadvantages. All potentially go on in a workplace, but without aligning and synergising these kinds of learning, many opportunities for appropriate learning are lost.

In the paramedic study, for example, Lovin (1991) pointed out how mandated continuing education for recertification was often wasted time because it was either boring or, more likely, was a repeat of what people already knew. When in-service was conducted by shift, even when the information was not new, paramedics reported that it could be fun and it contributed to team building (incidental learning) even if the information provided was likewise not new. How much more value could have been gained if continuing education had, for example, been built around storytelling with appropriate resources brought in to help paramedics go more deeply into their learning and role play situations for which they needed knowledge.

Health care situations such as this study of paramedics do reinforce the value of reflection before, during, and after action. But many workplaces (including those in which professionals are based) have a bias for action that typically excludes reflection that might be needed – before, during, or after action – to ensure that people are learning from experience rather than repeating the same experiences without the benefit of understanding when and how action is effective. When people act, and learn only incidentally, they may well NOT be learning. Learning requires some effort to understand and make tacit knowing explicit so that it can be better understood and thought about in relationship to past and future situations where circumstances, driving values, or cause–effect chains need to be clarified so that success can be attained and/or repeated.

Informal learning strikes a balance between action and reflection, but whether or not, and how, a person learns is left largely to the individual in terms of needed awareness of the opportunity to learn and organisation of the learning experience. This stands in contrast to formal training, which rests on an elaborate needs assessment and design process intended to ensure relevance and fit for the learner. But as we could see in the Lovin study, sometimes mechanisms put in place by the organisation spur and support informal learning – for example, the report made out after each call that requires reflection on what happened and may spur further review and rehearsal of lessons learned for future cases.

Much incidental learning also goes in when informal learning occurs. The challenge around incidental learning is that no one, the organisation or the individual, may be very aware that incidental learning is occurring because it is largely tacit and unobservable. Lovin (1991), for example, reports that incidental learning through storytelling sometimes resulted in embedded error, as we had noted when we first developed our thinking about our model. She provides an example of a paramedic who had found a way to bring a patient out of a drug overdose, but who was then reprimanded for not following accepted procedure. He at first apologised and indicated he had not known the correct procedure but would know the next time. But after thinking about it, he began to think his way had been better. So he started to consult others to find out what they thought. He talked to the training officer who thought either way would be OK as long as it worked. He talked to every paramedic he could approach to find out, if confronted by the situation, what they would have done. Many confirmed they would have done the same thing, which reinforced his belief that he should follow his way rather than procedure. Storytelling, in this case, was used to reinforce a belief that he did not have to follow procedure if he felt he knew better rather than seeing that while it had worked out for the best in that situation, it might not always work that way. Lovin talked to other paramedics who found themselves in similar circumstances, but recognised that perhaps their pursuit of others to learn what they would have done was less pursuit of truth and more pursuit of confirmation that others might have made the same mistake in similar circumstances (ibid., pp. 147–148).

Formal learning thus benefits from opportunities for reflection, but if these opportunities are too separated – in time, place, or relevance – from real life action, then learners may not see the point, or worse, may not feel motivated enough to engage seriously in learning from experiences (their own, those of others, or activities designed to simulate reality).

There are tensions, then, in how providers can best design and support informal and incidental learning in ways that make it easier to carry out and relevant to their agendas. The challenges that the provider faces involve shifting control of the experience to the learner and providing structure and resources to support his/her pursuit of learning goals in interaction with others. Professionals should be especially comfortable with this model because it suits their natural and/or socialised preferences for intrinsic motivation and commitment to developing their own expertise within the context of a larger body of shared expertise. Typically, however, organisations have been less satisfied with this approach because of an inherent need to control and predict towards certain desired goals and outcomes. While it is true that these goals and outcomes can be specified, and then leeway provided to reach these goals in a variety of ways, there is often a gap between a stated desire that employees (professionals or non-professionals) be self-directed in their learning and the reality of the way the workplace is structured. That gap is due, in part, to the fact that paradigms for organising and supporting work and learning are shifting in light of demographic shifts in the workforce, globalisation, and knowledge work. Companies, and professionals within them, can find that this provides a fruitful climate for experimentation with new models of work and learning. But it is also true that many of the people in a chain of command may not yet have shifted their thinking to these new paradigms, and while leadership at the top of an organisation may signal a shift in direction, the reality of interpreting what that direction means falls to these many people who act as the organisation's interpreters and negotiators of change.

References

Allen, P. B. (1995). *Art is a way of knowing*. Boston: Shambhala Press.
Argyris, C., & Schön, D. (1974). *Theory in practice: Increasing professional effectiveness*. San Francisco: Jossey-Bass.

Argyris, C., & Schön, D. (1978). *Organisational learning: A theory of action perspective*. San Francisco: Jossey-Bass.

Cleermans, A. (1995). No matter where you go there you are. *American Journal of Psychology, 108*(4), 589–599.

Cseh, M. (1998). *Managerial learning in the transition to a free market economy in Romanian private companies* (Doctoral dissertation).Athens: The University of Georgia. Dissertation Abstracts International, 59/06, 1865.

Cseh, M., Watkins, K. E., & Marsick, V. J. (1999). Re-conceptualizing Marsick and Watkins' model of informal and incidental learning in the workplace. In K. P. Kuchinke (Ed.), *1999 Proceedings of the Academy of HRD* (pp. 349–355). Baton Rouge: Academy of Human Resource Development.

Damasio, A. R. (1995). *Descartes' error: Emotion, reason, and the human brain*. New York: Avon Books.

Dewey, J. (1938). *Experience and education*. New York: Collier Books.

Goleman, D. (1995). *Emotional intelligence: Why it can matter more than IQ*. New York: Bantam Books.

Heron, J. (1992). *Feeling and personhood: Psychology in another key*. London: Sage.

Larson, B. K. (1991). *Informal workplace learning and partner relationships among paramedics in the prehospital setting*. (Doctoral dissertation, Teachers College, Columba University. Dissertation Abstracts International 52/02B, 0732.

LeDoux, J. (1996). *The emotional brain: The mysterious underpinnings of emotional life*. New York: Simon & Schuster.

Lewin, K. (1947). Frontiers in Group Dynamics. *Human Relations, 1*, 5–41.

Marsick, V. J., & Watkins, K. E. (1990). *Informal and incidental learning in the workplace*. New York: Routledge.

Marsick, V. J., Watkins, K. E., Callahan, M., & Volpe, M. (2008). Informal and Incidental Learning in the Workplace. In Smith, M. C. & DeFrates-Densch, N. (Eds.), *Handbook of Adult Learning and Development*. Routledge.

Nonaka, I., & Takeuchi, H. (1995). *The knowledge-creating company: How Japanese companies create the dynamics of innovation*. New York: Oxford University Press.

Poell, R. F., Chivers, G. E., van der Krogt, F. J., & Wildemeersch, D. A. (2000). Learning-network theory: organizing the dynamic relationships between learning and work. *Management Learning, 31*(1), 25–49.

Polanyi, M. (1967). *The tacit dimension*. New York: Doubleday & Company.

Schön, D. A. (1987). Educating the reflective practitioner: Toward a new design for teaching and learning in the professions. San Francisco: Jossey-Bass.

Seger, C. A. (1994). Implicit learning. *Psychological Bulletin, 115*(2), 163–196.

Simon, H. A. (1965). Administrative decision making. *Public Administration Review, 25*(1), 31–37.

Watkins, K., & Cervero, R. (2000). Organisations as contexts for learning: A case study in certified public accountancy. *Journal of Workplace Learning, 12*(5), 187–194.

Wenger, E. (1998). *Communities of Practice: Learning, meaning, and identity*. Cambridge: Cambridge University Press.

Yorks, L., & Kasl, E. (2002). Toward a theory and practice for whole-person learning: Reconceptualizing experience and the role of affect. *Adult Education Quarterly, 52*, 176–192.

Chapter 5
Making It Safe: The Effects of Leader Inclusiveness and Professional Status on Psychological Safety and Improvement Efforts in Health Care Teams

Ingrid M. Nembhard and Amy C. Edmondson

In today's complex organisations, teams are increasingly valued for their potential to innovate, solve problems and implement change. A growing literature on team learning identifies factors that allow teams to experiment, reflect and improve across a range of industry settings (Bunderson 2003a, 2003b; Edmondson, 1999; Gibson & Vermeulen, 2003). Few industries have more at stake when teams learn – or fail to learn – than health care. Increasingly, cross-disciplinary teams are responsible for delivering care to patients in settings ranging from primary care to critical acute care, chronic care, geriatrics and end-of-life care (Institute of Medicine, 2001). These teams face not only a daunting expansion of medical knowledge, but also increasing specialisation that divides critical knowledge among individuals – knowledge that must be integrated for the delivery of *quality* care, as well as for improving care.

In this environment, the combined challenges of teamwork and learning are emerging as central to the health care delivery enterprise, in particular because research has shown that 70–80% of medical errors are related to interactions within the health care team (Schaefer, Helmreich, & Scheideggar, 1994). This chapter seeks to advance theory in organisational behaviour and health care management by proposing and testing a model of engagement in team-based quality improvement work. In the next section, we review critical trends in health care delivery to set the stage for our model and empirical research.

Dynamic Trends in Health Care

Health care professionals today face a staggering rate of change in medical knowledge. Whereas in 1966, only 100 published articles reported on randomised control

I.M. Nembhard (✉)
Yale University, New Haven, USA
e-mail: ingrid.nembhard@yale.edu

This paper was first published in *Journal of Organizational Behaviour*, 27, 941-966 (2006). It is re-published here with kind permission of the authors and the copyright holders, John Wiley & Sons, Ltd trials – in medicine, the "gold standard" for recognising new knowledge – 1995 brought more than 10,000 (Chassin, 1998). In terms of sheer volume of new information, the Medline bibliographic database adds 30,000 new references each month, and the Federal Drug Administration reviews thousands of applications for new devices and drugs annually (Shine, 2002). No single individual can absorb all of this new knowledge in a timely manner. Nevertheless, new knowledge must be absorbed for continued effectiveness in health care delivery.

A second crucial trend is the increasing specialisation of health care professionals (Hafferty & Light, 1995). Prior to 1930, there were only two broad medical specialties (ophthalmology and otolaryngology). Today, there are 26 specialties and 93 subspecialties within the major specialties, 8 of which were approved during the 2002–2003 accrediting year (Accreditation Council for Graduate Medical Education, 2004). Thus, the scope of an individual physician's domain of expertise has diminished, while depth of expertise has increased. At the same time, a growing number of non-physician professions have joined the patient care enterprise. Specialists in nutrition, respiratory therapy, physical therapy, phlebotomy, and so on, have joined nurses as non-physician caregivers, playing vital roles in the health care system. In 1900, the ratio of physicians to non-physicians was 1:3; by 2000, it had exploded to 1 in 16 (Shine, 2002), implicating greater fragmentation of expertise, and more hand-offs in the patient care process (Leape et al., 1995). Today, an increasing number of different caregivers treat each patient at the bedside. Each brings information necessary and relevant for development of a cohesive care plan.

A third trend – almost a necessary outcome of the first two – is increasing interdependence. Many new technologies and care practices involve reciprocal (as opposed to sequential) interactions. Caregivers cannot simply do their jobs and assume others will come along at some point to do theirs. Instead, their knowledge and efforts must be integrated to deliver quality care.

These trends – increasing knowledge, specialisation and interdependence – which are more prominent in health care than in other industries, together imply a need for collaborative learning in groups of professionals from different disciplines. The modern intensive care unit (ICU) is said to exemplify the confluence of these factors (Wachter, 2004), but all health care settings have been touched by these trends. Collaboration – defined as "physicians and nurses [and other caregivers] working together, sharing responsibility for solving problems, and making decisions to formulate and carry out plans for patient care" (Baggs et al., 1999, p. 1991) – requires open communication and mutual respect in addition to collective decision making (Baggs et al., 1999; Brown, Ohlinger, Rusk, Delmore, & Ittmann, 2003; Zimmerman et al., 1993) and is critical to care delivery. Health professionals themselves have recognised the imperative for teamwork in clinical care and quality improvement, even suggesting that the latter needs to be based in cross-disciplinary teams (Donaldson & Mohr, 2000), a suggestion that has been embraced by many (e.g., Berwick, Godfrey, & Roessner, 1990; Horbar, 1999).

Barriers to Collaborative Learning in Health Care

Despite the need for collaborative learning in cross-disciplinary teams in the health care setting, team-based quality improvement efforts may stall for a number of reasons. First, the stakes are undeniably high. Human life is at risk when processes fail, creating understandable risk aversion that can inhibit willingness to engage in the chaos and uncertainty of team brainstorming and experimentation. It is noteworthy that studies of other high stress environments have shown that improvement efforts tend to be centralised and hierarchical rather than collective and democratic (Driskell & Salas, 1991; Fourshee & Helmreich, 1988; Hermann, 1963; Klein, 1976; Staw, Sandelands, & Dutton, 1981).

Second, cross-disciplinary teamwork – intended to integrate knowledge and expertise from different sources – is difficult to carry out in practice (e.g., see Edmondson, Roberto, & Watkins, 2003 for a review). Improving the quality of care delivery processes necessarily requires different viewpoints, each grounded in deep knowledge of a different aspect of the process. Physicians possess specialised medical expertise, while nurses and allied health workers (e.g., respiratory therapists and dietitians) have greater knowledge of daily patient-interaction processes. In combination, they contain a more comprehensive information base. However, information often goes unshared. A recent study showed that, although nurses witness and experience a variety of problems and employ a number of creative solutions to resolve emergent issues, they generally do not communicate these to others in the hierarchy (Tucker & Edmondson, 2003). Thus, despite its importance for improving care delivery, collaborative learning does not occur naturally in health care.

Third, and a central focus of this chapter, a well-entrenched status hierarchy exists in medicine, making it difficult to speak across professional boundaries (e.g., physician versus nurse versus therapists) to collaborate for learning (Edmondson, 2003). The medical training that instils a culture of autonomy for action can diminish professionals' tendencies to seek opportunities to learn to communicate, share authority and collaborate in problem solving and quality improvement (Institute of Medicine, 1999, 2001). Unfortunately, this reluctance can adversely affect patient care. Patient outcomes are significantly correlated with the degree of hierarchy in health care team interactions (Feiger & Schmitt, 1979). According to a recent report, *Keeping Patients Safe: Transforming the Work Environment of Nurses*, "counterproductive hierarchical communication patterns that derive from status differences" are partly responsible for many medical errors (Institute of Medicine, 2003, p.361). In a content analysis of medical malpractice cases from across the country, physicians (the high-status members of the team) were shown to have ignored important information communicated by nurses (the low status members of the team), and nurses also withheld relevant information for diagnosis and treatment from physicians (Schmitt, 1990). In this status-consciousness environment, opportunities for learning and improvement can be missed because of unwillingness to engage in quality-improving communication due to fear of reprisal by high-status others.

Aims of the Present Study

The present study investigates factors that promote engagement in quality improvement work when status differences are present in teams. We examine the relationship
between status and psychological safety, and introduce the construct of *leader
inclusiveness*, defined below, as a moderator of the status–psychological safety relationship. We then assess whether psychological safety mediates the relationship
between leader inclusiveness and engagement in improvement efforts. At a time
when quality improvement in health care is viewed as imperative, we aim to provide
insight into how to overcome an important barrier to quality improvement learning
efforts.

   The implications of this study extend beyond the health care industry, however.
With customer heterogeneity, a high need for customisation, and a highly specialised
workforce, hospitals present a challenging, but by no means unique, service setting.
Furthermore, the use of cross-disciplinary teams continues to rise across industries as organisations seek to learn and innovate to remain competitive (Griffin,
1997; Sarin & Mahajan, 2001; Wind & Mahajan, 1997). The salience of status in
health care though provides an opportunity to investigate its effects on team-based
improvement efforts and reveal implications for other organisations that use teams
encompassing status differences to improve products or services. Therefore, our
aim is to contribute to knowledge of the role of status in shaping perceptions of psychological safety and, more broadly, the conditions that support improvement and
learning in cross-disciplinary teams.

Collaborative Learning in Cross-Disciplinary Health Care Teams

Status in Professional Hierarchies as a Determinant of Psychological Safety

Status refers to the level of prominence, respect and influence associated with an
individual as a result of some characteristic (Anderson, John, Keltner, & Kring,
2001), such as age, education, ethnicity, gender, organisational position, profession
and wealth (Bacharach, Bamberger, & Mundell, 1993; Benoit-Smullyan, 1944).
According to status characteristics theory, personal characteristics affect self- and
other-assessments and beliefs about the individual and his or her performance abilities (Berger, Cohen, & Zelditch, 1972; Berger, Rosenholtz, & Zelditch, 1980). Status
characteristics can be "diffuse", meaning they are applicable over a range of settings
(e.g., age, gender, or ethnicity) or "specific", meaning they provide cues about a person's expertise relative to a task (e.g., education or professional training). In either
case, individuals that possess the esteemed characteristic or more of that characteristic are judged superior to those with less of that attribute. Thus, status indicates
relative position within a social hierarchy (Benoit-Smullyan, 1944).

In the United States, social status is often role- or profession-based. Status differences are thus "*most* salient in the work context where they often have practical implications (e.g., education level determining pay level)" (Bacharach et al., 1993, p. 24). Higher status individuals receive more tangible and intangible benefits in the workplace than their lower ranked coworkers. They gain power over the actions of others (e.g., determining co-worker schedules and tasks), prestige or the right to occupy honorary places (e.g., a windowed corner office), a reputation for significant contributions leading to greater solicitations of their opinions, the benefit of the doubt in ambiguous situations, and financial rewards (e.g., higher salary and department budgets).

The allocation of benefits which favours high-status individuals over lower-status individuals shapes the environment they share as well as interpersonal interactions (e.g., Alderfer, 1987). Individual awareness or beliefs that membership in a particular group (e.g., profession) bestows a certain level of status creates feelings of superiority or inferiority that consistently govern behaviour so as to preserve the hierarchy (Tajfel & Turner, 1986; Webster & Foschi, 1988). Compared to high-status individuals, those with low status are more likely to suffer low self-efficacy and underestimate their contribution to work tasks (Berger, Fisek, Norman, & Zelditch, 1985), and therefore withhold valid information (Argyris, 1985), defer decision rights to higher status others (Driskell & Salas, 1991), limit their organisational citizenship behaviour (Stamper & van Dyne, 2001) and speak less (Kirchler & Davis, 1986; Pagliari & Grimshaw, 2002; Vinokur, Burnstein, Sechrest, & Wortman, 1985; Weisband, Schneider, & Connolly, 1995). Consequently, organisations rely heavily on high-status individuals, which is beneficial when status corresponds to the expertise required for the task. However, empirical research suggests that individuals often fail to recognise the expertise held by multiple team members – to the detriment of group and organisational goals (e.g., see Littlepage, Robison & Reddington, 1997). Organisational innovation and improvement, in particular, suffer when minority opinions are ignored (Nemeth, 1986). Nevertheless, inadequate identification of the valid contributions continues because social hierarchy leads to the domination of high-status individuals and self-censoring by low-status individuals. The latter relates to perceptions of risk to self and fear of negative repercussions (e.g., public reprimand or assignment to a "bad" work shift).

Research on organisational silence indicates that sense of threat and/or risk is a key determinant of employees' willingness to speak up freely (Ashford, Rothbard, Piderit, & Dutton, 1998; Detert & Edmondson, 2005; Edmondson, 2003; Milliken, Morrison, & Hewlin, 2003; Morrison & Phelps, 1999; Ryan & Oestreich, 1991). Speaking up freely occurs when people are not constrained by the possibility of others' disapproval and/or the negative personal consequences that might accrue to them as a result – a state of psychological safety. In most organisations, those with high status have more control over formal appraisals and resources than those with low status, and thus may experience a certain freedom of self-expression in front of others, that low status individuals do not enjoy. Research on politeness shows that those with low status employ more "facework" (face saving verbal strategies) when addressing those with higher status than the other way around (Brown &

Levinson, 1987). With increased status, people exercise less concern about damaging others' face; such opinions can be freely voiced, and requests can be made of others without verbal compensation to convey apology, humility, or deference. This well-documented inverse relationship between status and politeness suggests corresponding differences in psychological safety across different status groups.

In general, high-status individuals tacitly assume that their voice is valued. People with high status – role-based and demographic – are more likely to be asked for their opinion than those with low status. Accustomed to having their opinions sought – often in formal capacities – they learn to offer them freely. They thus do not perceive the same level of interpersonal risk associated with self-expression experienced by those with low status. Qualitative evidence of this difference in psychological safety according to status was found in Kahn's (1990) study of an architectural firm and a summer camp; informants described their interactions with those positioned higher in the hierarchy as more stifling and threatening than their interactions with peers. Lower status individuals in Kahn's study reported a lack of confidence that higher status individuals would not embarrass or reject them for sharing contradictory thoughts.

Individuals in lower positions in the medical hierarchy (Helmreich, 2000) may feel a similar sense of fear about speaking up across status boundaries, for example, to raise a concern or challenge a current practice. The existence of a professional hierarchy in medicine and the differential status accorded to those who occupy different positions within that hierarchy is well-known to health professionals and well established in the health care literature (Coburn, 1992; DeSantis, 1980; Dingwall, 1974; Friedson, 1970a, 1970b; Fuchs, 1974; Hafferty & Wolinsky, 1991; Shortell, 1974; Wolinsky, 1988). We know that surgeons garner more prestige than other specialty physicians, that specialty physicians rank above primary care physicians, that physicians possess more power than nurses, nurses than physical therapists, and so on. The hierarchy and related status differences exist within professional groups (e.g., physicians: specialists versus primary care) and between groups (e.g., physicians versus non-physicians), with between group status differences being most salient and largest. We therefore predict, based on prior research on the behaviours of different status groups, that non-physicians, as lower status health professionals, view the cross-disciplinary team climate as less psychologically safe than higher status individuals such as physicians:

> *Hypothesis 1 (H1)*: In cross-disciplinary teams, higher status individuals will experience greater psychological safety than lower status individuals. (In cross-disciplinary health care teams, physicians will experience more psychological safety than nurses, who will experience more psychological safety than respiratory therapists.)

The proposed main effect between status and psychological safety may vary depending on how status differences are handled in a work group. Prior research found that psychological safety can vary significantly across groups, even within the same strong organisational culture (Edmondson, 1996, 1999). Bringing together professionals with different backgrounds and expertise may exacerbate this variance, if some groups handle the challenge of managing these differences more skillfully than others (Bunderson, 2003b). When status differences are present in a team, team members must manage a tension between the norms of collaboration that underlie the notion of teamwork and the reality of status differences. Prior research showed that the degree of status derived from different professions can vary across cross-disciplinary work groups (Bunderson, 2003a). Similarly, the formal status associated with a given profession in health care may be treated differently in different work groups called "units" in health care. The unit is a cross-disciplinary care team, consisting of all of the staff, that participates in delivering a specific domain of clinical care – for example, intensive care or cardiac care. Differences in status handling across work groups in other settings suggest the effect of role-based professional status on psychological safety will also vary across cross-disciplinary unit teams – indicating an interaction effect between status and unit team membership on psychological safety:

Hypothesis 2 (H2): Status and unit team membership will interact to predict psychological safety.

Bunderson (2003a) identified two group attributes – average tenure and power centralisation – that helped explain differences in status effects across groups, and suggested that future research consider alternative moderators such as task interdependence (Wageman, 1995) and task uncertainty (van de Ven, Delbecq, & Koenig, 1976). Another research suggests that how work is organised affects status relationships. In their study of specialised AIDS units versus general medical units treating AIDS patients, Aiken and Sloane (1997) found that the relative status of nurses was increased after the conversion to specialised units. They attributed the elevation in status to an increased appreciation for nurses' specialised knowledge and client differentiation. We explore another possibility – that leader behaviour, particularly in its level of inclusiveness, can frame the meaning of status differently across units, even with similar structures or work design (Edmondson, 2003), helping to explain why status effects might vary across work groups.

Leader Inclusiveness

Team leader behaviours, in general, have been shown to affect the internal dynamics of a team, in particular influencing team climate and learning orientation (Baker, Murray & Tasa, 1995; Edmondson, 1999; Hult, Hurley, Guinipero, & Nicholas, 2000; Madhavan & Grover, 1998; Norrgren & Schaller, 1999; Shortell, Rousseau, Gillies, Devers, & Simons, 1991; Yukl, 1994; Zimmerman et al., 1993). Team members are highly attuned to the behaviour of leaders and examine leader actions for information about what is expected and acceptable in team interactions (Tyler & Lind, 1992). If a leader takes an authoritarian, unsupportive, or defensive stance, team members are more likely to feel that speaking up in the team is unsafe. In contrast, if a leader is democratic, supportive, and welcomes questions and challenges, team members are likely to feel greater psychological safety in the team and in their interactions with each other.

Preliminary evidence of leadership effects on psychological safety emerged in a study of medication errors in nursing teams (Edmondson, 1996). In some units, nurses described nurse managers as authoritarian and also expressed deep fears about being reprimanded for revealing mistakes. In contrast, nurses in other units felt safe speaking up about errors because their nurse manager had stressed the importance of using this information as a learning tool for the unit. In a later study of cardiac surgery teams, qualitative data suggested that teams with leaders who actively invited others' input had higher psychological safety than those in which this behaviour was absent. Qualitative data suggested that surgeon team leaders handled status differences within their teams differently (Edmondson, 2003). Although all teams comprised four professional roles, with clear traditional status differences, in some, the surgeons (those with the highest status) made an explicit effort to invite others' input to help the team implement a new technology. In other teams, the leaders were not similarly proactive.

Building on these qualitative insights, we propose the construct of *leader inclusiveness*, defined as words and deeds by a leader or leaders that indicate an *invitation* and *appreciation* for others' contributions. Leader inclusiveness captures attempts by leaders to include others in discussions and decisions in which their voices and perspectives might otherwise be absent. It is related to team leader coaching behaviour, which describes team leader behaviours that facilitate group process and provide clarification and feedback (Baron, 1990; Edmondson, 1999), and to participative leadership, which describes leaders that consult with workers, participate in shared decision-making and delegate decision-making authority to subordinates (Bass, 1990; McGregor, 1960; Yukl, 1994). Leader inclusiveness differs from these constructs in that it directly pertains to situations characterised by status or power differences *and* pertains more narrowly to behaviours that invite and acknowledge others' views. The established constructs did not capture sufficiently the difficulty of lower social position, nor the behaviour of explicit invitation designed to overcome communication boundaries.[1]

Leader inclusiveness describes behaviour that, through direct invitation, should create psychological safety for speaking up. We suggest that both invitation and appreciation are needed to convey the inclusiveness that helps people believe that their voices are genuinely valued. Without a recognisable invitation, impressions derived from the historic lack of invitation will prevail. And without appreciation (i.e., a positive, constructive response), the initial positive impact of being invited to provide input will be insufficient to overcome the subsequent hurdle presented by status boundaries. Defining leader inclusiveness in this way, we hypothesise that

Hypothesis 3 (H3): Leader inclusiveness is positively associated with psychological safety.

---

[1]More specifically, team leader coaching describes the leader as an operational facilitator; participative leadership emphasises harnessing employee motivation to maximise productivity. Thus, neither construct is intended – as is leader inclusiveness – to address status salient environments, nor to identify the two-pronged strategy of invitation and appreciation.

Finally, we predict that leader inclusiveness will alter the status–psychological safety relationship as follows. When leaders demonstrate inclusiveness, lower status others are likely to feel supported and believe the leaders see them as important members of the team. An atmosphere of mutual respect across the different professions may develop, in which the specialised expertise held by those with low status is seen as valuable to the team's shared task. This helps to equalise the value associated with all members' contributions, promoting an egalitarian context. These efforts may increase the level of psychological safety felt by everyone in the team, but the effect is likely to be greater for low status individuals who have less prior experience with others expressing interest in their input than it will be for those with high status. In contrast, when leader inclusiveness is low, a lack of opportunity to overcome traditional status barriers allows them to prevail, such that low status individuals fail to experience an elevation in psychological safety, leaving high-status individuals more advantaged in this respect. Thus, we hypothesise

Hypothesis 4 (H4): Leader inclusiveness moderates the relationship between status and psychological safety.

Engagement in Quality Improvement

The need for active quality improvement in health care has been widely recognised since the Institute of Medicine released its 1999 report documenting rampant failures in the health care system. Improving the quality of work processes and outcomes requires effort and engagement – which we define, drawing on Kahn (1990), as being physically, cognitively, and/or emotionally connected to the improvement work. Engagement is essential for overcoming powerful barriers to quality improvement that exist in the health care setting, as well as in other busy and chaotic service contexts. Health care professionals are often stretched thin, barely able to complete their required tasks in the workday, let alone devote time to improving the system (Tucker & Edmondson, 2003). Participating in quality improvement efforts thus requires deliberate and effortful allocation of time. Yet, despite time and resource constraints, many in health care are embracing quality improvement projects, because of what is at stake when systems fail. The construct of engagement captures the commitment and effort these individuals devote to quality improvement.

We argue that engagement in quality improvement in health care is likely to be enabled by psychological safety. First, engaging in quality improvement requires team members to be willing to try new technologies and procedures, remaining cognitively "mindful" of relationships between tasks and team members (Weick, 2002) and emotionally open to giving and receiving feedback in these states of transition. These behaviours can be interpersonally risky and thus more likely to be found when psychological safety is present. In a psychologically safe environment, team members do not feel they must be guarded in their behaviour, instead feeling encouraged to question current practices and to share what may be regarded as provocative ideas, challenging the group to develop more innovative solutions. Without psychological safety, suggesting new procedures, overstepping professional status boundaries (Kahn, 1990), or offering unsolicited feedback would seem overly risky.

Second, in a related vein, researchers have argued and shown that individuals' willingness to participate in problem-solving activities diminishes significantly when they view the team as hostile (e.g., Dutton, 1993; MacDuffie, 1997). In fact, they are more likely to act in ways that diminish learning behaviour (Argyris & Schön, 1978). One such way is to withdraw from the team and its work. Kahn (1990) described this as personal *dis*engagement. We thus expect an association between psychological safety and engagement in quality improvement work in health care. Psychological safety creates the willingness to change personal habits (Schein & Bennis, 1965), and should allow team members to be enthusiastic about improvement and their role in that process.

Hypothesis 5 (H5): Psychological safety is positively associated with engagement in quality improvement work.

Combining Hypotheses 5 and 3, we predict that psychological safety will mediate a relationship between leader inclusiveness and engagement:

Hypothesis 6 (H6): Psychological safety mediates a relationship between leader inclusiveness and engagement in quality improvement work.

Together, our hypotheses comprise a model of engagement in quality improvement work that includes antecedents and consequences of psychological safety for health care improvement teams (see Fig. 5.1). We hypothesise that professional status (H1) and its interaction with unit team membership (H2) explain variance in psychological safety. Moreover, the magnitude of the status influence is moderated by leader inclusiveness (H4), an additional predictor of psychological safety (H3). Finally, psychological safety enables engagement in quality improvement work (H5), and mediates between leader inclusiveness and engagement (H6).

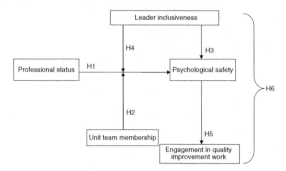

Fig. 5.1 A model of professional status on psychological safety as a precursor to engagement in quality improvement work: the moderating effect of leader inclusiveness and the mediating effect of psychological safety

Organisational Context

The Quality Improvement Imperative in Health Care

In 1998, the National Roundtable on Health Care Quality issued a statement, *The Urgent Need to Improve Quality of Care,* which documented significant quality problems in the American health care system, problems ranging from overuse of antibiotics to underuse of beta blockers following heart attack to misuse inherent in medical error (Chassin, Galvin, & the National Roundtable on Health Care Quality, 1998). Shortly thereafter, the Institute of Medicine published *To Err is Human* (1999) and *Crossing the Quality Chasm* (2001), which further quantified the extent of preventable medical error and identified the systemic nature of quality problems. In response to these reports, health care organisations across the country from individual providers to community health centers to hospital systems bolstered their efforts to improve the quality of care they delivered (Wachter, 2004). Continuous quality improvement became a community ideal, to which every organisation strove to achieve. The health care organisations we studied were no different.

Profile of Participating Unit Teams

We collected data for this study from NICUs in the United States and Canada. NICUs provide care for premature infants, infants weighing less than 1500 grams and infants born with complications. All of the NICUs studied were members of the 2-year 44-member Neonatal Intensive Care Quality improvement Collaborative (NIC/Q, 2002). Collaboratives such as this, which are intended to facilitate improvement by facilitating the transfer of knowledge across health care organisations (Kilo, 1999), are a growing phenomenon in health care (Mittman, 2004). In the one we studied, cross-disciplinary teams were encouraged to work together on specified improvement areas (e.g., infection control, respiratory care management, or discharge planning) to develop and test clinical, organisational, and operational changes for improving neonatal care. As such, this setting was particularly attractive for our study of how status relationships that exist between professional disciplines relate to psychological safety and engagement in quality improvement in cross-disciplinary teams. To craft and execute their quality improvement projects in-house, team members from different disciplines had to work together. Development of a new or better delivery room plan for infant resuscitation, for example, required physicians, nurses, and respiratory therapists to share their expertise and recommendations with one another to ensure that the developed plan included accurate and up-to-date practices from each group, and accounted for their interactions.

Methods

Sample and Procedure

We conducted data collection in three phases.

First, we visited 4 of the 44 neonatal intensive care units (NICUs) in the collaborative. We toured the units, observed unit functioning and interviewed 23 staff members (5–7 members per NICU) for 30 to 90 minutes using open-ended questions about the NICU work climate and quality improvement efforts. We selected the four NICUs to include differences in demographic variables (teaching status, size, etc.) and improvement efforts (e.g., improvement focus areas and prior collaborative participation) and selected interviewees to capture multiple professional groups (i.e., physicians, nurses and respiratory therapists). This increased our understanding of NICUs and facilitated the design of a meaningful survey for this population. In the second phase, we developed and pilot-tested a survey with these four NICUs. Descriptive statistics and psychometric tests indicated no need to alter the survey. Further, the survey results accorded with our site visit observations, supporting the validity of the instrument.

In the third and final phase, we invited the 40 remaining, non-pilot site NICUs in the collaborative to participate in the survey via phone and electronic mail directed to the leader of each NICU's collaborative improvement team. Twenty-three NICUs agreed, for a NICU response rate of 58%. When we compared participating sites to non-participating sites, we found no significant differences between the two groups on a variety of structural, clinical and patient acuity measures. For example, there were no significant differences based on hospital ownership type (not-for-profit, for-profit, government), teaching status, level of severity of the care provided in the NICU, volume of extremely low birth weight babies (ELBW, less than or equal to 1000 g), number of times the site participated in prior collaboratives (0, 1, or 2), length of stay, percentage of ELBW babies with Apgar scores less than or equal to 3 one minute after birth, percentage of babies transported from another hospital ("outborn"), average birth weight and gestational age (see Tucker, Nembhard, & Edmondson, 2006).

As soon as a NICU received the permission of its hospital Institutional Review Board (IRB), its team leader provided us with a count of the number of staff and patient beds in the unit. We then invited all team members in the NICU to participate in our survey by an invitational letter distributed in accordance with the procedures outlined in the hospital IRB approval. In 18 NICUs, the collaborative team leader electronically mailed or placed in team mailboxes our letter to team members, which provided instructions on where to retrieve a paper copy of the survey in the unit, if interested. In the remaining five NICUs, the team leader distributed our letter along with a paper copy of the survey to team mailboxes. The invitational letter described the purpose of the study, assured respondents' anonymity, and included instructions for completion of the paper as well as an online version of the survey. We offered two versions to allow participants to choose their preferred format. All individuals returned the survey directly to us through self-addressed stamped envelope or online submission.

In all, 1,440 health care professionals (46% of team members contacted) from 23 NICUs in the United States and Canada completed the survey between July 2003 and May 2004. Of the respondents, 1,375 persons declared their profession: 100 as physicians (83 neonatologists, 13 attending physicians and 4 neonatology fellows), 998 as nurses (65 neonatal nurse practitioners, 16 Master's prepared nurses, 8 clinical nurses specialists, 867 registered nurses, 14 licensed nurse practitioners and 28 other nursing functions), 131 as respiratory therapists, and 146 as other types of health care professionals (e.g., social workers and dietitians). Excluding individuals in the latter group (because the presence and recognition of their discipline as part of the NICU team varied across units), NICUs averaged 60 respondents, ranging from 10 to 164. The average number of respondents per NICU was 3 physicians, 15 nurses and 5 respiratory therapists.

We regarded the professionals in each NICU from medicine, nursing and respiratory therapy as the "unit team" because these interdependent professionals unquestionably work together in the unit on a daily basis. Their patients generally stay in the NICU for an extended period of time, often months, to receive the care that only a team of neonatal-trained practitioners can deliver. These teams and members are so specialised that they work exclusively in the NICU.[2]

Measures

Professional status. Professional status was inferred from occupational category because prior research had demonstrated that status in the medical field derives from role or position in the professional hierarchy (Friedson, 1970a, 1970b, 1994; Mechanic, 1991; Wolinsky, 1988). The numerous professional roles reported in the survey were combined into three major categories for the purposes of these analyses: (1) physicians (neonatologists, other attending physicians and neonatal fellows); (2) nurses; and (3) respiratory therapists. Further, because physicians – as "captains of the health care team" (Fuchs, 1974) – garner higher status than all other health care professionals (Hafferty & Light, 1995), an additional dichotomous professional status variable was created to reflect that (0 = low status = nurses and respiratory therapists, 1= high status = physicians).

Unit team membership. Unit team membership, a categorical variable, refers to the specific NICU in which an individual respondent worked ($N = 23$).

---

[2]There is one possible exception to the exclusivity of the NICU teams. Some hospitals do use "rotating" respiratory therapists, who work exclusively on the unit for a defined period of time periodically (e.g. 2 months every 2 months), then rotate to other units when not assigned to the NICU. That said, we believe that "unit teams" are accurately represented in our sample since we asked team leaders to distribute the survey to NICU staff. We abided by team leader judgement of team membership.

Psychological safety. Four items from Edmondson's (1999) psychological safety scale adapted to this context were used to assess the extent to which respondents felt safe to speak up about issues or ideas regarding the NICU. Examples of these items are "Members of this NICU are able to bring up problems and tough issues" and "People in this unit are comfortable checking with each other if they have questions about the right way to do something." Respondents' agreement (1 = strongly disagree, 7 = strongly agree) with these items formed a single scale (Chronbach alpha = .73).

Leader inclusiveness. In the hospital context, physicians are both high-status technical experts and leaders who are responsible for directing the efforts of others in delivering care to patients. Thus, although the construct of leader inclusiveness is more general, in this setting it refers to behaviours and attitudes of the physicians-in-charge. A three-item scale assessed the extent to which NICU leaders' words and deeds indicated an invitation and appreciation for others as contributing members in a team endeavour. The first two items, "NICU physician leadership encourages nurses to take initiative" and "Physicians ask for the input of team members that belong to other professional groups," were adapted from Shortell et al.'s (1991) physician leadership scale. The third item, "Physicians do not value the opinion of others equally" (reversed scored), was developed by us for this research. The level of agreement with each statement (1 = strongly disagree, 7 = strong agree) was averaged to provide a single perception for each respondent (Chronbach alpha = 0.75).

In this study, we assessed leader inclusiveness with data from non-physicians only, for two reasons. First, prior research suggested that nurses provide a more accurate assessment of organisational culture and leadership practices than physicians. One study showed that while nurses' reports of the culture showed appropriate variance, physicians' reports were more uniform across different contexts, as well as more positive; further, only the nurse data predicted performance outcomes (Leonard, Frankel, Simmonds, & Vega, 2004), affirming earlier studies' findings that nurses' perceptions of the work environment are more predictive of the risk of adverse outcomes (e.g., Baggs et al., 1999) and quality of care (e.g., Shortell et al., 1991) than physicians. Second, and more important, conceptually, those with low status are in a better position to assess the degree to which high-status leaders are including them than are those with high status – who may rate themselves as inclusive even when others would not do so. More simply, physician ratings of their own inclusiveness towards others are unlikely to be as externally valid as the ratings of those others will be.

Engagement in quality improvement work. Engagement in quality improvement work was measured using a four-item scale adapted from Baker and colleagues (2003). Sample items are "A growing number of staff in this NICU are participating in improvement efforts" and "In the coming year, I would like to be very involved in our NICU's quality improvement efforts." Respondents rated their agreement with these statements on a seven-point scale (1 = strongly disagree to 7 = strongly agree). Chronbach's alpha was 0.79.

Control variables. We included gender, years working in any NICU, years as an employee of the hospital, years working in the current NICU and hours per week in the NICU as control variables since these demographic variables are potential predictors of psychological safety at the individual level. These control variables were excluded from the group-level analyses performed to test psychological safety as a mediator between leader inclusiveness and engagement in quality improvement work (H6).

Table 5.1 provides the means, standard deviations and intercorrelations between the variables. We assessed the adequacy of our survey measures through tests of internal consistency reliability and discriminant validity. The results supported the use of these measures for analysis. Chronbach's alpha for all survey scales exceeded the 0.70 threshold proposed by Nunnally (1978) for internal consistency, and factor analysis, in which the planned constructs emerged, confirmed discriminant validity.

Analysis and Results

To test Hypotheses 1 and 2, that status and its interaction with unit team membership explain variance in psychological safety; we used a univariate general linear model (GLM) with professional status (three groups: physicians, nurses and respiratory therapists) and unit team membership as independent variables and the reflected, logarithmic transformation of psychological safety as the dependent variable.[3] We also included the above mentioned control variables. Results shown in the upper portion of Table 5.2 indicate that two of the five control variables were significant and that our first two hypotheses were supported. The number of years spent working in any NICU and the number of years spent working in the current NICU significantly predicted psychological safety ($F(4, 1111) = 3.54$, $p = 0.01$ and $F(4, 1111) = 3.09$, $p = 0.02$): More time spent in NICUs in general as well as an intermediate amount of time spent in the current NICU (5 to less than 10 years) both were associated with higher psychological safety. The number of years as an employee of the current hospital was only marginally predictive ($F(4, 1111) = 2.09$, $p = 0.08$), and gender and hours worked per week not at all ($F(1, 1111) = 0.01$, $p = 0.93$ and $F(1, 1111) = 0.24$, $p = 0.62$).

Consistent with Hypothesis 1, professional status was positively associated with psychological safety ($F(2, 67) = 8.46$, $p = 0.001$). Physicians felt significantly more psychological safety than nurses ($t(1111) = -0.33$, $p < 0.001$) who in turn reported more psychological safety than respiratory therapists ($t(1111) = -.11$, $p = 0.02$); the overall planned contrast was significant ($F(2, 1111) = .14.11$, $p < 0.001$).

---

[3]The reflected, logarithmic transformation corrected for heterogeneity of variance and non-normality (i.e. negative skewness) in the dataset (Tabachnick & Fidell, 2001).

Table 5.1 Summary statistics and intercorrelations for individual-level data

Variable	Mean	S.D.	1	2	3	4	5	6	7	8	9
1. Professional status – 3 groups: Physicians v. nurses v. therapists	2.03	0.43									
2. Professional status – 2 groups: High v. low status	0.08	0.27	0.71**								
3. Psychological safety	5.31	1.08	0.15**	0.14**							
4. Leader inclusiveness	4.62	0.55	< 0.01	−0.01	0.29**						
5. Engagement in quality improvement work	5.45	1.06	0.12**	0.17**	0.48**	0.21**					
6. Gender	1.10	0.30	0.23**	0.56**	0.05	−0.04	0.02				
7. Years in any NICU[a]	4.17	1.19	0.08**	0.10**	−0.05	0.09**	−0.03	0.08**			
8. Years as a hospital employee[a]	3.97	1.26	0.03	0.01	−0.04	0.02	−0.02	0.07*	0.73**		
9. Years in current NICU[a]	3.84	1.31	0.05	0.03	−0.04	0.02	−0.02	0.08**	0.81**	0.94**	
10. Hours per week in NICU	33.84	13.46	0.35**	0.38**	0.05	−0.03	0.10**	0.12**	−0.06*	−0.08**	−0.08**

[a]This is a categorical variable: 1 = less than 1 year, 2 = 1 to less than 2 years, 3 = 2 to less than 5 years, 4= 5 to less than 10 years, 5 = 10 or more years
* $p < 0.05$
** $p < 0.01$

Table 5.2 Results of general linear model analysis

Model	Independent variables	F-ratio	p
Y = Ln(psychological safety)	Gender	$F(1, 1111) = 0.01$	0.93
	Years in any NICU	$F(4, 1111) = 3.54$	0.01
	Years as a hospital employee	$F(4, 1111) = 2.09$	0.08
	Years in current NICU	$F(4, 1111) = 3.09$	0.02
	Hours per week in NICU	$F(1, 1111) = 0.2$	0.62
	Professional status − 3 groups	$F(2, 67) = 8.46$	0.001
	Unit team membership	$F(22, 41) = 2.08$	0.02
	Professional status (3) x unit team membership	$F(31, 1111) = 2.22$	<0.001
Y = Ln(psychological safety)	Gender	$F(1, 1126) = 0.10$	0.76
	Years in any NICU	$F(4, 1126) = 3.98$	0.003
	Years as a hospital employee	$F(4, 1126) = 1.66$	0.16
	Years in current NICU	$F(4, 1126) = 2.43$	0.05
	Hours per week in NICU	$F(1, 1126) = 0.001$	0.97
	Professional status − 2 groups	$F(1, 1126) = 11.58$	0.001
	Leader inclusiveness	$F(21, 1126) = 4.27$	<0.001
	Professional status (2) x leader inclusiveness	$F(18, 1126) = 1.78$	0.02

To determine whether the effect of professional status on psychological safety varied across multidisciplinary teams, as predicted in Hypothesis 2, we examined the interaction term composed of professional status and unit team membership. The interaction was significant ($F(31, 1111) = 2.22$, $p < 0.001$), indicating that the difference in psychological safety felt across status groups varied across teams, even as the main effect of status on psychological safety remained significant. In some teams, status differences were less important, such that members of different professional groups felt similarly safe. In others, professional status differences led to larger disparities in psychological safety among groups.

Hypotheses 3 and 4 that leader inclusiveness predicts psychological safety, and moderates the relationship between status and psychological safety, were tested using GLM analyses. First, however, we assessed the properties of leader inclusiveness, as a new construct. Just as prior work (Edmondson, 1999; Shamir, Zakay, Breinin, & Popper, 1998) has shown convergent perceptions of leadership behaviour in teams, we anticipated that views of leader inclusiveness would be shared in the NICUs studied. To test this, we performed a one-way analysis of variance with unit team membership as the independent variable and leader inclusiveness (rated by non-physicians only) as the dependent variable. The ANOVA results showed significant variance at the group level of analysis for leader inclusiveness as reported by low status individuals ($F(22, 1095) = 9.44$, $p < 0.001$), and an intraclass correlation that was positive and significant ($r_{ICC} = 0.35$), confirming leader inclusiveness as a group-level measure (Kenny & LaVoie, 1985). We therefore entered the team's leader inclusiveness score (the team average) as the individual's score for each member of the team in the individual-level dataset.

We used this dataset and a GLM to test Hypotheses 3 and 4 that leader inclusiveness is positively associated with psychological safety and moderates the relationship between professional status and psychological safety. The dichotomous professional status variable (high status, if physician and low status, if nurse or respiratory therapist), leader inclusiveness and their interaction served as independent variables, along with all of the control variables. Again, the reflected, logarithmically transformed psychological safety measure served as the dependent variable. The results shown in the lower section of Table 5.2 support the hypothesised relationships. When physician leaders were perceived as inclusive and welcoming of others' ideas and efforts, psychological safety was greater ($F(21, 1126) = 4.27$, $p < 0.001$) (Hypothesis 3). Also, as predicted in Hypothesis 4, leader inclusiveness moderated the relationship between status and psychological safety, as indicated by a significant interaction term ($F(18, 1126) = 1.78$, $p = 0.02$). Low leader inclusiveness was associated with a greater disparity in psychological safety between high and low status individuals to the disadvantage of low status individuals. In contrast, high leader inclusiveness was associated with a lower difference in psychological safety between the two groups, raising the psychological safety of low status individuals closer to that of their high-status team members (see Fig. 5.2).

To test Hypothesis 5, that psychological safety is positively associated with engagement in quality improvement work, we conducted a regression analysis on the group level dataset. Using this dataset, allowed us to not only test our hypothesis, but also as important, examine the relative influence of a competing group-level variable on engagement: staff workload or busyness of the work environment. Prior work has identified staff workload as a predictor of quality-related behaviour (Oliva,

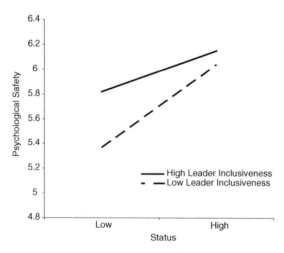

Fig. 5.2 Psychological safety as a function of professional status and leader inclusiveness

2001; Tucker & Edmondson, 2003). Overburdened employees facing competing priorities are less likely to further quality goals. Therefore, to continue with our model of engagement in quality improvement work, the question of relative influence had to be addressed to provide assurance that our model was not mis-specified in emphasising psychological safety as a determinant of engagement. We first performed one way analysis of variance and intraclass correlations for psychological safety ($F(22, 1366) = 8.62$, $p < 0.001$; $r_{ICC} = 0.21$) and engagement in quality improvement work ($F(22, 1352) = 7.67$, $p < 0.001$; $r_{ICC} = 0.81$) to confirm the group level status of the variables before proceeding with the analysis. We then regressed engagement on psychological safety and the ratio of staff-to-patient beds (mean $= 3.31$, S.D. $= 0.91$), our measure of staff workload. The results provided support for our hypothesis that the more members feel they work in a team characterised by interpersonal trust and respect, the more enthusiastic and devoted they are to participating in quality improvement efforts, which often require the interpersonally risky act of collaborative learning ($B = 0.62$, $p = 0.001$). We found this relationship, even after accounting for the competing influence of staff busyness, which was an insignificant predictor of engagement ($B = -0.14$, $p = 0.09$) and thus eliminated from further analyses.

To test Hypothesis 6, that psychological safety mediates the relationship between leader inclusiveness and engagement in quality improvement work, we estimated three regression equations to satisfy the conditions for mediation (Baron & Kenny, 1986). The first condition is that the independent variable must significantly affect the mediator; second, the independent variable must predict the dependent variable; and third, the mediator must significantly predict the dependent variable when entered in the same regression equation as the independent variable, while the independent variable drops in significance or becomes insignificant. We assessed whether these conditions were satisfied using group-level data because leader inclusiveness (our independent variable), psychological safety (our proposed mediator) and engagement in quality improvement work (our dependent variable) are conceptually meaningful and empirically demonstrated as group-level variables. We measured leader inclusiveness at the aggregate non-physician level for reasons explained above, and analyses related to testing Hypothesis 5 confirmed psychological safety and engagement as group-level constructs as well.

As shown in Table 5.3, the results support all three mediation conditions: (1) leader inclusiveness predicts psychological safety (B $= 0.53$, $p < 0.001$), (2) leadership inclusiveness predicts team engagement at the group level (B $= 0.41$, $p = 0.004$), and (3) when included in the same model, leader inclusiveness becomes insignificant (B $= 0.11$, $p = 0.52$), while psychological safety remains significant (B $= 0.57$, $p = 0.03$). Thus, the data support psychological safety as a mediator of the relationship between leader inclusiveness and team engagement in quality improvement work.

In sum, all of our hypotheses were supported by the data. Not only do high-status individuals differ from low status individuals in psychological safety, but also there is an interaction between status and unit team membership, and between status and leader inclusiveness. Greater inclusiveness minimises the effect of status

Table 5.3 Tests of psychological safety as a mediator between leader inclusiveness and engagement in quality improvement work ($N = 23$)

Conditions to demonstrate mediation[a]	Independent variable	B	t	p	R^2
1. Does leader inclusiveness predict *engagement in quality improvement work*?	Leader inclusiveness	0.41	3.19	0.004	0.33
2. Does leader inclusiveness predict *psychological safety*?	Leader inclusiveness	0.53	5.02	<0.001	0.55
3. Does the effect of leader inclusiveness drop substantially or become insignificant when psychological safety (the mediator) is included in the model for *engagement in quality improvement work*?	Psychological safety	0.57	2.32	0.03	0.47
	Leader inclusiveness	0.11	0.65	0.52	

[a]Dependent variables are in italics

on psychological safety in the team, and vice versa. Moreover, with more leader inclusiveness comes greater psychological safety, which in turn predicts greater team engagement in quality improvement work.

Discussion and Conclusions

Towards a Theory of Role-Based Status and Psychological Safety in Teams

This chapter empirically examined the effect of professional status on psychological safety in health care teams, motivated both by the theoretical role of psychological safety in team learning (Edmondson, 1999) and by the practical need for team learning in today's hospitals. As anticipated, psychological safety was significantly associated with professional status in these data. The results thus suggest that, in health care, professional status influences beliefs about how easy or appropriate it is to speak up to offer ideas, raise concerns, or ask questions. At the same time, our results showed significant differences across groups in the strength of the association between status and psychological safety, suggesting that this relationship need not be deterministic. In some teams, members with high (i.e., physicians) and low (i.e., nurses and respiratory therapists) status reported more similar levels of safety than in other teams, in which relatively large disparities in psychological safety between professional groups were found. This finding provides reassurance that the effects of traditional status differences in health care may be overcome, facilitating full participation in cross-disciplinary team improvement efforts.

Unlike in other industries, where employees may advance in the hierarchy – moving from sales assistant to sales associate or from analyst to consultant to principal, for example – medical professionals cannot rely on professional mobility to confer greater status. Professions tend to be stable over a career. Nurses and respiratory therapists generally do not become doctors. As a result, the opportunity for natural status gains by lower status individuals can be rare. With history and industry structure as perpetuators, profession-related status differences continue. And, the growing interdependence among professions only heightens intergroup tensions. According to social psychological (Alderfer, 1977; Alderfer & Smith, 1982; Messick & Mackie, 1989) and ethnographic (Dougherty, 1992) research, this is natural.

Our results suggest leader inclusiveness – words and deeds by leaders that invite and appreciate others' contributions – can take nature off its course, helping to overcome status' inhibiting effects on psychological safety. In cross-disciplinary teams with high leader inclusiveness, the status–psychological safety relationship was weakened. We thus suggest that active, inclusive behavior on the part of physician leaders may be an essential means of facilitating others' meaningful engagement in team-based quality improvement work. Thus, a key contribution of this study is the identification of an interpersonal strategy for improving the climate for learning within cross-disciplinary teams in health care. This extends prior work that has shown psychological safety consistently to be related to leader behavior (Edmondson, 1999; 2003; Hult et al., 2000; Lovelace, Shapiro and Weingart, 2001; Norrgren & Schaller, 1999), by narrowing and sharpening the nature of leader behaviors that promote psychological safety.

Recent studies of psychological safety and communication in the health care environment have also highlighted the role of the leadership in cultivating a culture of safety, but have not articulated the actual practices of leaders that are needed, other than *training staff* to speak up (Leonard et al., 2004; Maxfield, Grenny, McMillan, Patterson, & Switzler, 2005). Our research suggests that *training leaders* to invite team members' comments and to appreciate those comments overtly is as important. As we did not test any training methods, we cannot draw conclusions about what training strategies will work. However, training that includes instruction in the timing and phrasing of invitation and appreciation may be useful. Boyle and Kochinda (2004) tested a training intervention to improve communication between nurse and physician leaders,[4] and found that staff perceptions of leadership, communication and problem solving between professional groups improved in the post-intervention period, affirming that leadership training is promising route to improved team climate. Our results also suggest it is route to increasing engagement in quality improvement.

---

[4]The "collaborative communication intervention" employed by Boyle and Kochinda (2004) consisted of multiple learning activities, small group skill practice and problem-solving decisions; feedback and reinforcement of newly learned skills; a planning assignment for on-the-job applications; and assessment and feedback after the intervention. Participating ICU leaders spent a total of 23.5 hours learning communication and process skills (e.g., how to open a conversation and how to seek ideas from all involved, etc.).

A More Nuanced Look at Team Learning for Health Care Improvement Efforts

The study also provides insight into a more focused type of team learning than has been investigated in prior related research: team learning for quality improvement. First, we found evidence that psychological safety, in combination with leader inclusiveness, promotes team engagement in quality improvement work. Second, the finding that psychological safety mediates between leader inclusiveness and engagement in quality improvement extends prior work that showed psychological safety to be a mediator between the broader construct of team leader coaching behaviour and team learning behaviour, more generally (Edmondson, 1999). Finally, our model and findings shed light on the important but rarely studied phenomenon of engagement in discretionary, effortful quality improvement activities. Although our emphasis was on the effects of psychological safety, we also acknowledge that there may be other processes that contribute to engagement (e.g., psychological availability) (Kahn, 1990) that we have not addressed. Future research should explore additional mechanisms by which teams become actively engaged in quality improvement work.

The challenge of engaging busy, overworked professionals and service workers – already burdened by the heavy demands of their "real jobs" – in quality improvement activities should not be underestimated. In the course of a day, health care professionals are continuously called upon to immediately address the many needs of patients and co-workers. The requests are so many that nurses often sacrifice their personal breaks (e.g., lunchtime) and work overtime without compensation in order to complete their daily clinical care tasks (Tucker & Edmondson, 2003). The time pressure to complete tasks is so great that the most burdened frequently neglect to wash their hands, despite almost universal awareness that hand hygiene is a cornerstone of good clinical practice (Institute of Medicine, 2003).

In this challenging work environment, competing demands could surely relegate the perceived extra-role work of participating in quality improvement efforts to the background unless engagement ignites a counter response. Our analyses – using staff-to-patient beds as a measure of workload – suggest that the engagement needed to motivate such efforts is related more to psychological safety within the unit team than the burden created by competing demands and workload. This is good news for health care because it suggests that improvement efforts need not be delayed until greater slack is created; rather engagement in improvement efforts may occur in unit teams once a climate of psychological safety for learning is cultivated. Thus, another contribution of the present study is to illuminate organisational antecedents of engagement, which can be a difficult state to elicit naturally.

Limitations

This study is not without limitations. First, our use of a sample consisting exclusively of NICUs and their professionals may limit the generalisability of the findings. While NICUs are similar to other health care units in exemplifying the trend towards cross-disciplinary teams mentioned at the outset (associated with increasing knowledge, specialisation and interdependence), one could argue that these trends are heightened in NICUs, making the setting unusual. Moreover, the fragility of the (infant) patient and the importance of timely communication and action are also special characteristics of the NICU. These contextual variables may foster an appreciation for teamwork and recognition of each discipline's contribution such that leader inclusiveness is more prevalent in NICUs than in other health care settings, and more likely to elicit responsiveness. Other unit types (e.g., outpatient units) may be slower to realise the unique contributions of traditionally lower status team members and the interdependency among disciplines. Therefore, status differences may be greater in those unit teams compared to those in the NICU environment, and leadership's achievement of inclusiveness may be more difficult. Our data do not allow us to make a comparison based on unit type. However, the presence of significant variance between NICUs with respect to leader inclusiveness suggests that leader inclusiveness is not a universal NICU attribute. Some NICU leaders experience significant difficulty behaving inclusively. Whether this relationship varies across unit types will have to be investigated in future work.

Future work should also address imperfections of our data. We received completed surveys from only 58% of the NICUs in the collaborative and only 46% of unit team members contacted (excluding survey pilot sites). Although demographic comparison of participating and non-participating NICUs showed no differences between the two groups and our response rates are similar to other studies in hospitals (Edmondson, 1996; Jacob & Deshpande, 1997; Kaissi et al., 2004), we cannot ignore the possibility of non-response bias at the group and individual levels. The latter is a most serious concern if individual non-respondents are those who did not feel psychologically safe and included. The absence of their responses biases their unit data upward, incorrectly giving the appearance of units that have managed to minimised status differences in psychological safety and that are inclusive. Subsequent studies with higher response rates are needed to address this concern. Additionally, those studies are advised to examine a relationship we were unable to test with our dataset – whether specialisation among nurses is associated with differences in psychological safety. Nurse respondents did indicate their professional training (e.g., neonatal nurse practitioner versus Master's prepared nurse) in their survey responses; however this was not enough information to accurately identify different specialties within the nursing populations across units. We urge scholars in this area to collect information about daily tasks and specific care delivery roles to further assess the effects of specialisation and status *within* a professional group on psychological safety.

Finally, we must acknowledge that team engagement in quality improvement work is an intermediary outcome. The ultimate goal of health professionals involved in quality improvement work is to close the gap between current and evidence-based practice to produce the highest quality care possible in a consistent manner (Shojania, McDonald, Wachter, & Owens, 2004). Although we lack data in this study to test the relationship between engagement in quality improvement work and team learning as evidenced by quality improvement outcomes, past research shows a positive relationship between employee engagement and other organisational outcomes, including customer satisfaction, productivity, profit and safety (Buckingham & Coffman, 1999), and future research should further test this relationship.

Practical Implications

In sum, this study extends a stream of research on creating psychological safety for learning within cross-disciplinary teams, and begins the discussion about team engagement in quality improvement work. At a time when much attention is centered on how to advance quality improvement efforts in health care, this chapter offers initial theoretical and practical insight. Specifically, training leaders to be inclusive to foster psychological safety may be a critical antecedent of effective quality improvement, because it may create the engagement that is necessary for teams to participate in the specific learning activities required for quality improvement. We find, in related work, that psychological safety enables the performance of "learn-how" activities – experimental activities such as pilot projects, dry runs and problem-solving cycles – which are interpersonally risky yet often required for the implementation success of quality improvement projects in health care (Tucker, Nembhard, & Edmondson, 2006). Together, these findings imply a focus on team leader behaviour to create the conditions (i.e., psychological safety) and then the opportunities (i.e., learn-how activities) for team quality improvement efforts.

We do not intend to suggest that the development of inclusive leaders within NICUs would affect psychological safety or engagement in other parts of hospital systems. NICU leaders rarely interact with other clinical units, thus the opportunities for their inclusive nature to shape the climate of other multidisciplinary care delivery teams directly is limited. Likewise, NICU team members typically do not work on other care teams, so any habit of collaborative interactions is mostly NICU-contained.

Although this research took place in the health care context, the findings may apply to other organisational contexts as well. In particular, in other organisations with cross-disciplinary teams, status diversity and a need for teams to continuously improve the services or products the organisation produces, the model developed in this chapter may be highly relevant. A growing number of industries are characterised by these features, as organisations realise that individuals in different functions, locations and stations of life possess specialised knowledge that can be valuable for problem solving and innovation, *if* shared and combined with the knowledge of other employees through teamwork. Therefore, our model may have wider relevance than just health care, but health care, with its prevalence of cross-disciplinary teams, salient status differences, and many quality improvement efforts is particularly conducive for exploring and developing these ideas.

Acknowledgements This research benefited greatly from the expert help of health care management and operations researchers Anita L. Tucker and Dr. Richard Bohmer (also a physician), as well as the superb research assistance of Laura Feldman. We thank the participants in the Leadership and Groups seminar at Harvard University, Denise Rousseau and two anonymous reviewers for their constructive comments on earlier versions of this manuscript. We also appreciate the invitation to conduct this research provided by Dr. Jeffrey Horbar, Kathy Leahy, Paul Plsek and the Vermont Oxford Network, as well as the willingness of nurses, physicians, respiratory therapists and other staff members of the participating hospitals to engage in this research. Their time, effort, and honesty provided an invaluable contribution, for which we are deeply appreciative. The Harvard Business School Division of Research provided generous financial support.

References

Accreditation Council for Graduate Medical Education. (2004). *2002–2003 Annual Report.* Retrieved December 14, 2004, from http://www.acgme.org/acWebsite/about/ab_2002-03AnnRep.pdf.

Aiken, L. H., & Sloane, D. M. (1997). Effects of specialisation and client differentiation on the status of nurses: The case of AIDS. *Journal of Health and Social Behaviour, 38,* 203–222.

Alderfer, C. P. (1977). Group and intergroup relations. In J. R. Hackman & J. L. Suttle (Eds.), *Improving life at work: Behavioural science approaches to organisational change* (pp. 227–296). Santa Monica, CA: Goodyear.

Alderfer, C. P. (1987). An intergroup perspective on organisational behaviour. In J. W. Lorsch (Ed.), *Handbook of Organisational Behaviour* (pp.190–222). Englewood Cliffs, NJ: Prentice-Hall.

Alderfer, C. P., & Smith, K. K. (1982). Studying intergroup relations embedded in organisations. *Administrative Science Quarterly, 27,* 35–65.

Anderson, C., John, O. P., Keltner, D., & Kring, A. M. (2001). Who attains social status? Effects of personality and physical attractiveness in social groups. *Journal of Personality and Social Psychology, 81,* 116–132.

Argyris, C. (1985). *Strategy, change, and defensive routines.* Boston, MA: Pitman.

Argyris, C., & Schön, D. A. (1978). *Organisational learning: A theory of action perspective.* Reading, MA: Addison-Wesley.

Ashford, S. J., Rothbard, N. P., Piderit, S. K., & Dutton, J. E. (1998). Out on a limb: The role of context and impression management in selling gender-equity issues. *Administrative Science Quarterly, 43,* 23–57.

Bacharach, S. B., Bamberger, P., & Mundell, B. (1993). Status inconsistency in organisations: From social hierarchy to stress. *Journal of Organisational Behaviour, 14,* 21–36.

Baggs, J. G., Schmitt, M. H., Mushlin, A. I., Mitchell, P. H., Eldredge, D. H., Oakes, D., et al. (1999). Association between nurse-physician collaboration and patient outcomes in three intensive care units. *Critical Care Medicine, 27,* 1991–1998.

Baker, R. G., King, H., MacDonald, J. L., & Horbar, J. D. (2003). Using organisational assessment surveys for improvement in neonatal intensive care. *Pediatrics, 111,* e419–e425.

Baker, R. G., Murray, M., & Tasa, K. (1995, December). *Quality in action: An instrument for assessing organisational culture for quality improvement.* Paper presented at the First International Scientific Symposium on Improving Quality and Value in Health Care, Orlando, FL.

Baron, R. M., & Kenny, D.A. (1986). The moderator-mediator variable distinction in social psychological research: Conceptual, strategic and statistical considerations. *Journal of Personality and Social Psychology, 51,* 1173–1183.

Baron, R. A. (1990). Countering the effects of destructive criticism: The relative efficacy of four interventions. *Journal of Applied Psychology, 73,* 199–207.

Bass, B. M. (1990). *Bass and Stogdill's handbook of leadership.* New York: Free Press.

Benoit-Smullyan, E. (1944). Status, status types, and status interrelations. *American Sociological Review, 9*, 151–161.

Berger, J., Cohen, B. P., & Zelditch, M. (1972). Status characteristics and social interaction. *American Sociological Review, 8*, 241–255.

Berger, J., Fisek, H., Norman, R. Z., & Zelditch, M. (1985). The formation of reward expectations in status situations. In J. Berger & M. Zelditch (Eds.), *Status, Rewards, and Influence.* San Francisco, CA: Jossey-Bass.

Berger, J., Rosenholtz, S. J., & Zelditch, M. (1980). Status organizing processes. In A. Inkeles, N. J. Smelser & R. H. Turner (Eds.), *Annual Review of Sociology* (Vol. 6, pp. 479–508). Palo Alto: Annual Reviews.

Berwick, D. M., Godfrey, A. B., & Roessner, J. (1990). *Curing health care: New strategies for quality improvement.* A report on the National Demonstration Project on Quality Improvement in Health Care. San Francisco, CA: Jossey-Bass.

Boyle, D. K., & Kochinda, C. (2004). Enhancing collaborative communication of nurse and physician leadership in two intensive care units. *Journal of Nursing Administration, 34*(2), 60–70.

Brown, M. S., Ohlinger, J., Rusk, C., Delmore, P., & Ittmann, P., on Behalf of the CARE Group. (2003). Implementing potentially better practices for multidisciplinary team building: Creating a neonatal intensive care unit culture of collaboration. *Pediatrics, 111*(Suppl.). e482–e488.

Brown, P., & Levinson, S. C. (1987). *Politeness: Some universals in language usage.* New York: Cambridge University Press.

Buckingham, M., & Coffman, C. (1999). *First, Break All the Rules.* New York: Simon and Schuster.

Bunderson, J. S. (2003a). Recognizing and utilizing expertise in work groups: A status characteristics perspective. *Administrative Science Quarterly, 48,* 557–591.

Bunderson, J. S. (2003b). Team member functional background and involvement in management teams: Direct effects and the moderating role of power centralisation. *Academy of Management Journal, 46*, 458–474.

Chassin, M. R. (1998). Is health care ready for six sigma quality? *Milbank Quarterly, 76,* 575–591.

Chassin, M. R., Galvin, R. W., & National Roundtable on Health Care Quality. (1998). The urgent need to improve health care quality. *Journal of the American Medical Association, 280,* 1000–1005.

Coburn, D. (1992). FriEdson then and now: An 'internalist' critique of Friedson's past and present views of the medical profession. *International Journal of Health Services, 22,* 497–512.

DeSantis, G. (1980). Realms of expertise: A view from within the medical profession. In J. A. Roth (Ed.), *Research in the sociology of health* (pp.179–236). Greenwich, CT: JAI.

Detert, J. R., & Edmondson, A.C. (2005). No exit, no voice: The bind of risky voice opportunities in organisations." *Harvard Business School Working Paper, No. 05-049.*

Dingwall, R. W. (1974). Some sociological aspects of 'nursing research''. *The Sociological Review, 22,* 45–55.

Donaldson, M. S., & Mohr, J. J. (2000). *Exploring innovation and quality improvement in health care microsystems: A cross case analysis.* Washington, D.C.: Institute of Medicine, National Academy Press.

Dougherty, D. (1992). Interpretive barriers to successful product innovation in large firms. *Organisation Science, 3,* 179–202.

Driskell, J. E., & Salas, E. (1991). Group decision making under stress. *Journal of Applied Psychology, 76,* 473–478.

Dutton, J. E. (1993). The making of organisational opportunities: an interpretive pathway to organisational change. In L. L. Cummings & B. M. Staw (Eds.), *Research in organisational behaviour* (pp. 195–226). Greenwich, CT: JAI Press.

Edmondson, A. (1999). Psychological safety and learning behaviour in work teams. *Administrative Science Quarterly, 44,* 350–383.

Edmondson, A. C. (1996). Learning from mistakes is easier said than done: group and organisational influences on the detection and correction of human error. *Journal of Applied Behavioural Science, 32,* 5–32.

Edmondson, A. C. (2003). Speaking up in operating room: how team leaders promote learn interdisciplinary action teams. *Journal of Management Studies, 40,* 1419–1452.

Edmondson, A. C., Roberto, M. A., & Watkins, M. D. (2003). A dynamic model of top management team effectiveness: managing unstructured task streams. *Leadership Quarterly, 219,* 1–29.

Feiger, S. M., & Schmitt, M. H. (1979). Collegiality in interdisciplinary health teams: Its measurement and its effects. *Social Science & Medicine, 13A,* 217–229.

Fourshee, H. C., & Helmreich, R.L. (1988). Group interaction and flight crew performance. In E. L. Wiener, D. C. Nagel, & M. P. Friedman (Eds.), *Human Factors in Aviation* (pp.189–227). San Diego, CA: Academic.

Friedson E. (1970a). *The profession of medicine.* New York: Dodd, Mead.

Friedson, E. (1970b). *Professional dominance: the social structure of medical care.* Chicago, IL: Aldine.

Friedson, E. (1994). *Professionalism reborn: Theory, prophecy, and policy.* Chicago, IL: University of Chicago Press.

Fuchs, V. (1974). *Who shall live? Health, economics and social choice.* New York: Basic Books.

Gibson, C. B., & Vermeulen, F. (2003). A health divide: Subgroups as stimulus for team learning behaviour. *Administrative Science Quarterly, 48,* 202–239.

Griffin, A. (1997). PDMA research on new product development practices: Updating trends and benchmarking best practices. *The Journal of Product Innovation Management, 14,* 429–458.

Hafferty, F. W., & Light, D. W. (1995). Professional dynamics and the changing nature of medical work. *Journal of Health and Social Behaviour, 35,* 132–153.

Hafferty, F. W., & Wolinsky, F. D. (1991). Conflicting characterisations of professional dominance. *Current Research on Occupations and Professions, 6,* 225–249.

Helmreich, R. L. (2000). On error management: Lessons from aviation. *British Journal of Management, 320,* 781–785.

Hermann, C. F. (1963). Some consequences of crisis which limit the viability of organisations. *Administrative Science Quarterly, 8,* 61–82.

Horbar, J. D. (1999). The Vermont Oxford Network: Evidence-based quality improvement for neonatology. *Pediatrics, 103,* 350–359.

Hult, G. T. M., Hurley, R. F., Guinipero, L. C., & Nichols, E. L. (2000). Organisational learning in global purchasing: A model and test of internal users and corporate buyers. *Decision Sciences, 31,* 293–325.

Institute of Medicine. (1999). *To err is human: Building a safer health system.* In L.T. Kohn, J. M. Corrigan, & M.S. Donaldson (Eds.), Washington, DC: National Academy Press.

Institute of Medicine. (2001). *Crossing the quality chasm: A new system for the 21st century.* Washington, DC: National Academy Press.

Institute of Medicine. (2003). *Keeping patients safe: Transforming the work environment of nurses.* Washington, DC: National Academy Press.

Jacob, J., & Deshpande, S. P. (1997). The impact of ethical climate on job satisfaction of nurses. *Health Care Management Review, 22,* 76–80.

Kahn, W. A. (1990). Psychological conditions of personal engagement and disengagement at work. *Academy of Management Journal, 33,* 692–724.

Kaissi, A., Kralewski, J., Curoe, A., Dowd, B., & Silversmith, J. (2004). How does the culture of medical group practices influence the types of programs used to assure quality of care? *Health Care Management Review, 29,* 129–138.

Kenny, D. K., & LaVoie, L. 1985. Separating individual and group effects. *Journal of Personality and Social Psychology, 48,* 339–348.

Kilo, C. M. (1999). Improving care through collaboration. *Pediatrics, 103*(Suppl.). 384–393.

Kirchler, E., & Davis, J. H. (1986). The influence of member status differences and task type on group consensus and member position change. *Journal of Personality and Social Psychology, 51,* 83–91.

Klein, A. L. (1976). Changes in leadership appraisal as a function of the stress of a simulated panic situation. *Journal of Personality and Social Psychology, 34,* 1143–1154.

Leape, L. L., Bates, D. W., Cullen D. J., Cooper, J., Demonaco, H. J., Gallivan, T., et al. (1995). Systems analysis of adverse drug events. *Journal of the American Medical Association, 274,* 35–43.

Leonard, M. S., Frankel, A., Simmonds, T., & Vega, K. B. (2004). *Achieving safe and reliable healthcare: Strategies and solutions.* Ann Arbor, MI: Health Administration Press.

Littlepage, G., Robison, W., & Reddington, K. (1997). Effects of task experience and group experience on group performance, member ability, and recognition of expertise. *Organisational Behaviour and Human Decision Processes, 69,* 133–147.

Lovelace, K., Shapiro, D. L., & Weingart, L. R. (2001). Maximizing cross-functional new product teams' innovativeness and constraint adherence: A conflict communication perspective. *Academy of Management Journal, 44,* 779–793.

MacDuffie, J. P. (1997). The road to "root cause": Shop-floor problem-solving at three auto assembly plants. *Management Science, 43,* 479–502.

Madhavan, R., & Grover, R. (1998). From embedded knowledge to embodied knowledge: New product development as knowledge management. *Journal of Marketing, 62,* 1–12.

Maxfield, D., Grenny, J., McMillan, R., Patterson, K., & Switzler, A. (2005). *Silence Kills: The Seven Crucial Conversations for Healthcare.* Provo, UT: VitalSmarts, L.C.

McGregor, D. (1960). *The Human Side of Enterprise.* New York: McGraw Hill.

Mechanic, D. (1991). Sources of countervailing power in medicine. *Journal of Health Politics, Policy and Law, 16,* 485–498.

Messick, D. M., & Mackie, D. M. (1989). Intergroup relations. *Annual review of psychology, 40,* 45–81.

Milliken, F. J., Morrison, E.W., & Hewlin, P.F. (2003). An exploratory study of employee silence: Issues that employees don't communicate upward and why. *Journal of Management Studies, 40,* 1453–1476.

Mittman, B. S. (2004). Creating the evidence base for quality improvement collaboratives. *Annals of Internal Medicine, 140,* 897–901.

Morrison, E. W., & Phelps, C. C. (1999). Taking charge at work: Extrarole efforts to initiate workplace change. *Academy of Management Journal, 42,* 403–419.

Nemeth, C. J. (1986). Differential contributions of majority and minority influence. *Psychological Review, 93,* 23–32.

Norrgren, F., & Schaller, J. (1999). Leadership style: Its impact on cross-functional product development. *The Journal of Product Innovation Management, 16,* 377–384.

Nunnally, J. 1978. *Psychometric theory* (2nd Ed.), New York: McGraw-Hill.

Oliva, R. (2001). Tradeoffs in response to work pressure in the service industry. *California Management Review, 43,* 26–42.

Pagliari, C., & Grimshaw, J. (2002). Impact of group structure and process on multidisciplinary evidence-based guideline development: An observational study. *Journal of Evaluation in Clinical Practice, 8*(2). 145–153.

Ryan, K.D., & Oestreich, D.K. (1991). *Driving fear out of the workplace: How to overcome the invisible barriers to quality, productivity, and innovation.* San Francisco: Jossey-Bass.

Sarin, S., & Mahajan, V. (2001). The effect of reward structures on the performance of cross-functional product development teams. *Journal of Marketing, 65,* 35–53.

Schaefer, H. G., Helmreich, R.L., & Scheideggar, D. (1994). Human factors and safety in emergency medicine. *Resuscitation, 28,* 221–225.

Schein, E. H., & Bennis, W. (1965). *Personal and organisational change through group methods: a labouratory approach.* New York: Wiley.

Schmitt, M. H. (1990). Medical malpractice and interdisciplinary team dynamics. *Proceedings of the 12th Annual Interdisciplinary Health Care Team Conference* (pp. 53–66). Indianapolis, IN: Indiana University.

Shamir, B., Zakay, E., Breinin, E., & Popper, M. (1998). Correlates of charismatic leader behaviour in military units: Subordinates' attitudes, unit characteristics and superiors' appraisals of leader performance. *Academy of Management Journal, 41*, 387–409.

Shine, K. I. (2002). Health care quality and how to achieve it. *Academic Medicine, 77*, 91–99.

Shojania, K.G., McDonald, K. M., Wachter, R. M., & Owens, D. K. (2004). *Closing the quality gap: A critical analysis of quality improvement strategies.* AHRQ Publication No. 04-0051-1.

Shortell S. M. (1974). Occupational prestige differences within the medical and allied health professions. *Social Science and Medicine, 8*, 1–9.

Shortell, S. M., Rousseau, D. M, Gillies, R. R., Devers, K. J., & Simons, T. L. (1991). Organisational assessment in intensive care units (ICUs): construct development, reliability, and validity of the ICU nurse-physician questionnaire. *Medical Care, 29*, 709–726.

Stamper, C. L., & Van Dyne, L. (2001). Work status and organisational citizenship behaviour: a field study of restaurant employees. *Journal of Organisational Behaviour, 22*, 517–536.

Staw, B. M., Sandelands, L. E., & Dutton, J. E. (1981). Threat-rigidity effects in organisational behaviour: a multilevel analysis. *Administrative Science Quarterly, 26*, 501–524.

Tabachnick, B. G., & Fidell, L. S. (2001). *Computer-assisted research and design.* Boston: Allyn and Bacon.

Tajfel, H., & Turner, J. C. (1986). The social identity theory of intergroup behaviour. In S. Worchel & W. G. Austin (Eds.), *Psychology of intergroup relations* (pp. 7–24). Chicago: Nelson-Hall.

Tucker, A. L., Nembhard, I. M., & Edmondson, A. C. (2006). *The effects of learn-what and learn-how on the implementation success of improvement projects.* HBS Working Paper No. 06-049.

Tucker, A.L., & Edmondson, A. C. (2003). Why hospitals don't learn from failures: Organisational and psychological dynamics that inhibit system change. *California Management Review, 45*, 55–72.

Tyler, T. R., & Lind, E.A. (1992). A relational model of authority in groups. In M. P. Zanna (Ed.), *Advances in experimental social psychology* (Vol 25 pp.115–191). New York: Academic.

van de Ven, A. H., Delbecq, A. L., & Koenig, R., Jr. (1976). Determinants of coordination modes within organisations. *American Sociological Review, 41*, 322–338.

Vinokur, A., Burnstein, E., Sechrest, L., & Wortman, P. M. (1985). Group decision-making by experts: Field study of panels evaluating medical technologies. *Journal of Personality and Social Psychology, 49*, 70–84.

Wachter, R. M. (2004). The end of the beginning: Patient safety five years after 'To Err is Human'. *Health Affairs, W4*, 534–545.

Wageman, R. (1995). Interdependence and group effectiveness. *Administrative Science Quarterly, 40*, 145–180.

Webster, M., & Foschi, M. (1988). *Status generalisations.* Stanford, CA: Stanford University Press.

Weick, K. E. (2002). The reduction of medical errors through mindful interdependence. In M. M. Rosenthal & K. M. Sutcliffe (Eds.), *Medical error: What do we know? What do we do?* (pp. 177–199). San Francisco, CA: Jossey-Bass.

Weisband, S. P., Schneider, S. K., & Connolly, T. (1995). Computer-mediated communication and social information: Status salience and status differences. *Academy of Management Journal, 38*, 1124–1151.

Wind, J., & Mahajan, V. (1997). Issues and opportunities in new product development: An introduction to the special issue. *Journal of Marketing Research, 34*(February), 1–12.

Wolinsky, F. D. (1988). The professional dominance perspective, revisited. *The Milbank Quarterly, 66*, 33–47.

Yukl, G. (1994). *Leadership in organisations* (3rd Ed.). Englewood Cliffs, NJ: Prentice Hall.

Zimmerman, J. E, Shortell, S. M, Rousseau, D. M, Duffy, J., Gillies, R. R, Knaus, W.A., et al. (1993). Improving intensive care: Observations based on organisational case studies in nine intensive care units: A prospective, multicenter study. *Critical Care Medicine, 21*, 1443–1451.

Chapter 6
Making Sense of Curriculum Innovation and Mathematics Teacher Identity

Candia Morgan

The professional environment in which teachers work has been changing in recent years through centralised governmental interventions in a number of countries. This has involved the introduction or elaboration of national curricula, testing regimes and measures of school effectiveness. All these interventions, characteristic of mar-ketisation of education and the new regime of performativity (Ball, 2003) have the effect to "erode teachers' autonomy and challenge teachers' individual and collective professional and personal identities" (Day, 2002). In England, teach-ers' traditional professional independence has been substantially diminished by the introduction of the National Curriculum (DES/WO, 1988; DfEE, 1999), with its prescription of curriculum content and its associated assessment, followed more recently by the National Primary and Secondary Strategies' definition and prescrip-tion of pedagogy (DfES, 1999, 2001) and accompanied by a punitive regime of published "league tables" of schools and inspections by the Office for Standards in Education (Ofsted). Yet such increased regulation of teachers' practices, while possibly successful in the short term in achieving its desired changes and raising achievement of pupils on specific measures, contains within itself the risk of damag-ing the quality of teaching and of the teaching profession, thus negating any benefits that might ensue from the reforms. As Beck and Young (2005) argue, "genuine ethi-cal responsibility" in professional practice can only occur if practitioners themselves are responsible for the quality of the service they provide. In this chapter, I intend to explore this dilemma for regulation in the English context, examining the ways in which documents supporting the changes in curriculum and pedagogy endorsed by the *National Strategy* for Key Stage 3[1] work to recruit mathematics teachers

C. Morgan (✉)
Institute of Education, University of London, London, UK
e-mail: C.Morgan@ioe.ac.uk

An earlier version of this chapter (Morgan, 2005) was presented at the Fourth International Mathematics Education and Society Conference. I am grateful for the stimulating discussion with conference participants

[1] Key Stage 3 refers to the first 3 years of secondary school, consisting of pupils in Years 7, 8 and 9 (age 11–14). The National Strategy, itself an expansion of the National Literacy and Numeracy

C. Kanes (ed.), *Elaborating Professionalism*, Innovation and Change in Professional Education 5, DOI 10.1007/978-90-481-2605-7_6,
© Springer Science+Business Media B.V. 2010

to acceptance of the reforms, while allowing them to maintain their professional identities.

The notion of identity itself is subject to considerable debate and is used and defined in a variety of ways. I do not intend to engage in detail here with the question of what constitutes identity and acknowledge that my own use of the term is proba- bly insufficiently rigorously defined. Nevertheless, my use of *identity* is underpinned by the following principles:

- Identity is not monolithic but multiple and dynamic.
- Discourses construct subject positions and ascribe these to participants.
- Individuals participate in multiple discourses with different resources and sets of subject positions available.
- Individuals' positioning at any point is constrained, though not determined, by the roles and subject positions available to them within the discourses at play and by the ways in which other participants relate to them. But they also posi- tion themselves. This occurs through the choices (conscious or unconscious) they make between the resources available to them as they seek to account for their practices.
- This accounting has both "external" and "internal" aspects, consisting of how others conceive of the subject and how subjects conceive of themselves.

"Professional identity" is taken to refer to the ways in which teachers account for their practices as teachers and their positionings within official and unofficial discourses of teaching and of their subject.

At a time of change in the discourses of education, there is potential for conflict between teachers' existing positionings and accounting strategies and those avail- able or ascribed to them by the new regimes. For example, Woods and Jeffrey's (2002) study of primary teachers undergoing Ofsted inspection identifies the way in which the monitoring regime creates conflicts for the teachers, describing this in terms of inconsistencies between the "social identities" ascribed to them exter- nally by newly introduced competence-based official definitions of good teaching and their "personal identities" and "self concepts", shaped in part by their experi- ences of teaching and of their initial training that had been framed by child-centred philosophies of education and previously officially endorsed notions of good teach- ing based on personal qualities. While Woods and Jeffrey show how some of the teachers studied worked to position themselves in ways that allowed them to cope

---

Strategies introduced into primary schools in the late 1990 s, has expanded its scope considerably since its inception in 2001. From an initial focus on the core curriculum subjects, it now intervenes in all subject areas and many other aspects of pedagogy and school management, including, for example, assessment, behaviour management and truancy. Most recently it has been renamed the Secondary Strategy, to incorporate Key Stage 4 (Years 10 and 11). In this chapter, however, I focus only on the mathematics component of the Strategy, specifically the *Framework for Teaching Mathematics: Years 7, 8 and 9* (DfES, 2001), the key definition of mathematics and mathematics teaching in the lower secondary school.

with the fragmentation of their social and self-identities, others were unable to establish coherent positions within the new discourse of teaching, eventually leaving the profession.

It is perhaps inevitable that such fragmentation and conflict should occur as teachers have to engage with new discourses that redefine their roles and introduce different criteria for evaluating their practice as well as changing structures and locations of authority and accountability. Newly introduced discourses, however strongly regulated and officially endorsed, do not simply displace old discourses. Rather, they add new sets of resources to those already available for participants to draw on in making sense of their practice and establishing their identities and they realign existing resources in ways that may disrupt existing sets of values and ways of accounting. In an earlier study of mathematics teachers engaged in assessing pupils' written work as part of a recently introduced system of national high stakes assessment, teachers were seen to position themselves in different ways in relation to official and unofficial discourses of mathematics teaching, learning and assessment (Morgan, Tsatsaroni, & Lerman, 2002) and to shift between different positions as they sought to resolve the conflicts between the values and concepts of the various discourses (Morgan, 1996). Such conflicts between the discursive resources and positions available to participants in a situation create spaces within which emotional experiences may arise (Evans, Morgan, and Tsatsaroni, 2006), driving participants to work to establish some form of coherence in their positioning and to account for their practices in ways that are positively valued within one or more of the discourses at play.

For mathematics teachers, establishing a positive professional identity involves positioning themselves within discourses of education in general and mathematics teaching in particular in ways that allow them to be seen by others and by themselves as "good" teachers of mathematics.[2] They must thus be able to demonstrate that they have the qualities that are valued within the relevant discourses as qualities of good teachers of mathematics and that their teaching practices are consistent with those that are valued as "good practice". But what is good teaching? Stronach, Corbin, McNamara, Stark, & Warne (2002) argue that performative discourses in education have relocated notions of "good". Judgements of what is good may once have been based on psychological or ethical grounds, making use of theories about how children learn or principles of social justice. Current curriculum discourse, in contrast, defines it normatively. Teaching and learning are presented as two sides of the same coin: good or effective teaching is that which leads to good learning, which is itself defined in terms of test results. Curricula tend to be defined in terms of what pupils should learn or what they should be taught – these two being presented as essentially the same – or in some cases the kinds of experiences they should have. For example, the National Curriculum for England contains "Programmes of Study"

---

[2] Some may instead (or additionally) choose to position themselves in relation to other aspects of their professional practice (e.g. management or pastoral care), but I am concerned here only with the aspects of teachers' professional identity in relation to their teaching of mathematics.

consisting of lists of what "Pupils should be taught" to do, while the "Attainment Targets" against which achievement is measured consist of parallel lists expressed in terms of what pupils themselves have learnt to do (DfEE, 1999). Traditionally, *how* to teach has generally been considered a matter of professional judgement, to be debated among teachers and others with a professional concern with education but not to be explicitly prescribed. Now, however, teaching in England is regulated not only by specification of content and assessment regimes but also by increasingly detailed descriptions of teaching methods. In this chapter, I begin to examine the ways in which the nature of mathematics teaching is constructed within this official discourse and the resources it provides for mathematics teachers to account for their practices and to position themselves as "good" teachers.

The Context of Curriculum Innovation

Since the late 1980s, the UK curriculum in general, and the curriculum for state-maintained schools in England in particular, have been subject to increasing degrees of state regulation through specification of what must be taught; imposition of mandatory testing regimes with high stakes for pupils, teachers and schools; regular and frequent inspection of individual teachers and schools; and, more recently, the introduction of performance management schemes to control teachers' careers. Until relatively recently, however, what actually happened in individual classrooms was regulated only indirectly, primarily through the design of assessment instruments intended to encourage teachers to adopt specific teaching practices in order to prepare their pupils for the tests and examinations they would have to take. The introduction of the statutory National Curriculum in 1988 was accompanied by Non-Statutory Guidance (NCC, 1989) about approaches to teaching but this guidance faded quietly into the background as teachers and schools concentrated on ensuring that they fulfilled their statutory obligations and achieved the highest possible results in national tests.[3]

While schools are still legally bound only by the specification of the content they must teach, increasing pressure has been exerted on both primary and secondary schools and on teachers to organise the "delivery" of the curriculum and to teach in officially approved ways. What started as a curriculum development project to improve standards of literacy and numeracy at primary level, especially in schools considered to be under-achieving, has expanded to become a *"National*

---

[3] Apart from the fact that this guidance was non-statutory and unenforced, its neglect may be explained as the result of the mismatch between its dominant discourse and that of the statutory curriculum and its accompanying assessment. A prime example of this is the notion, prominent in the guidance, that "Using and Applying Mathematics" should "permeate" the curriculum – in contrast to its clear separation in the statutory curriculum, defined as a separate program of study and assessed independently. It is interesting to note that there was an intersection between the sets of authors of the National Curriculum and of the Non-Statutory Guidance, yet the voices represented in the two documents are largely distinct.

Strategy" addressing an ever-widening range of aspects of schooling from discussion of mental calculation strategies, through approaches to formative assessment, to behaviour management.[4] For mathematics teachers in secondary schools, the *National Framework for Teaching Mathematics*, a key document of the *National Strategy*, describes and exemplifies an approach to organising and teaching the content of the National Curriculum for pupils in Years 7, 8 and 9 (age 11–14). Though schools are not required to use the *Framework*, they "are expected to ... be able to justify not doing so by reference to what they are doing" (DfES, 2001). Individual teachers are not required to teach in the ways described but are obviously subject to pressure from managers within their schools to comply. Moreover, support materials, resources and training, whether provided by government agencies or independent sources, including teachers' professional associations, increasingly assume compliance with the model of teaching presented in the *Framework*.

Unity and Diversity

Evaluations of the implementation of the *National Strategy* have indicated that it has had some influence in the vast majority of classrooms in primary and secondary schools in England (Earl et al., 2003; Ofsted, 2003). However, they also report that the nature of the changes implemented has not always matched the intentions of the strategy (Ofsted, 2002, 2003, 2005; Stoll et al., 2003) and that many teachers have been "'tweaking' rather than radically changing practice" (Stoll et al., 2003) – a finding supported by studies of the practices of primary teachers that have identified qualitative differences in the nature of activities implemented (Askew, Denvir, Rhodes, & Brown, 2000) and persistence of "traditional" forms of classroom interaction (Hardman, Smith, Bramald, & Mroz, 2002).

Explanations of problems in implementation of curriculum development tend to focus on teachers' resistance to or transformation of new curricula (e.g., Fullan & Hargreaves, 1992), while evaluations of the *National Strategy* have identified "teacher capacity" as a concern (Earl et al., 2003; Ofsted, 2003). Such identification of teacher deficit as a major barrier to successful development focuses attention on intervention at the level of training and support structures for teachers but fails to take into account other factors that may affect the success of curriculum development, including those related to the form of the development itself. The sets of concepts and values expressed in the dissemination of a curriculum development may not constitute straightforward guidance for practice. For example, Brown et al. (2000) identify ambiguities in the discourse of the primary *National Strategy*, allowing alternative interpretations of recommended pedagogy. Further, Jones and Tanner (2002) report that secondary mathematics teachers involved in a development and

---

[4]The panoptic nature of the National Numeracy Strategy, the forerunner of the National Strategy, was identified at an early stage by Tansy Hardy (Hardy, 2000). The extent of surveillance of both teachers and pupils is now even greater.

research project, implementing "whole class interactive teaching" as recommended by the *National Strategy*, differed in their practices, in spite of training, support and apparent consensus and commitment to the overall values of the program. Nevertheless, it is interesting to note that, in spite of this evidence of diversity in teachers' implementation or interpretation of the *National Strategy*, the external evaluation of the early years of implementation in primary schools[5] has hailed it as a remarkable example of successful large scale reform (Earl et al., 2003).

Part of my job as a teacher educator involves visiting a variety of secondary schools in the Greater London area, observing trainee[6] mathematics teachers in the classroom and talking about teaching with them and with the teachers who mentor them. With the introduction of the *National Strategy*, my own work with trainees has been shaped by its discourse and regulated by a curriculum for Initial Teacher Training that demands that new teachers should demonstrate that they "use the relevant frameworks, methods and expectations set out in the *National Strategy*" (DfES, 2002). Thus, however critical our discussions may be, we certainly make use of the *Framework* and part of our joint work is to find ways of demonstrating that we are doing so. A feature of this experience that has struck me as both interesting and puzzling has been the extent to which the *Framework* has been accepted as a guide to practice by mathematics departments and teachers. While some teachers may object to the slight to their professionalism offered by official recommendations about teaching methods, few challenge the validity of the methods themselves and those who claim not to pay much attention to the document often justify themselves by saying "I'm doing that already", thus claiming compliance by default. It appears that these mathematics teachers have found ways of accounting for their practices that avoid conflict between the new developments and their established professional identities. This is in stark contrast to the conflict displayed by the primary teachers studied by Woods and Jeffrey (2002).

Organisational aspects of the *National Strategy*, including planning and record keeping formats and the idea that a lesson should have a three-part structure, have been widely adopted in ways that show direct relationship to the official guidance. Yet the teaching practices observed in schools appear as diverse as they did before the introduction of the *National Strategy*. Even where teachers are explicitly implementing what is referred to in the *Framework* as the "oral and mental starter" component of a lesson, there is considerable variation in the objectives, the type

---

[5]Though Ofsted reports each year, evaluating the impact of the Strategy in secondary schools, no independent external evaluation at secondary level has been undertaken since the evaluation of the pilot year (Stoll et al., 2003).

[6]The term *trainee* is a part of the new official discourse of pre-service teacher education/training/development, reflecting the culture of performativity in education. Many of those working in Higher Education with pre-service teachers attempt to contest the official discourse and to preserve liberal discourses of education and professionalism by continuing to refer to *students* and to name their occupation as *teacher education*. I have chosen to use the official *trainee* to indicate the fact that, however critical the experience offered within the HE institution may be, its prime function is nevertheless to induct trainees/students into the official discourse of schooling.

of activity and the extent and form of interaction between teacher and pupils. For example, while in one classroom the starter may take the form of a set of calculation problems read out by the teacher or even written on the board for pupils to solve individually in written form and then be allocated a private "mark out of ten", in another classroom the teacher may pose an open question and orchestrate a public sharing and discussion of pupils' alternative responses, and in yet another classroom a game-like format may be used to engage pupils in multiple rapid responses. This variation persists, even into what is now the fifth full year of implementation, suggesting that the recommendations have been understood and implemented in substantially different ways by different teachers and schools. This raises the question, therefore, how can it be that such widespread consensus about the legitimacy of the teaching methods recommended by the *National Strategy* and claimed compliance with its recommendations can coexist with continued diversity in classroom practices? I will address this question by examining the resources the new curriculum discourse provides that may allow these teachers to account for their diverse practices in coherent ways.

A Discourse Analytic Approach

In a previous study of teachers implementing curriculum development in the context of high stakes assessment (Morgan, 1998), I identified different practices and different ways in which teachers were positioned in relation to their task of assessing pupils' texts. A systematisation of these findings by Morgan, Tsatsaroni and Lerman (2002), drawing on Bernstein's theory of pedagogic discourse (Bernstein, 1996), related the positions to a variety of educational and everyday discourses on which teachers were able to draw as they recontextualised the official discourse of the curriculum. Moreover, the official discourse itself could be seen to be a recontextualisation of other discourses drawn from various fields, resulting in tensions among the various concepts and values of the curriculum development. In order to understand the ways in which teachers may be making sense of implementing the *National Strategy* and establishing coherent professional identities, I have chosen to start by analyzing the official discourse of the curriculum development itself, aiming in particular to identify the nature of teaching and the qualities and practices associated with the subject position of a "good teacher" as they are presented within the texts available to teachers.

An initial problem in attempting to study the discourse of a curriculum innovation such as the *National Strategy* is the wealth of sources available, including documents produced both by government agencies and by commercial publishers; videos; Internet based resources; and training sessions. In order to make the initial task manageable I have chosen to focus on limited selections from one key document, the *National Framework for Teaching Mathematics* (DfES, 2001). This is probably the most widely distributed and well known of the official materials, provided free of charge to all serving and trainee secondary mathematics teachers.

It contains detailed guidance for mathematics teachers as well as definitive lists of learning objectives for pupils in each year of the lower secondary school and extensive exemplification of how these might be interpreted in practice. While the guidance contained in this document has been supplemented and revised by more recent publications, the *Framework* itself is still regarded as core to the *National Strategy*.

The "Guide to the *Framework*" is divided into the following sections:

- Introduction, which outlines the policy level context of the document;
- Mathematics at Key Stage 3, which has sub-sections related to each of the components of the mathematics curriculum and to cross-curricular links and ICT;
- Teaching strategies;
- Inclusion and differentiation;
- Assessment and target setting;
- Planning.

Like many curricular documents, the *Framework* is addressed to multiple audiences, including school managers and heads of departments as well as teachers themselves. I have chosen to analyse Section 3 *Teaching Strategies* initially, as this most explicitly addresses teachers themselves about the nature of teaching.

The analytic approach is that of critical discourse analysis (Chouliaraki & Fairclough, 1999; Fairclough, 1995), drawing on the grammatical tools of Halliday's functional systemic linguistics (Halliday, 1985) and interpreting the features thus identified in relation to the social context in which the texts are used and other discourses commonly available to mathematics teachers (Morgan, 2006). In order to analyse how the nature of teaching and of teachers is constructed, I have focused on those grammatical features that perform ideational (or experiential) functions, identifying in particular the ways in which teachers and teaching are involved in the text as actors and the processes in which they are presented as agents. At the same time, I have taken account of interpersonal aspects of the text, in particular mood and modality, in order to consider the ways in which its teacher-readers may be positioned in relation to the text and its authority.

Teaching and Teachers in the *Framework*

The section entitled "Teaching strategies" is marked by a distinct lack of any space for readers to question or debate its description of teaching. Thus the section starts by stating the following:

The recommended approach to teaching is based on ensuring

- sufficient regular teaching time for mathematics, including extra support for pupils who need it to keep in step with the majority of their year group;
- a high proportion of direct, interactive teaching;

- engagement by all pupils in tasks and activities which, even when differentiated, relate to a common theme;
- regular opportunities to develop oral, mental and visualisation skills.

The nominal phrase "recommended approach to teaching" succeeds in obscuring who is doing the recommending, thus preventing the teacher-reader from questioning their authority or the validity of their recommendation. The frequent use of unqualified intensive relational statements (of the form "A is B"), characteristic of scientific writing (Halliday, 1998), constructs the text as a straightforward description of the way things are. The modality, as throughout the document, is high, providing no room for doubt about the truth of this description.

It is interesting to note the preponderance of procedural components in this list, emphasising the amount of time to be given to teaching (as yet undefined) and the organisation of the class as a whole rather than as individuals or groups. The emphasis on time and structure is achieved both by the position of the list at the beginning of the text and by the position of temporal and structural components at the beginning of each of the bullet points: "sufficient regular teaching time"; "a high proportion" (of teaching time); "regular opportunities". The guidance thus prioritises procedural aspects rather than addressing principles of the nature of teaching. This may provide less challenge to teachers' existing practices in that it is only the balance and organisation of various aspects of the practice that need to be adjusted rather than the qualities of these aspects. At the same time, the quantification of these components is indefinite ("regular", "sufficient", "a high proportion"), and thus open to a considerable degree of interpretative variation. Dowling (1998) makes a distinction between procedural and principled aspects of mathematics textbooks, identifying these as distributing "dependent" and "apprenticed" voices, respectively, to low- and high-attaining groups of pupils. In the case described by Dowling, dependency, rather than apprenticeship, excludes some groups of pupils from high status "esoteric" mathematics. In contrast, I would argue that, in the context of guidance to teachers, a relative absence of apprenticing strategies allows experienced teachers to maintain their existing positioning as expert professionals with no need to be apprenticed into new principles and their associated teaching practices, merely needing to adopt new procedures.

After this initial introduction, the authoritative presentation is reinforced by addressing the teacher-reader with imperative instructions:

> *Aim* to spend a high proportion of each lesson in direct teaching, often of the whole class, but also of groups and of individuals (my emphasis).

and by the use of modifiers that strengthen the value judgements implicit in the text:

> *High-quality* direct teaching is oral, interactive and lively, and *will not* be achieved by lecturing the class, or by *always* expecting pupils to teach themselves indirectly from books (my emphasis).

The only type of teaching identified in this "recommended approach" or, indeed, named in this section of the document as a whole is "direct interactive teaching" (valued as good), defined by contrasting it with "lecturing" or expecting pupils to teach themselves (bad). While only a "high proportion" of each lesson is recommended to be occupied by this type of teaching, no mention is made of any other approved kind of teaching that might happen in any other part of the lesson. The value attached to "direct interactive teaching" is heightened by being modified by qualifiers "high-quality" and "good" at several points in the text – the possibility that there might be bad examples (or even indifferent ones) is never raised, while lecturing and expecting pupils to teach themselves are constructed as practices other than teaching. The absence of exemplification of bad teaching means that no position of "bad teacher" is constructed explicitly in the text, thus avoiding forcing teachers to resist such a negative positioning by denying the validity of the text itself.

A list of "teaching strategies" is then presented:

Good direct teaching is achieved by balancing different teaching strategies:

- Directing and telling [...]
- Demonstrating and modelling [...]
- Explaining and illustrating [...]
- Questioning and discussing [...]
- Exploring and investigating [...]
- Consolidating and embedding [...]
- Reflecting and evaluating [...]
- Summarising and reminding [...]

It is interesting to note how the *Framework*'s characterisation of recommended teaching contrasts with the corresponding section of the Cockcroft Report, previously the United Kingdom's best known and most influential recommendations about teaching approaches, also presented in the form of a list.

242 ... We are aware that there are some teachers who would wish us to indicate a definitive style for the teaching of mathematics, but we do not believe that this is either desirable or possible. Approaches to the teaching of a particular piece of mathematics need to be related to the topic itself and to the abilities and experience of both teachers and pupils. Because of differences of personality and circumstance, methods which may be extremely successful with one teacher and one group of pupils will not necessarily be suitable for use by another teacher or with another group of pupils. Nevertheless, we believe that there are certain elements which need to be present in successful mathematics teaching to pupils of all ages.

243 Mathematics teaching at all levels should include opportunities for

- exposition by the teacher;
- discussion between teacher and pupils and between pupils themselves;
- appropriate practical work;
- consolidation and practice of fundamental skills and routines;
- problem solving, including the application of mathematics to everyday situations; investigational work (DES, 1982, p.71).

Here, however, the modality in the first paragraph is low, presenting teaching methods as contingent on mathematics, teachers and pupils. The recommendations are presented as the beliefs of the authors rather than as fact and the tentative voice of the authors is in sharp contrast to the anonymous authority of the *Framework*'s "factual" presentation. The elements of teaching mentioned in the first paragraph of the extract are transformed in paragraph 243 into a list of "opportunities" to be included. It thus does not focus, as the *Framework* does, on the actions of teachers but more generally on what might happen in the classroom.

In the *Framework*, the lack of explicit agency expressed by the passive *is achieved* and the authoritative presentation of the list of nominalised strategies again make it hard to question, but simultaneously introduce some ambiguity about who is doing these things. This ambiguity is compounded by the mixture of types of processes included in the list. Although all are presented as aspects of teaching, some, especially those involving non-verbal processes, are glossed in ways that suggest the pupils are the actors. (Each point in the list is expanded by a further, more elaborated list, expressed in similar nominalised form.) For example, the point headed "Exploring and investigating" continues:

> asking pupils to pose problems or suggest a line of enquiry, to investigate whether particular cases can be generalised, to seek counterexamples or identify exceptional cases; encouraging them to consider alternative ways of representing problems and solutions, in algebraic, graphical or diagrammatic form, and to move from one form to another to gain a different perspective on the problem . . .

Leaving aside the question of whether the activities listed may be considered to constitute exploring and investigating, it is clear that the teacher's role in this is to *ask* and *encourage* pupils rather than to explore or investigate themselves. This pattern is apparent in considering the types of processes ascribed to teachers and to pupils throughout this section of the *Framework*. These are summarised in Table 6.1, using Halliday's categorisation of process types to distinguish between the types of activities that are presented as appropriate for teachers and for pupils. The proportion of verbal processes in the table under-represents the emphasis on teachers "telling" as a significant number of the material processes also involve giving information, for example, "using blackboard instruments to demonstrate a geometric construction, using a thermometer to model the use of negative numbers".

Table 6.1 Processes involving teachers and pupils: "Teaching Strategies", *National Framework for Teaching Mathematics*

Type of process	Teachers		Pupils	
	N	%	N	%
Behavioural	1	2	2	6
Material	27 (of which 8 are related to communication)	52 (15)	16 (of which 3 are related to communication)	46 (9)
Mental	3	6	10	29
Verbal	21	40	7	20
All	52	100	35	101[a]

[a]Does not sum to 100 due to rounding

In spite of the statement that "High-quality direct teaching ... will not be achieved by lecturing the class", a very high proportion of the processes in this list of its components involve talking by the teacher. Even "Reflecting and evaluating" involves "using [pupils' errors] as positive teaching points by talking about them" and "giving [pupils] oral feedback on their written work". The description of teaching thus comprises contradictory messages; the contradiction is even incorporated into its name – it is both *direct* and *interactive*. On the one hand, it is not lecturing. Lecturing is not itself defined but belongs to a discourse that contrasts the pair teaching-learning with the pair lecturing-listening. The lecturer (according to this contrast) delivers a lecture without interaction with the audience or concern for their understanding; the teacher ensures learning. On the other hand, teaching is "direct", involving telling, demonstrating, explaining and so on.

The recommended approach to teaching is thus constructed as

- *Unquestionable*: There is no author to debate with and the qualities of good teaching are presented as scientific facts, though without any reasoning that would allow space for disagreement or debate.
- *Unitary*: Only one type of teaching is named. This is contrasted and opposed to "lecturing" (which is not teaching) and to pupils teaching themselves (which again is not teaching).
- *Verbal*: and, to a high degree
- *Teacher-centred*.

But it is simultaneously constructed as

- *All encompassing*.

The headings of the list of teaching strategies succeed in incorporating aspects such as exploring, investigating, discussing and consolidating, which might be thought to belong to a more pupil-centred philosophy like that associated with the recommendations of the Cockcroft Report (and which, indeed, echo the list of opportunities listed in paragraph 243 of that report). On closer examination it may be seen that the terms are transformed here to allow them to be accommodated to a teacher-centred approach. Discussing, for example, is constructed as a teacher-led activity within "Questioning and discussing", glossed as

> questioning in ways which match the direction and pace of the lesson to ensure that all pupils take part (if needed, supported by apparatus, a calculator or a communication aid, or by an adult who translates, signs or uses symbols); using open and closed questions, skillfully framed, adjusted and targeted to make sure that pupils of all abilities are involved and contribute to discussions; asking for explanations; giving time for pupils to think before inviting an answer; listening carefully to pupils' responses and responding constructively in order to take forward their learning; challenging their assumptions and making them think ...

The possibility that, for example, pupils might discuss among themselves is absent from the text. Yet this very absence allows space for teachers to continue to include such activities within their teaching; it is not negated (as "lecturing" is). Indeed the ellipsis at the end of each of the glossing lists of activities allows potentially infinite space for teachers to insert concepts of teaching drawn from the resources of other discourses.

For the teacher who was previously most comfortable with a teacher-centred approach, the *Framework* offers few challenges. Although other materials provided by the *National Strategy* suggest that a traditional "chalk-and-talk" approach may not be compatible with the intentions of at least some of the agents behind the innovation, it is certainly possible to read the description of teaching offered in this key document in ways that provide justification for the claim "I am doing it already". At the same time, for the teacher comfortable with pupil-centred approaches, aspects of compatible discourses are also present in the *Framework* text, allowing readings that involve valuing approaches to teaching and learning such as discussion, investigation, exploration and problem solving.

Conclusion

The anonymous authors of the *Framework* have managed to perform the difficult task of presenting a picture of mathematics teaching that is simultaneously

- authoritative, consistent with the assumption of current government and media discourse that teachers need to be forced to change their practice and that debate is a feature of sixties libertarianism and the airy-fairy theorising of the "educational establishment";
- new, satisfying the political demand for reform; and
- familiar enough and open enough that a majority of teachers is likely to be able to identify with it in some degree, ensuring that most teachers and schools will be positioned as compliant and that hence a success may be claimed for the *National Strategy*.

This analysis suggests that the resources provided by the new official discourse of mathematics teaching not only recruit resources from other, potentially oppositional discourses, but also allow space for alternative voices to be incorporated without significant conflict. This offers a possible explanation for the widespread acceptance of the *National Strategy* and its diverse manifestation in classrooms. Returning to the concept of identity outlined at the beginning of this chapter, teachers' professional identities are constructed in the context of multiple discourses of teaching. The official discourse is not the only source of resources and possible subject positions available to teachers in the United Kingdom to account for their professional practices. However, its recruitment of potentially oppositional discourses and openness to alternative voices allow teachers to position themselves positively as "good" teachers and to account for their practices by drawing simultaneously upon the resources of this discourse and of those alternative discourses they had drawn upon prior to the introduction of the reform. Their identity work can thus be achieved without substantial conflict for individual teachers as they relate their practice to that described, interpreting the components of teaching specified in the *Framework* by drawing on other discourses of teaching. Moreover, while the procedural aspects of the reform, dealing with timing and structure, are presented as non-negotiable, these do not challenge teachers' existing principles and ways of accounting for their teaching practices. Because the *Framework* does not explicitly present principles or theories of teaching and learning to underpin the proposed teaching methods, teachers can position themselves as compliant with the official prescribed approach to teaching while simultaneously maintaining a positive identity as expert professionals, justifying their practices by reference to pre-existing principles rather than merely by the need to comply.

The UK government is thus able to claim the *National Strategy* as a major success: a victory for modern ways of thinking over the dinosaurs of the educational establishment. Perhaps this is a thoroughly post-modern victory as the new discourse of mathematics teaching is universally incorporated into teachers' ways of accounting for their practices while the practices themselves arguably remain much as they were. Mathematics teachers are overwhelmingly implementing the pedagogy as defined in the *Framework* but still keep enough coherence and apparent autonomy in their professional identities to avoid the loss of ethical responsibility which is feared by Beck and Young (2005). The question of whether and to what extent the implementation of the *National Strategy* has led to genuine changes in pedagogy remains open.

While I have argued that experienced teachers can maintain their professional autonomy, the same may not be true for new teachers who do not have the same established basis of alternative discourses to draw on as they make sense of the prescriptions of the *Framework*. I suggested earlier that the dominance of procedural discourse and consequent lack of apprenticing strategies allow experienced teachers to maintain an "expert" positioning. New teachers, however, in the absence of introduction to principles of pedagogy, are more likely to become positioned as dependent followers of procedures. Of course, their interactions with experienced teachers, with mathematics educators involved in pre-service and in-service courses and with other sources such as professional associations and publications may introduce them to alternative discourses of mathematics teaching, including ones which offer them principled rather than procedural ways of conceiving of teaching. However, such unofficial agents are themselves being recruited to speak with the voice of the official discourse. Higher education, also subject to increased regulation, is compelled to prepare new mathematics teachers to use the *Framework*. Many leading teachers and their organisations have been recruited to become agents of the *National Strategy* both literally, as employees providing training or "consultancy" to schools, and less formally through publications which take its existence, its language, concepts and values as given. While the discursive strategy of the *Framework* may thus have successfully negotiated the risks posed by the challenges of performative curriculum reform to professional identity and the quality of teaching in the short term, the longer-term prospects for the development of the teaching profession are more problematic.

The discussion of professional identity offered in this chapter has been located within a particular national and temporal context, considering the ways in which the newly introduced official discourse of reform of teaching in the United Kingdom may interact with teachers' existing ways of accounting for their practices. More generally, I would suggest that the theoretical orientation and analytical approach used here, applied to key texts of other curriculum development initiatives, can provide insight into the ways teachers respond to the recommendations of such reforms. Where reforms do not have the intended impact on teachers' practices, rather than calling immediately for training and support, it may be useful to consider the ongoing work teachers must do to maintain a positive professional identity, and how they may reconcile the principles and values of a new discourse with those of other more familiar discourses as they seek to justify their practices to themselves as well as to others.

References

Askew, M., Denvir, H., Rhodes, V., & Brown, M. (2000). Numeracy practices in primary schools: Towards a theoretical framework. In T. Rowland & C. Morgan, (Eds.), *Research in Mathematics Education Volume 2: Papers of the British Society for Research into Learning Mathematics* (pp. 63–76). London: British Society for Research into Learning Mathematics, London.

Ball, S. J. (2003). The teacher's soul and the terrors of performativity. *Journal of Educational Policy, 18*(2), 215–228.

Beck, J., & Young, M. F. D. (2005). The assault on the professions and the restructuring of academic and professional identities: a Bernsteinian analysis. *British Journal of Sociology of Education, 26*(2), 183–197.

Bernstein, B. (1996). *Pedagogy, symbolic control and identity: Theory, research, critique.* London: Taylor & Francis.

Brown, M., Millett, A., Bibby, T., & Johnson, D. C. (2000). Turning our attention from the what to the how: the National Numeracy Strategy. *British Educational Research Journal, 26*(4), 457–472.

Chouliaraki, L., & Fairclough, N. (1999). *Discourse in late modernity: Rethinking critical discourse analysis.* Edinburgh: Edinburgh University Press.

Day, C. (2002). School reform and transitions in teacher professionalism and identity. *International Journal of Educational Research, 37,* 677–692.

DES. (1982). *Mathematics counts: Report of the committee of inquiry into the teaching of mathematics in schools under the chairmanship of Dr W. H. Cockcroft.* London: HMSO.

DES/WO. (1988). *Mathematics in the national curriculum.* London: HMSO.

DfEE. (1999). *Mathematics: The national curriculum for England.* London: Department for Education and Employment.

DfES. (1999). *Framework for teaching mathematics: Reception to Year 6,* London: Department for Education and Skills.

DfES. (2001). *Key Stage 3 national strategy – framework for teaching mathematics: Years 7, 8 and 9.* London: Department for Education and Skills.

DfES. (2002). *Qualifying to teach: Professional standards for qualified teacher status and requirements for initial teacher training.* London: Teacher Training Agency.

Dowling, P. (1998). *The sociology of mathematics education: Mathematical myths/pedagogic texts.* London: The Falmer.

Earl, L., Watson, N., Levin, B., Leithwood, K., Fullan, M., & Torrance, N. (2003). *Watching and Learning 3: Final report of the external evaluation of England's national literacy and numeracy strategies*. Toronto: Ontario Institute for Studies in Education, University of Toronto.

Evans, J., Morgan, C., & Tsatsaroni, A. (2006). Discursive positioning and emotion in school mathematics practices. *Educational Studies in Mathematics, 63*(2), 209–226.

Fairclough, N. (1995). *Critical discourse analysis: The critical study of language*. Longman, Harlow.

Fullan, M., & Hargreaves, A. (1992). Teacher development and educational change. In M. Fullan & A. Hargreaves, (Eds.), *Teacher development and educational change*. London: The Falmer.

Halliday, M. A. K. (1985) *An introduction to functional grammar*. London: Edward Arnold.

Halliday, M. A. K. (1998). Things and relations: Regrammaticising experience as technical knowledge. In J. R. Martin & R. Veel (Eds.), *Reading science: Critical and functional perspectives on discourse of science* (pp. 186–235). London: Routledge.

Hardman, F., Smith, F., Bramald, R., & Mroz, M. (2002). *Whole class teaching in the literacy and numeracy hours* (Final report ESRC grant no. R000 239213). Newcastle: University of Newcastle.

Hardy, T. (2000). Tracing Foucault's power in the mathematics classroom. In T. Rowland & C. Morgan, (Eds.), *Research in Mathematics Education Volume 2: Papers of the British Society for Research into Learning Mathematics* (pp. 207–224). London: British Society for Research into Learning Mathematics.

Jones, S., & Tanner, H. (2002). Teachers' interpretations of effective whole–class interactive teaching in secondary mathematics classrooms. *Educational Studies, 28*(3), 265–274.

Morgan, C. (1996). Teacher as examiner: the case of mathematics coursework. *Assessment in Education, 3*(3), 353–375.

Morgan, C. (1998). *Writing mathematically: the discourse of investigation*. London: The Falmer.

Morgan, C. (2005). Making sense of curriculum innovation: a case study. In M. Goos, C. Kanes & R. Brown, (Eds.), *Mathematics Education and Society, Proceedings of the 4th International Mathematics Education and Society Conference* (pp. 258–267). Brisbane: Centre for Learning Research, Griffith University.

Morgan, C. (2006). What does social semiotics have to offer mathematics education research? *Educational Studies in Mathematics, 61*(1/2), 219–245.

Morgan, C., Tsatsaroni, A., & Lerman, S. (2002). Mathematics teachers' positions and practices in discourses of assessment. *British Journal of Sociology of Education, 23*(3), 445–461.

NCC (1989). *Mathematics non-statutory guidance*. New York: National Curriculum Council.

Ofsted (2002). *The Key Stage 3 Strategy: Evaluation of the First Year of the Pilot*. London: Office for Standards in Education.

Ofsted (2003). *The Key Stage 3 Strategy: Evaluation of the Second Year*. London: Office for Standards in Education.

Ofsted (2005). *The Key Stage 3 Strategy: Evaluation of the Fifth Year*. London: Office for Standards in Education.

Stoll, L., Stobart, G., Martin, S., Freeman, S., Freedman, E., Sammons, P., et al. (2003). *Preparing for change: Evaluation of the implementation of the Key Stage 3 Strategy Pilot – Executive Summary*. Nottingham: Department for Education and Skills.

Stronach, I., Corbin, B., McNamara, O., Stark, S., & Warne, T. (2002). Towards an uncertain politics of professionalism: teacher and nurse identities in flux. *Journal of Educational Policy, 17*(1), 109–138.

Woods, P., & Jeffrey, B. (2002). The reconstruction of primary teachers' identities. *British Journal of Sociology of Education, 23*(1), 89–106.

Chapter 7
Working with Learner Contributions: A Key Dimension of Professional Practice

Karin Brodie

This chapter deals with the professional practice of teachers interacting with learners'[1] contributions in mathematics classrooms. Working with learners' mathematical ideas is key to curriculum change and teacher development in many countries. In the United States, standards for professional development (National Council of Teachers of Mathematics, 1991) explicitly describe the teacher's role in classroom discourse as eliciting, listening to, engaging and challenging each student's thinking. In South Africa, curriculum documents ask teachers to focus on learners' thinking and ways of knowing, to respect their diversity and to build on what they know (Department of Education, 1996).

Research on mathematics teachers' interactions with learner thinking has established three main findings:

1. Instances of teachers seriously engaging with and transforming learners' mathematical ideas are extremely rare, across a range of contexts (Brodie, Lelliott, & Davis, 2002b; Chisholm et al., 2000; Fraivillig, Murphy & Fuson, 1999; Jansen, 1999; Kawanaka & Stigler, 1999; Stigler & Hiebert, 1999; Taylor & Vinjevold, 1999);
2. When teachers do engage with learners' thinking, there is some evidence of better and more equitable learner achievement in mathematics, and that learners develop more motivated and positive identities as mathematics learners (Boaler, 1997, 2003; Boaler & Greeno, 2000; Hickey, Moore, & Pelligrino, 2001; Schoenfeld, 2002); and
3. Learning to engage in such practice is extremely difficult and requires extensive professional development of particular kinds (Brodie, 2002; Brodie, Lelliott, & Davis, 2002a; Brodie et al., 2002b; Franke, Fennema, & Carpenter, 1997; Stocks & Schofield, 1997).

K. Brodie (✉)
School of Education, University of the Witwatersrand, Johannesburg, South Africa
e-mail: Karin.Brodie@wits.ac.za

[1] In South Africa the word "learner" is used instead of student so as not to distinguish learners in different sites of learning. I use the terms "learner" and "student" interchangeably, as appropriate in context, to refer to school mathematics learners.

C. Kanes (ed.), *Elaborating Professionalism*, Innovation and Change in Professional
Education 5, DOI 10.1007/978-90-481-2605-7_7,
© Springer Science+Business Media B.V. 2010

In this chapter I engage with the question of how teachers interact with their learners' mathematical contributions from the perspective of their professional practice. I argue, that as with all professional practice, there is a texture and complexity to such work and that developing a language of description (Bernstein, 2000) is important in helping teachers learn to do this work. Using the language of description that I develop, I present a detailed study of the ways in which two South African teachers interacted with learner contributions. These teachers worked in vastly different South African contexts but were both grappling with the demands and practices of the new curriculum, [2] in particular how to engage with learners' mathematical reasoning. I argue that contextual constraints entered into their practices in important ways and that the teachers' knowledge was central to how they made sense of and worked with learner contributions.

Professional Practice

Scribner and Cole (1981) define a practice as follows:

> By a practice we mean a recurrent, goal-directed sequence of activities using a particular technology and particular systems of knowledge. We use the term "skills" to refer to the coordinated sets of actions involved in applying this knowledge in particular settings. A practice, then, consists of three components: technology, knowledge, and skills. We can apply this concept to spheres of activity that are predominantly conceptual (for example, the practice of law) as well as to those that are predominantly sensory-motor (for example, the practice of weaving). All practices involve interrelated tasks that share common tools, knowledge base, and skills. But we may construe them more or less broadly to refer to entire domains of activity around a common object (for example, law) or to more specific endeavours within such domains (cross-examination or legal research). Whether defined in broad or narrow terms, practice always refers to socially developed and patterned ways of using technology and knowledge to accomplish tasks. Conversely, tasks that individuals engage in constitute a social practice when they are directed to socially recognised goals and make use of a shared technology and knowledge system (p. 236).

This definition resonates with many other conceptualisations of practice. Practices involve patterned, coordinated regularities of action directed towards particular goals or goods (MacIntyre, 1981); they are simultaneously practical and more than practical (Cochran-Smith & Lytle, 1999); they involve particular forms of knowledge and skills; they are always located in historical and social contexts that give structure and meaning to the practice – "practice is always social practice" (Wenger, 1998, p. 47), and they involve social and power relations among people and interests (Kemmis, 2005). For Wenger practice entails community, meaning and learning – practices learn and people learn in practice. McIntyre's notion of a practice is as a means whereby internal goods and standards of excellence are realised and "human powers to achieve excellence ... are systematically extended" (p. 175).

The notion of professional practice adds to the above that professionals practise in situations of uncertainty, are called upon to make considered judgements in

---

[2] South Africa has a national curriculum so the reforms are presented to teachers as a new curriculum.

such situations and are expected to be accountable for their decisions and actions (Shulman, 1998). Professionalism involves service to others, and autonomy and accountability to "clients" (Shulman, 1983). Such autonomy and accountability can only be accomplished on the basis of a systematic and technical knowledge base, and continuous learning and development of this knowledge base (Cochran-Smith & Lytle, 1999; Shulman, 1987).

The roles of knowledge and contexts in professional practice deserve explicit attention. I draw on Cochran-Smith and Lytle's (1999) notion of "knowledge of practice", where "knowledge making is understood as a pedagogic act, constructed in the context of use, intimately connected to the knower, and although relevant to immediate situations, also inevitably a process of theorising" (p. 272–273). [3] Such knowledge brings together theory and practice and suggests that learning happens both in practice and through thoughtful reflection on and distancing from practice (Ball & Cohen, 1999; Slonimsky & Shalem, 2004). Ball and Cohen argue that such knowledge includes knowledge of students, how they learn, where their strengths and weaknesses with particular mathematical ideas might be, and knowledge of contexts, specifically the constraints and affordances of particular school contexts.

The focus of this chapter is on a particular form of professional practice, where teachers attempt to hear and take seriously learners' mathematical meanings and respond to these in appropriate ways, both building on learners' current knowledge and transforming it into new mathematical knowledge. Such professional practice works towards particular goods, of developing learners' conceptual and connected understandings of mathematical ideas. I argue that such practice includes coordinated and patterned ways of responding to learners' contributions in order to achieve these goods. In order to analyse the regularities in teachers' responses, I develop a language of description for learner contributions. This language might also help teachers to explore and better understand their own patterns of response to learners' ideas. I also argue that teachers' ways of responding will be located in their pedagogical content knowledge, in learners' ways of making sense of mathematical ideas and the contexts in which teachers and learners interact. I will show that teachers' knowledge of, orientations towards and ways of working with their learners' mathematical ideas are both deeply situated within their own contexts and show regularities across contexts.

The Teachers and Their Contexts

This chapter is drawn from a larger study with five teachers: 3 in Grade 11 and 2 in Grade 10. Here I focus on the two Grade 10 teachers, who worked in vastly different school contexts.

---

[3] Cochran-Smith and Lytle contrast this notion with two others: 1. knowledge for practice, where knowledge is generated outside of practice in general terms and applied to it; and 2. knowledge in practice, where knowledge is generated in practice, is entirely local, predominantly tacit and difficult to theorise outside of particular practices.

Mr. Peters taught in a government school that has only black[4] learners, the majority of whom come from very poor homes. Most parents and caregivers of learners
are unskilled workers, with many unemployed. The Grade 10 class in which the
research took place had 45 learners and was not streamed. The classroom had "old
style" desks with adjoined chairs for each learner. There was a chalkboard and chalk,
no overhead projector and screen and no electricity, so on rainy days the classroom
was dark. Some windows were broken and the paint was peeling off. The school
is located in an area where there is gang activity and some of this spills into and
involves learners at the school.

Ms. King taught in a private school, where most learners are from extremely
wealthy homes, with the exception of the teachers' children and a few learners on
scholarships. Almost all learners are white. Many parents are professionals or company executives. The Grade 10 class in which the research took place had 27 learners
and was the second highest of seven streamed classes. The classroom was part of a
newly built wing of the school, was carpeted and had air-conditioning. There was a
big table and chair for each learner, which could easily be arranged for group work.
There were whiteboards and pens, cupboards and tables for storing paper and work-
sheets, an overhead projector and screen, and a television set that could be used for
presentations from a computer.

As part of the research study, Mr. Peters and Ms. King worked together to develop
a set of tasks that would elicit mathematical reasoning from their learners and
planned how they would go about working with learners' responses to these tasks.
The task that is the subject of the analysis in this chapter is

Consider the following conjecture: $x^2 + 1$ can never be 0. Use a logical argument to
convince someone else why the conjecture is either true or false for any real value of x.

This can be thought about empirically by trying out numbers in the expression
x^2+1 and noticing that x^2 will always give a number greater than or equal to zero. It
can be solved theoretically by drawing on the property that as a perfect square, x^2
will always have to be greater than or equal to zero and therefore x^2+1 will always be
positive. I observed and videotaped the lessons where the two teachers used the task,
interviewed both teachers a number of times and conducted task-based interviews
with the learners.

At the time of the study, Mr. Peters had 13 years mathematics teaching experience
and Ms. King had 11. Both have extremely good mathematical content knowledge
and pedagogical content knowledge. At the time they were both enrolled on an in-
service mathematics education programme where they reflected on and grappled
with issues in the new curriculum. As part of their in-service programme, Mr. Peters
and Ms. King had to complete a mini-research project. Their projects took the form
of an analysis of some of the video data of their own classroom collected for the bigger research project. The five teachers in the project worked together with me as a

---

[4] 'Black' refers to the apartheid categories: 'Black African', 'Coloured' and 'Indian'. People
classified as such were systematically disadvantaged under the apartheid system.

collaborative action research team to analyse their teaching drawing on the theoretical concepts from the programme (Brodie, Coetzee, Modau, & Molefe, 2005; Lauf, 2003; O'Brien, 2003). The focus of these projects was on using tasks and classroom interaction to develop learners' mathematical reasoning. So the teachers were simultaneously working on developing their practice, reflecting on this development as subjects in a research study, reflecting on their development through an analysis of their own teaching, and developing the theoretical tools to do the above – that is, in Cochran-Smith and Lytle's terms they were using and developing knowledge of practice. This chapter focuses on my analysis of the lessons and the teachers' reflections on them in their interviews and projects.

A key aspect of the way in which the teachers' contexts enter into their practices is through their learners' knowledge. On the basis of the learner interviews and my observations it was clear that the two sets of learners had very different knowledge bases: Mr. Peters' learners were operating far below Grade 10 level, while Ms. King's learners were at Grade 10 level, with a significant number who were advanced for Grade 10. A key aspect of these teachers' practices, which brings together knowledge and context, is how they are oriented towards their particular learners' knowledge. In order to understand how the teachers responded in patterned ways to their learners' mathematical ideas, I needed to develop a way in which to describe the range of learner contributions in the classrooms. This language of description works across the classrooms and in so doing illuminates the differences between the classrooms in terms of learner knowledge. This then provides a basis to show how the teachers responded to their learners' contributions, both similarly and differently, in ways determined by their knowledge of their learners' knowledge.

Learner Contributions

In traditional mathematics pedagogy teachers tend to work with the categories of "right" and "wrong". They affirm correct answers and methods and negatively evaluate incorrect ones (Edwards & Mercer, 1987; Mehan, 1979). The internal goods (MacIntyre, 1981) of such practice are to promote correct answers. Thus teacher engagement with incorrect answers aims for the production of correct answers and methods, rather than an understanding of why the answers are incorrect and why the learners might be making errors. Curriculum reforms are attempting to shift the internal goods of mathematics teaching so that teachers actively elicit learner ideas in order to develop conceptual links, promote discussion and extend learner thinking. When teachers do this, they are often confronted by a broader range of learner contributions. These contributions might be correct, incorrect or partially correct, well or poorly expressed, relevant or not relevant to the task or discussion, and productive or unproductive for further conversation and development of mathematical ideas. Interacting with a range of learner contributions makes teachers' decisions about how to proceed and when and how to evaluate learner thinking extremely complex and calls upon their knowledge of mathematics and of learners in particularly deep ways. In order to understand the ways in which teachers respond to learners' ideas, it is necessary to describe the range of contributions. I developed the following set of categories for learner contributions in my data: Basic Errors, Appropriate Errors, Missing Information, Partial Insights, Complete and Correct and Beyond Task. [5]

A first important distinction is between contributions that could count as complete and correct responses to a task, and those that were partial responses, along either of two dimensions: completeness or correctness. Complete and Correct contributions are those that provide an adequate answer to a particular task or question. For example, in response to the task "can $x^2 + 1$ equal 0 if x is a real number", the response "no, because as a perfect square x^2 must be greater than or equal to zero and therefore $x^2 + 1$ must be positive", is a Complete and Correct contribution.

Partial contributions are those that are either incomplete or incorrect in some way. There are three kinds of partial contributions, one of which is incorrect, one of which is incomplete, and one of which is both. An Appropriate Error is an incorrect contribution that mathematics teachers would expect at the particular grade level in relation to the task. For example, a claim that $-x$ represents a negative number, coming from a Grade 10 learner would be classified an Appropriate Error, because if x is negative, $-x$ is positive. Appropriate Errors are distinguished from Basic Errors, which will be discussed below. A contribution that is Missing Information is correct but incomplete, when a learner presents some of the information required by the task, but not all of it. For example, if a learner says that x^2 is always greater than zero, she is missing the information that x can be zero and therefore x^2 is always greater than or equal to zero. A Partial Insight contribution is one where a learner is grappling with an important idea, which is neither quite complete, nor correct. An example of a Partial Insight would be when a learner argued that as she substituted lower numbers, the value of $x^2 + 1$ decreased. Therefore, if she tried a negative number for x, she would obtain zero for $x^2 + 1$.

A second distinction that is important is between Appropriate Errors and Basic Errors. Basic Errors are errors that one would not expect at the particular grade level – for example, errors in multiplying 1/2 by 1/2 in a Grade 10 classroom. Basic errors are in a different relation to the task than Appropriate Errors, because they indicate that the learner is not struggling with the concepts that the task is intended to develop, but rather with other mathematical concepts that are necessary for completing the task and have been taught in previous years.

Finally, contributions that go Beyond Task requirements are contributions that are related to the task or topic of the lesson but go beyond the immediate task and/or make some interesting links between ideas. For example, in response to the task

---

[5] I use the term *error* very carefully. I prefer it to the term *misconception* in that it indicates a performance, rather than an underlying conceptual structure (Nesher, 1987; Smith, DiSessa, & Roschelle, 1993). While such errors may indicate appropriate thinking, as is the case in the category 'appropriate error', I found it important to talk about errors, as teachers orient towards them in particular ways.

"can $x^2 + 1$ equal 0 if x is a real number", the response "if x is -1, then x^2 can equal 0" goes beyond the task because it brings complex numbers into the discussion.

These codes could account for all of the learner contributions in the lessons except for a small number that were so unclear that I could not make out the learner's meaning. [6] This classification scheme is useful in a number of ways. First, it provides a way to characterise what happens in lessons. A lesson with many Complete and Correct contributions looks very different from one with many partial contributions, and both of these look different from a lesson with many Basic Errors. Second, the kinds of contributions suggest the level of learner participation in the lesson and indicate how learner knowledge is implicated in lesson participation. Third, they provide a basis on which to understand how teachers respond similarly and differently to similar and different learner contributions.

Table 7.1 shows the distribution of learner contributions across the two classrooms.

The biggest differences across the two classrooms are in the Basic Errors and Complete and Correct contributions. This difference can be accounted for largely by the differential knowledge of the learners. Given the substantial differences among the learners' knowledge, the small differences between Partial Insights and Beyond Task contributions are of interest. The fact that Mr. Peters' weaker learners showed more Partial Insights and some Beyond Task contributions is particularly interesting. Finally, the fact that Appropriate Errors and Missing Information contributions are similar across the classrooms suggests that these are not only related to learner knowledge. In the rest of this chapter I focus on the similarities and differences in the ways in which Mr. Peters and Ms. King responded to Basic and Appropriate Errors. In so doing, I show similarities and differences in their practices of responding to learner contributions, which are related to their knowledge of practice and their learners' knowledge. The discussion illuminates more general aspects of their different pedagogies, which in turn can account for the unexpected differences in Partial Insights in the two classrooms.

Table 7.1 Distribution of learner contributions (percents of total)

	Mr. Peters	Ms. King
Basic errors	21	1
Appropriate errors	19	17
Missing information	11	10
Partial insights	8	3
Complete and correct	35	59
Beyond task	3	7
Unclear	4	2

---

[6]The codes work across all five teachers, not only the two who are the focus of this chapter.

Appropriate Errors

As shown above, there were a similar number of Appropriate Errors in Mr. Peters' and Ms. King's lessons. The nature of the appropriate errors in the two classrooms was also similar, which suggests that these cannot only be accounted for by the specific contexts. As will be seen below, they are strongly task-related, although the ways in which they occurred in the two classrooms and the ways in which the teachers responded to them is strongly context related. Although the number and kinds of Appropriate Errors that arose in the two classrooms were similar, in Mr. Peters' class many more learners made these errors and made a number of Basic Errors at the same time. This difference in the learners' knowledge in the two teachers' classrooms afforded different pedagogies.

In response to the task (stated above) the vast majority of Mr. Peters' learners argued that it is true, that $x^2 + 1$ could not equal zero because $x^2 + 1$ would always equal $x^2 + 1$. Their reasoning was that because x^2 and 1 are unlike terms, the expression $x^2 + 1$ could not be simplified. [7] They did not think about the possibility that if x was given a value, then $x^2 + 1$ could be simplified and would have a value. Mr. Peters put the solution of one group on the board and asked them to explain their thinking by using probing questions (Boaler & Brodie, 2004):

> Mr. Peters: Grace and Rethabile. And most of you belong in this group (writes Grace and Rethabile's solution on board). Grace, do you want to say something about that? What were you thinking? What were the reasons that you (inaudible)?
> Grace: Sir, because the $x^2 + 1$ ne sir, you can never get the 0 because it can't be because they unlike terms. You can only get, the answers only gonna be $x^2 + 1$, that's the only thing that we saw because there's no other answer or anything else.
> Mr. Peters: How do you relate this to the answer not being 0? Because you say there it's true, the answer won't be 0, because $x^2 + 1$ is equal to $x^2 + 1$. You say they're unlike terms. Why can't the answer never be 0, using that explanation you are giving us?
> Grace: *(Sighs and pinches Rethabile)*
> Mr. Peters: Rethabile, do you wanna help her?
> Rethabile: Yes, sir.
> Mr. Peters: Come, let's talk about it.
> Rethabile: Sir, what we wrote here, I was going to say that the x^2 is an unknown value and the 1 is a real number, sir. So making it an unknown number and a real number and both unlike terms, they cannot be, you cannot get a 0, sir. You can only get $x^2 + 1$.
> Mr. Peters: It can only end up $x^2 + 1$?
> Rethabile: Yes, sir. There's nothing else that we can get, sir. But the 0, sir.
> Mr. Peters: So you can't get a value, you can't get a value?
> Rethabile: That's how far we got sir
> Mr. Peters: Come, Lesedi, lets listen so you can contribute, so it will only give you $x^2 + 1$, it won't give you another value, 0. Will it give us the value of 1? Will it give us the value of 2? $x^2 + 1$.
> Rethabile: It will give us only 1, sir, because x is equal to 1, sir.

---

[7]This is a standard rule for manipulating algebraic expressions taught in Grade 8. The fact that learners tried to use it here shows that although they know the rule, they cannot distinguish circumstances in which it can be appropriately applied, and so they applied it inappropriately.

In the above extract, we see Mr. Peters' probing questions moving from very general "what were you thinking", "what were the reasons", to the more specific "how do you relate this to the answer not being zero" and "So it will only give you $x^2 + 1$, it won't give you another value, 0. Will it give us the value of 1? Will it give us the value of 2?" Even these two final probes, which could have enabled learners to think about $x^2 + 1$ as taking several values depending on the value of x, did not help. In fact they led Rethabile directly into a Basic Error, that x is equal to 1 (this will be discussed below). Mr. Peters responded to Appropriate Errors by spending considerable time discussing the particular contribution, probing learners' thinking and trying to get them to clarify their ideas. The discussion on the above Appropriate Error went on for about another forty turns. Mr. Peters elicited and made public different learners' ideas, both those that were correct and those that were not, and held up different ideas for discussion. He did not immediately move to correcting Appropriate Errors.

As the discussion on the above Appropriate Error progressed, it became clear that the learners were not seeing $x^2 + 1$ as a variable expression that could take on a range of values depending on the value of x. Mr. Peters spoke about this often in his interviews. The following comment was typical:

"they don't see x squared as, you know, being a certain value, when can I get it to zero, you know, or can I ever get it to zero by substitution? They just look at it physically. . . . they're not looking at x as a variable."

When Mr. Peters says learners just look at it physically, he means that they look at the superficial (syntactic) features of the expression and make decisions about it based on these features; they do not think about the underlying conceptual meaning of the expression. This is the original distinction between procedural and conceptual reasoning (Davis, 1988; Hiebert & Lefevre, 1986). Mr. Peters spent a lot of time trying to help learners to generate conceptual meanings for algebraic expressions. A related appropriate error that also occurred in this classroom was when learners claimed that an expression like $-x$ or $-2x$ is a negative number because of the negative sign, showing very clearly how they focus on the syntactic elements of the expression rather than its meaning. Mr. Peters commented on this as well:

"During and after the first lesson I discovered that many learners were saying that x^2 is positive and their justification was linked to the fact that if a sign of a number is not displayed, we accept that the number is positive. The learners' logic was based on the parallel that 5 is positive and -5 is negative, therefore x^2 is positive and $-x^2$ is negative . . . [In] this task . . . the sign in front of the x^2 is not the determining factor of the expression being positive, negative or zero."

Mr. Peters' practice and his reflections on his learners' thinking illuminate a number of elements of his professional practice. First, he was clearly developing and using his knowledge of practice (Cochran-Smith & Lytle, 1999), and particularly his knowledge of his learners' mathematical thinking (Ball & Cohen, 1999). He thought carefully about the errors that his learners made, related these to his broader knowledge of mathematics and learners' potential misconceptions in this area, and he worked to develop appropriate meanings. He knew that his learners had weak mathematical knowledge and were prone to making errors that often suggested underlying misconceptions. He therefore did not evaluate such errors negatively; rather he brought them into the public domain for discussion.

There were similarities in Appropriate Errors in Ms. King's and Mr. Peters' lessons, particularly in relation to the meaning of x and x^2. In Ms. King's class some learners had difficulty representing x^2 when $x = -1$, arguing that $-(1)^2$, rather than $(-1)^2$ is an appropriate instantiation of x^2. They did not understand that in this context the square applies to the whole of x, which is -1, rather than to the 1 only. This is a somewhat subtle issue relating to the order of operations. Other learners wrote that $-x$ represented a negative number. It is clear that the learners in both classrooms were struggling to make meaning of negative numbers written algebraically – a difficulty that is strongly related to the particular task. A major difference between the two classrooms was that these errors were widespread among Mr. Peters' learners while very few learners in Ms. King's class made them. Ms. King was able to draw on other learners for a range of correct responses and explanations, which came very quickly and were accepted by the learners who had made the error. For example, Clive had written that if -1 was not in brackets, then the expression could equal zero – for example, $-1^2 + 1 = 0$. Ms. King asked the class to comment on this contribution and a learner remarked:

> Learner: He's squaring the 1, but not the negative.
> Ms. King: Right, He's squaring the 1, but not the negative. Now, what does, what do you think of that?
> Gordon: That's wrong, its wrong.
> Jimmy: That doesn't work because when you've got $x = -1$, it's supposed to be the whole of -1.
> Ms. King: Yes
> Jimmy: The minus is with the 1, you can't just times 1 and leave it out.

In the transcript we see three learners who immediately got to the core of Clive's difficulty and explained his mistake. This did not happen in Mr. Peters' classroom and is related to the level of knowledge and confidence of Ms. King's learners. Even so, after this Clive still struggled with the idea and Ms King worked to help him:

> Clive: But Mam, can't -1 be -1 times 1?
> Ms. King: Yes, you can have a sum -1 times 1, but is that x squared?
> Clive: No
> Ms. King: What does x squared mean? What does x squared mean, Clive?
> Clive: That number whatever x is times itself.
> Ms. King: That number times itself. So, over here, Clive, if x is -1, tell me what is x squared?
> Clive: Uh, 1
> Ms. King: The long way, the whole thing
> Clive: Minus 1 times minus 1
> Ms. King: Minus 1 times minus 1 – what's the answer?
> Clive: 1

In the above, Ms. King worked quickly to correct Clive's error. She did not probe his misunderstanding rather she used the correct ideas expressed above to help her to correct the error. In our interview she commented on why she had done this:

"I think that this issue had been going on for so long now. Virtually everybody was convinced except for one or two now and I think I was just getting tired of this issue dragging on for so long now that I didn't think that there was much to be gained."

So she judged that for most learners it was time to move on. Ms. King worked to understand Appropriate Errors, asked other learners to comment on them in the hope that they would correct them, and if this did not work, moved quite quickly to correct them herself. This shows Ms. King's knowledge of her learners' knowledge and the pacing that was required to maintain their interest. Ms. King reflected less on the actual mathematics involved in the errors, perhaps because she has less need to than Mr. Peters. Her position was that Chris had in fact understood his error and was being a little "dogged" in insisting that he might still be right − that is, defending his position so as to not lose face among his peers.

The similarities and differences between Ms. King and Mr. Peters' responses to errors are illuminating of this practice. They both noticed and dealt with Appropriate Errors through discussion with the class, and this was clearly part of their knowledge of practice.

That Mr. Peters dealt with these more extensively has to do with the fact that they were more widespread in his classroom − that is, this decision is strongly contextually constrained and strongly related to the different mathematical knowledge of learners in the two classrooms. An analysis of Mr. Peters' responses to Basic Errors is further illuminating of similarities and differences across the two teachers.

Basic Errors

Basic Errors occurred throughout Mr. Peters' lessons. Mr. Peters dealt with these errors by trying to find out the exact nature of the errors and then working to correct them.

During the above discussion of Grace and Rethabile's Appropriate Error, a number of Basic Errors occurred in quick succession. Learners claimed that "x is equal to 1"; "x is equal to 1 because there is a 1 in front of the x"; "because there is a 1 in front of the x, $1x^2 + 1 = 2x^2$"; and "x has unknown value, so it can be taken to be 1 and adding the 1's gives $2x^2$". The way in which Mr. Peters worked with the last error is illuminating. In the transcript below, Ahmed states that $x^2 + 1$ does give an answer and Mr. Peters asked him to elaborate:

Ahmed: You can get an answer
Mr. Peters: So, what is the answer
Ahmed: Um, if you have $1x^2$ plus 1, sir
Mr. Peters: What's $1x^2$ plus 1
Ahmed: If I add it, if I add it sir, $1x^2$, would give me, plus 1 would give me $2x^2$
Mr. Peters: Would give you $2x^2$, right (pause), so $x^2 + 1$, because of the 1 there, Ahmed says, that's gonna be equal to $2x^2$ (writes on board $1x^2 + 1 = 2x^2$). Has anyone got something to say about this?

When Ahmed made a Basic Error in simplifying the unlike terms, Mr. Peters did not immediately negatively evaluate it (although he did later). Rather he asked other learners to comment. The second learner who he called on made a useful contribution:

> Lebo: Um, I disagree because $1x^2 + 1$, they are unlike terms because of the x^2, they are unlike terms, you can't add unlike terms
> Learner: Ja [yes]
> Mr. Peters: You can't add unlike terms
> Lebo: (*and some others*) Yes

Mr. Peters had expected Lebo to argue this. He said in his interview:

> "Lebo's hand is up for quite a while at this stage, she had ... Ahmed was talking already, she had, you know, saw it, no, this, it can't be added, so that's why I interrupt. I knew I'm going to be a little relieved there, you know. Ja, I could see she's just dying to say that you cannot add them, so that's why I moved to her so that she could come and clarify."

So, after some discussion, Mr. Peters specifically chose a learner who was likely to state the correct mathematics. He did not immediately affirm her position (evident in his tone when saying "you can't add unlike terms"), but asked other learners whether they agreed or disagreed. When he saw that the majority agreed, he continued to repeat and affirm Lebo's point. The above suggests Mr. Peters' knowledge of his learners and his willingness to call on a learner who might help the discussion. This technique did not always work, however; sometimes calling on a learner exacerbated the error and Mr. Peters would need to correct the mathematics. He did this in all cases of Basic Errors, suggesting that his approach to these was to bring them into the public domain, evaluate how many learners did hold these errors and work quite quickly to correct them.

So Mr. Peters' approach to both Basic and Appropriate Errors was to make them public, ask other learners to comment and to have some discussion about them. Although he did this with both Basic and Appropriate Errors, he moved to correct Basic Errors more quickly than Appropriate Errors, which he maintained for more extensive public discussion. This suggests the use of professional judgement in how to use limited time most appropriately. Mr. Peters' responses to Basic Errors were similar to Ms. King's responses to Appropriate Errors, working to make them public and then correcting them. There are significant differences related to their contexts however. Ms. King corrected these Appropriate Errors quickly because they were not shared and because she judged the need to move on. Mr. Peters first ascertained how widespread the Basic Errors were in his class. If they were not too widespread he could rely on learners to correct them, as Ms. King could for Appropriate Errors. If learners did not help him, then he did it himself, because he wanted to return to the discussion of the Appropriate Errors, which had given rise to the Basic Errors.

Mr. Peters' extensive discussion of Appropriate Errors suggests a pedagogical approach of trying to transform errors and misconceptions by discussion. This approach was not evident in his approach to Basic Errors, or in Ms. King's approach to Appropriate Errors. The two teachers' different approaches to Appropriate Errors suggest different pedagogical approaches, which can account for the other kinds of contributions in the two classrooms.

The Other Contributions

The fact that Ms. King worked to correct Appropriate Errors and Mr. Peters to correct Basic Errors accounts for the high number of Complete Correct responses in both classrooms. Ms. King's learners' stronger knowledge also accounts for the significantly higher number of Complete, Correct contributions in her lessons, as does her pedagogy, which was to move towards correct answers after some discussion.

In contrast, Mr. Peters' extensive discussion of Appropriate Errors led directly to some Partial Insights. In the case above, one learner argued "x^2 is already a value" and "there's already a number there". This suggests that he was thinking about the role of the x^2 in the expression $x^2 + 1$, although not necessarily that it has to be positive or zero. Another learner argued that they would not get to zero, because they were always adding 1. She was clearly working with the elements of the expression in relation to each other, but had not yet fully expressed the crucial part that x^2 could not be less than zero. Mr. Peters' response to Partial Insights was to discuss them in extended ways, similarly to how he discussed Appropriate Errors.

The Beyond Task contributions in Ms. King's lessons came predominantly from one set of contributions. Some learners had asked another teacher about the problem and he told them that $x^2 + 1$ can be zero if they considered complex numbers, and i as -1. Ms. King asked the learners to explain this to the class and they struggled. Ms. King tried to help them, but the rest of the class was still confused and so she provided a comprehensive, clear and inspired explanation, with no preparation, about complex numbers on the Cartesian plane as an extension of the number line. Ms King expressed contradictory feelings about beyond-task contributions. She enjoyed the learners' excitement about the idea of -1 but expressed concern and some insecurity about her own response, because she had to "wing it", she had not prepared for it. It is clear that in this situation her mathematical knowledge enabled her to respond in the way she did.

Conclusions and Implications

In this chapter I have illuminated the professional practice of working with learners' mathematical meanings. To do this, I developed a language of description for different kinds of learner contributions and then showed that two teachers responded to these in patterned ways, strongly afforded by their contexts[8].

The fact that there are patterned regularities across teachers as well as significant differences that can be related to local contexts in particular ways suggests that this professional practice can be both taught and learned. Theorising mathematics

---

[8]The original study included an additional two teachers and showed even more regularities across and within teachers in relation to their particular contexts.

learning and misconceptions were clearly helpful to Mr. Peters in understanding his learners' ideas, in relation to particular learner contributions. The language of description for learner contributions might be a helpful technology for developing teacher responsiveness to learner contributions. It can guide teachers' viewing of their own or others' practice, and help them to think about the patterned ways in which they respond to learners' contributions and the ways in which their responses are constrained by their knowledge, their learners' knowledge and other aspects of their contexts.

I have shown that the teachers' responses demonstrate professional judgement, drawing on their pedagogical content knowledge of mathematics and of their learners. The analysis shows up considerable texture in teachers' thinking and action. The contextual issue that most informed the two teachers' decisions was their learners' knowledge and the paper suggests that learner knowledge is a key element of teachers' knowledge and their ways of responding to learners. The different knowledge of the learners in the two classrooms supported different pedagogies suggesting that theories of pedagogical content knowledge and pedagogical change should take account of learner knowledge as a key variable. The teachers' knowledge in these two classrooms amounts to knowledge of practice, in that they combine knowledge of their particular learners with their knowledge of mathematics and mathematics learning. This chapter suggests initial mechanisms to both understand this knowledge more closely, and to help teachers to develop it.

References

Ball, D. L., & Cohen, D. K. (1999). Developing practice, developing practitioners: Towards a practice-based theory of professional education. In L. Darling-Hammond & G. Sykes (Eds.), *Teaching as the learning profession* (pp. 3–32). San Francisco: Jossey-Bass.

Bernstein, B. (2000). Pedagogy, symbolic control and identity: Theory, research, critique (revised edition). Lanham, ML: Rowman and Littlefield.

Boaler, J. (1997). Experiencing school mathematics: Teaching styles, sex and setting. Buckingham: Open University Press.

Boaler, J. (2003). Equitable teaching practices: The case of Railside. Paper presented at the Annual conference of the California Mathematics Council, Asilomar, California, December 2003.

Boaler, J., & Brodie, K. (2004). The importance, nature and impact of teacher questions. In D. E. McDougall & J. A. Ross (Eds.), *Proceedings of the 26th annual meeting of the North American chapter of the International Group for the Psychology of Mathematics Education* (Vol. 2, pp. 773–781). Toronto: Ontario Institute of Studies in Education/University of Toronto.

Boaler, J., & Greeno, J. G. (2000). Identity, agency and knowing in mathematics worlds. In J. Boaler (Ed.), *Multiple perspectives on mathematics teaching and learning* (pp. 171–200). Westport, CT: Ablex.

Brodie, K. (2002). Between the old and the new: A study of a mathematics teacher's changing practices in South Africa. In P. Valero & O. Skovsmose (Eds.), *Proceedings of the 3rd international Mathematics Education and Society conference (MES3)* (pp. 192–199). Helsingor: Centre for Research in Learning Mathematics, Danish University of Education.

Brodie, K., Coetzee, K., Modau, A. S., & Molefe, N. (2005). *Teachers and Academics Collaborating on Research on Mathematics Classroom Interaction.* Paper presented at the International Commission on Mathematics Instruction (ICMI) Africa Regional Conference, University of the Witwatersrand, Johannesburg.

Brodie, K., Lelliott, T., & Davis, H. (2002a). Developing learner-centred practices through the FDE programme. In J. Adler & Y. Reed (Eds.), *Challenges of teacher development: An investigation of take-up in South Africa* (pp. 94–117). Pretoria: Van Schaik.

Brodie, K., Lelliott, T., & Davis, H. (2002b). Forms and substance in learner-centred teaching: Teachers' take-up from an in-service programme in South Africa. *Teaching and Teacher Education, 18*, 541–559.

Chisholm, L., Volmink, J., Ndhlovu, T., Potenza, E., Mahomed, H., Muller, J., et al. (2000). *A South African curriculum for the twenty first century. Report of the review committee on Curriculum 2005.* Pretoria: Department of Education.

Cochran-Smith, M., & Lytle, S. (1999). Relationships of knowledge and practice: Teacher learning in communities. In A. Iran-Nejad & P. D. Pearson (Eds.). *Review of Research in Education* (Vol. 24, pp. 249–305).

Davis, R. B. (1988). The world according to McNeill. *Journal of mathematical behaviour, 7*, 51–78.

Department of Education. (1996). *Curriculum framework for general and further education and training.* Pretoria: National Department of Education.

Edwards, D., & Mercer, N. (1987). *Common knowledge: The growth of understanding in the classroom.* London: Routledge.

Fraivillig, J. L., Murphy, L. A., & Fuson, K. C. (1999). Advancing children's mathematical thinking in everyday mathematics classrooms. *Journal for Research in Mathematics Education, 2*, 148–170.

Franke, M. L., Fennema, E., & Carpenter, T. (1997). Teachers creating change: Examining evolving beliefs and classroom practice. In E. Fennema & B. S. Nelson (Eds.), *Mathematics teachers in transition* (pp. 255–282). Mahwah, NJ: Lawrence Erlbaum Associates.

Hickey, D. T., Moore, A. L., & Pelligrino, J. W. (2001). The motivational and academic consequences of elementary mathematics environments: Do constructivist innovations and reforms make a difference? *American Educational Research Journal, 38*(3), 611–652.

Hiebert, J., & Lefevre, P. (1986). Conceptual and procedural knowledge in mathematics: An introductory analysis. In J. Hiebert (Ed.), *Conceptual and procedural knowledge: the case of mathematics* (pp. 1–27). Hillsdale, NJ: Lawrence Erlbaum.

Jansen, J. (1999). A very noisy OBE: The implementation of OBE in Grade 1 classrooms. In J. Jansen & P. Christie (Eds.), *Changing curriculum: Studies on outcomes-based education in South Africa.* (pp. 203–217). Cape Town: Juta.

Kawanaka, T., & Stigler, J. W. (1999). Teachers' use of questions in eighth-grade mathematics classrooms in Germany, Japan and the United States. *Mathematical thinking and learning, 1*, 255–278.

Kemmis, S. (2005). Is mathematics education a pratice? Mathematics teaching? In M. Goos, C. Kanes, & R. Brown (Eds.), *Proceedings of the fourth International Mathematics Education and Society conference (MES4).* Brisbane: Centre for Learning Research, Griffith University.

Lauf, L. C. (2003). *Towards an holistic approach to teaching and learning mathematics.* Unpublished Research Project. Johannesburg: University of the Witwatersrand.

MacIntyre, A. (1981). *After Virtue.* London: Duckworth.

Mehan, H. (1979). *Learning lessons: Social organisation in the classroom.* Cambridge, MA: Harvard University Press.

National Council of Teachers of Mathematics. (1991). *Professional standards for teaching mathematics.* Reston, VA: NCTM.

Nesher, P. (1987). Towards and instructional theory: The role of students' misconceptions. *For the Learning of Mathematics, 7*(3), 33–39.

O'Brien, R. G. (2003). *Teaching through the practices of justification and explanation.* Unpublished Research Report. Johannesburg: University of the Witwatersrand.

Schoenfeld, A. H. (2002). Making mathematics work for all children: Issues of standards, testing, and equity. *Educational Researcher, 31*(1), 13–25.

Scribner, S., & Cole, M. (1981). *The psychology of literacy.* Cambridge, MA: Harvard University Press.

Shulman, L. S. (1983). Autonomy and obligation. In L. S. Shulman & G. Sykes (Eds.), *Handbook of teaching and policy* (pp. 484–504). Boston: Allyn and Bacon.

Shulman, L. S. (1987). Knowledge and teaching: Foundations of the new reform. *Harvard Educational Review, 57*(1), 1–22.

Shulman, L. S. (1998). Theory, pratice and the education of professionals. *The Elementary School Journal, 98*(5), 511–526.

Slonimsky, L., & Shalem, Y. (2004). Pedagogic responsiveness for academic depth. In H. Griesel (Ed.), *Curriculum responsiveness: case studies in higher education*. Pretoria: South African Vice-Chancellor's Association.

Smith, J. P., DiSessa, A. A., & Roschelle, J. (1993). Misconceptions reconceived: A constructivist analysis of knowledge in transition. *The journal of the learning sciences, 3*(2), 115–163.

Stigler, J. W., & Hiebert, J. (1999). The teaching gap: Best ideas from the world's teachers for improving education in the classroom. New York: Free Press.

Stocks, J., & Schofield, J. (1997). Educational reform and professional development. In E. Fennema & B. Scott Nelson (Eds.), *Mathematics teachers in transition*. Mahwah: Lawrence Erlbaum Associates.

Taylor, N., & Vinjevold, P. (Eds.), (1999). *Getting learning right: Report of the President's Education Initiative Research Project*. Johannesburg: Joint Education Trust.

Wenger, E. (1998). *Communities of practice: Learning, meaning and identity*. Cambridge: Cambridge University Press.

Chapter 8
What Is Professional Practice? Recognising and Respecting Diversity in Understandings of Practice

Stephen Kemmis

In this chapter, I explore a diversity of ways in which "practice" has been understood in various relevant literatures. Given the ubiquity of the term, however, I cannot hope to do justice to all views of practice. Much of what I have to say focuses on "professional practice", although a great deal is also relevant to the wider and more general concept of a "social practice" – an even more elusive concept in the literature, and still more difficult to unravel. My narrower purview may be permissible for a book on developing professional practice. I say little here about the concept of a "profession", though it seems so crucial in defining "professional practice". I am happy to leave that discussion in the background here. I use examples drawn principally from education (reflecting the origins of this paper in a conference of mathematics educators; Kemmis, 2005b), but also, in less depth, from some other professional settings. On the other hand, I am conscious that much of what I have to say about professional practice may have application to many situations and occupations not usually described as "professions". And I am not always sure that the usual kinds of criteria used to define professions (like their use of distinctive bodies of knowledge, or self-accreditation or self-regulation) are particularly helpful when it comes to understanding professional practice *qua* practice.

I begin by drawing attention to a range of individual and extra-individual features of practice mentioned in various different schools of theorising about practice, some of which (like Schatzki, 1996, 2002) explicitly understands itself as "practice theory". I do this by presenting a variety of "key features" of practice which I outline in a table intended to give a kind of "map" of the conversation-space between different kinds of theories of practice. The table aims to give a more encompassing view of practice than the views taken by some theorists and researchers, especially those who have focused on practice in terms of the knowledge and action of individual practitioners – that is, the individualistic view of practice against which I want to counterpose the extra-individual features that also constitute practice.

S. Kemmis (✉)
Charles Sturt University, Wagga Wagga, NSW, Australia
e-mail: skemmis@csu.edu.au

C. Kanes (ed.), *Elaborating Professionalism*, Innovation and Change in Professional Education 5, DOI 10.1007/978-90-481-2605-7_8,
© Springer Science+Business Media B.V. 2010

In the next section, before elaborating the table (the task of the penultimate section), I briefly discuss practitioner's and client's views of practice, aiming to show that practices are constructed in interaction – beyond the agency of professional practitioners alone. In particular, I aim to show that histories, cultural and discursive resources, social connections and solidarities, and locations in material-economic arrangements and exchanges are all implied in the construction of practices.

The penultimate section then elaborates my "practice table", showing how different theorists of practice emphasise different kinds of features in their theories of practice. Although only two-dimensional, I hope the "practice table" gives some sense of how the theoretical "conversation" about practice has employed different kinds of conceptual resources, configured differently in each case – and that there is not clear agreement in the field about what practice is and how it is to be understood. Of course my brief reference to different ideas employed by different theorists does not and cannot do justice to their views or the coherence of their accounts of practice. It is simply intended to suggest some "dimensionality" in the overall conversation or debate about what practice is. I hope this section suggests that the contributions of different theorists and theories to the larger debate can be recognised and respected as that – as contributions to a more encompassing understanding of practice.

The final section makes some brief comments about the limitations of the technicist view of practice that has become prevalent in public administration in recent decades, and suggestions about using the practice table in research on practice.

Towards a More Encompassing View of Practice

In this section, I elaborate a view of practice described in a paper I presented at a conference on "Knowing Practice" in Umeå, Sweden, in 2004 (Kemmis, 2005a; see also the contributions by Wilfred Carr (2005), Joseph Dunne (2005), Karin Rönnerman (2005), Tone Saugstad (2005) and Thomas Schwandt (2005)). In that paper, I argued that practice is not best understood in terms of "professional practice knowledge", as, for example, in the views presented by Eraut (1994) and Higgs, Titchen and Neville (2001) who suggest that professional practice knowledge can be described in terms of

1. propositional, theoretical or scientific knowledge – for example, the knowledge of pathology;
2. professional craft knowledge or knowing how to do something; and
3. personal knowledge about oneself as a person and in relationship with others (Higgs, Titchen & Neville, 2001, p.5).

Against the view that practice can best be understood from the perspective of practitioners' knowledge – that is, what is in the heads of individual practitioners – I argued that practice has a number of extra-individual features, and that neither practice itself nor the process of changing practice can be adequately understood without reference to these extra-individual features. I drew on a variety of theorists of practice (like MacIntyre, Bourdieu, Foucault and Habermas) to show that, beyond the individual person of the practitioner, practice is also socially, discursively, culturally and historically formed.

One reason for making this argument was to address the educators of professionals: to argue that we should not limit our teaching to instilling professional practice knowledge in the form of technical, craft and personal knowledge, but rather to insist that neophyte and developing professionals should understand how practices are constructed in the social and other dimensions just listed. If I might put it this way, understanding and changing practice requires work *outside* the heads of practitioners as well as *inside* them. In my Umeå paper, I argued for opening communicative spaces – public spheres constituted for public discourse (based on Habermas, 1996) – in which both communities of practice and practitioners and their clients could thematise and explore problems and issues of practice, and the effects and longer-term consequences of particular kinds of practice.

A second reason for arguing for a more encompassing view of practice is addressed to researchers studying practice in different fields. In our chapters for the second and third editions of *The Handbook of Qualitative Research* (Kemmis & McTaggart, 2000, 2005), Robin McTaggart and I argued that research on practice has frequently proceeded with impoverished views of practice as an object of study, and that to understand practice in a more multidimensional way it must be studied using multidisciplinary, multi-method approaches which allow it to be viewed from at least the five perspectives as sketched in Fig. 8.1, in part because they characteristically rely on the kinds of research methods and techniques as sketched in Fig. 8.2.

These characteristic approaches to the study of practice mean that the practice one researcher "sees" is likely to be very different from what is "seen" by a researcher from a different tradition. These differences may betray disagreements

Focus: Perspective:	The individual	The social	Both: Reflexive-dialectical view of individual–social relations and connections
Objective	(1) Practice as individual behaviour, seen in terms of performances, events & effects: behaviourist and most cognitivist approaches in psychology	(2) Practice as social interaction - e.g., ritual, system-structured: structure-functionalist and social systems approaches	
Subjective	(3) Practice as intentional action, shaped by meaning and values: psychological *verstehen* (empathetic understanding) and most constructivist approaches	(4) Practice as socially structured, shaped by discourses, tradition: interpretive, æsthetic-historical *verstehen* & post-structuralist approaches	
Both: Reflexive-dialectical view of subjective–objective relations and connections			(5) Practice as socially and historically constituted, and as reconstituted by human agency and social action: critical theory, critical social science

Fig. 8.1 Relationships between different traditions in the study of practice

Focus: Perspective:	The individual	The social	Both: Reflexive-dialectical view of individual–social relations and connections
Objective	(1) Practice as individual behaviour: Quantitative, correlational-experimental methods. Psychometric and observational techniques, tests, interaction schedules.	(2) Practice as social and systems behaviour: Quantitative, correlational-experimental methods. Observational techniques, sociometrics, systems analysis, social ecology.	
Subjective	(3) Practice as intentional action: Qualitative, interpretive methods. Clinical analysis, interview, questionnaire, diaries, journals, self-report, introspection	(4) Practice as socially structured, shaped by discourses and tradition: Qualitative, interpretive, historical methods. Discourse analysis, document analysis.	
Both: Reflexive-dialectical view of subjective–objective relations and connections			(5) Practice as socially and historically constituted, and as reconstituted by human agency and social action: Critical methods. Dialectical analysis (multiple methods).

Fig. 8.2 Methods and techniques characteristic of different approaches to the study of practice

about what *research* is, which in turn give rise to disagreements about what *practice* is – whether practice in general, or in the case of particular professions or occupations, or in the case of particular practitioners.

In our chapter for the second edition of the *Handbook*, we therefore argued for "symposium research" in the study of practice – research drawing on different disciplines and employing multiple methods.

In Fig. 8.3, I identify a range of different features of practice all of which seem to me significant in adequately understanding a practice. I would like to claim that there are no other interesting categories to consider about practice than the ones pointed to in my summary – but no doubt I have missed aspects of practice just as important as the ones identified here, and have inadequately expressed some of the ideas intended. Repairing some such omissions, the figure also includes aspects of practice not explicitly discussed in my Umeå paper – particularly the column referring to the material-technical aspects of practice as behaviour assumed and omitted in that paper. I hope the key words listed in each cell provide sufficient pointers to the work of other thinkers and theorists of practice; clearly, there is not space here to provide a comprehensive justification of all of the elements included – that task would require a large book.

Practitioners' and Clients' Perspectives on Practice

Before discussing Fig 8.3 in more detail, I would like to consider some further questions about practice which I believe are central to understanding them as practices – namely, that they involve social interactions in which "clients" are

(1) INDIVIDUAL FEATURES OF PRACTICE — CONSTITUTED IN A DIALECTICAL RELATIONSHIP →	(2) EXTRA-INDIVIDUAL FEATURES OF PRACTICE		
Cf. forms of knowledge: (a) cognitive: conceptual understanding [cf. cultural features]; (b) affective: values/emotions [cf. social features]; (c) psychomotor: skills [cf. material features].	(a) CULTURAL-DISCURSIVE FEATURES Medium: language/ discourse Generic social practice: communication	(b) SOCIAL FEATURES Medium: power, social relationship Generic social practice: social organisation/connection	(c) MATERIAL-ECONOMIC FEATURES Medium: work Generic social practice: production
A. Meaning & purpose — Practice is not just activity: it involves *meaning and intention*, and may draw on *professional practice knowledge* including *technical* (knowing that), *craft* ('know-how') and *personal knowledge* (Eraut; Giddens; Higgs et al; Oakeshott)	Practice is always meaningful in the sense that it has meaning to practitioners and usually those with whom they interact, and it is frequently 'theoretical' – i.e., it refers to theory that informs it (of which practitioners or others may or may not be aware) (Carr & Kemmis)	Practice involves and expresses *values* (it is value-laden) like the value of *care* (Noddings, 2003), *social norms* (it is guided by moral and ethical concerns) and *virtues* (MacIntyre; Taylor; Toulmin)	Practice involves *purposive action and interaction in and on the world* (with others and objects) (behaviourists, systems theorists to address identified *needs or problems* in pursuit of characteristic *goals and ends* (Althusser)
B. Structured — Practice is always *experientially-formed* – it realises and is realised in the *identity / subjectivity* of the practitioner as a practitioner (Benhabib, Giddens, Schatzki, Wenger). It expresses *agency* (and sometimes *resistance*). Participation in practices produces a structure of learned *dispositions* (*habitus*) towards the field of practice (Bourdieu).	Practice is always culturally and discursively formed and structured – it realises and is realised in languages and discourses (cf. Bourdieu's cultural capital: Bakhtin; Shotter; Vygotsky; Wittgenstein). It is represented in symbolic forms that codify it. It makes the nexus of power/knowledge (Foucault). Intersubjectivity is grounded in the logos of language (Habermas).	Practice is always socially (and politically) *formed and structured* (and *contested*, Gramsci) – it realises and is realised in social (and political) interactions and relationships (incl. characteristic practitioner-client role relationships) (cf. Bourdieu's *social field* and *social capital*: Bernstein; activity theory; e.g., Engeström, Leontiev, Vygotsky).	Practice involves the use of *learned skills and techniques* (that have themselves developed and evolved over time) (cf. behaviourists) in *structured systems of relationships* between people, and people and things (cf. systems theory, activity theory) which may include relations of *economic exchange* (cf. Bourdieu's *economic capital*)
C. Situated — Practice is always *embodied* (Foucault)– it is what particular people do, in a particular place and time –employing learned *capacities and competences*, and inevitably involving *identity work* and *emotional work* (e.g., as a painful consequence of caring) (Noddings, 2003; Schatzki)	Practice is grounded in agreements and debates that form culturally-embodied self-understandings and the discursive histories of communities of practice (Engeström; Kuhn; Lave & Wenger; Toulmin). It invites communicative action to reach intersubjective agreement, mutual understanding and consensus about what to do (Habermas).	Practice realises and is realised in characteristic *solidarities* (Habermas) and forms of *social integration* of people (practitioners, clients, others) in relation to one another (e.g., in care via nursing, in education via teaching, in sustenance of people and land via farming) (Giddens; Schatzki)	Practice involves *action on the material world in the material here-and-now* (particular times, places, objects, physical conditions) in the form of situated *work* or *labour* (Althusser; activity theory; behaviourists). It involves access to and the use and transfer (including redistribution) of *resources*.

Fig. 8.3 Individual and extra-individual features of practice

D. Temporally-located	Practice is always *dramaturgical* in character (Habermas) – it unfolds in human and social action, against the *narrative* background of individuals' lives (biographies) (Schatzki; also cf. MacIntyre's 'narrative unity of a human life')	Practice is always culturally-located against particular traditions of particular societies and groups (Foucault; Kuhn; MacIntyre; Toulmin; Wittgenstein). Practitioners can reach historical self-consciousness of their own perspectives as well as of the events they interpret (Gadamer, effective history).	Practice is always *historically formed and structured* – the product of local (in this situation, among these people) and more global history (Foucault; Giddens; MacIntyre; Schatzki). Practices are *reproduced and transformed over time.*	Practice occurs in/over *time* (Giddens), through processes (*transformation of raw materials into end products via labour*; Althusser), against a technical background of education, training and development
E. Systemic	Practices are frequently preserved, maintained and developed through the development of the *professional role and functions* of the practitioner (cf. role theory)	Practices are always discursively/linguistically justified through argument and frequently subject to discursive accreditation and regulation through law, policy, standards (Foucault, incl. on performativity; Habermas, incl. on system and lifeworld, colonisation, juridification)	Practices are frequently preserved, maintained, developed and regulated in *institutions and organisations*, and the cooperative *work of professions* (MacIntyre; sociology of professions).	Practices frequently involve systemically-structured *material interactions* (e.g., role related functions) and often *economic exchanges and transactions* (e.g., payment for services) (activity theory; systems theory)
F. Reflexivity & transformation	Practice is always *reflexive.* – bringing to mind the relationship between practitioners as subjects and the objects of their practice via their *praxis* (activity theory: Bourdieu; Giddens; Gouldner; Schatzki; Toulmin). It invites the practitioner to *historical self consciousness* (Gadamer). It stimulates the *reproduction and transformation of identities.*	Practice always invites communicative action (i.e. collaborative action oriented towards mutual understanding, inter-subjective agreement and consensus about what to do) (Habermas; Kemmis). Practices are always culturally/linguistically reproduced and culturally/linguistically transformed over time and place.	Practice always invites *opening communicative space* (and the creation of *public discourse in public spheres*) in which practitioners, and practitioners and clients and others, mutually explore issues and themes of common concern or interest (Habermas; Kemmis; Kemmis & McTaggart). Practices are always *socially reproduced and socially transformed* over time and place.	Practice is *materially or strategically reflexive*, not only in the sense that it makes transformations of the world (e.g., raw materials to end products), but also that the operations and interactions involved can them-selves be *materially reproduced and transformed* over time and place (redesigned, re-engineered, improved) (activity theory: Habermas; Toulmin)
G. Forms of reasoning about practice	Practice always involves *practical reasoning* (Aristotle; Gadamer; Gauthier; Schwab), using knowledge in the face of uncertainty (*exploratory action*) – guided by a *practical* knowledge-constitutive interest in acting wisely and prudently in given circumstances (Carr & Kemmis; Habermas	Practice invites aesthetic-expressive understanding and reasoning about practice as symbolic, and exploration of the aesthetics and poetics of practice (Shotter, Lyotard). Practice also invites critical reasoning about cultural-discursive aspects of practice (see the cell to the right)	Practice invites *critical reasoning* in which participants collaboratively explore the nature and consequences their actions against the criteria of comprehensibility, truth (accuracy), truthfulness (sincerity) and moral appropriateness – guided by an *emancipatory* knowledge-constitutive interest in identifying and overcoming incomprehensibility, irrationality, deception (incl. false consciousness, self-deception) and injustice (incl. suffering, domination and oppression) (Benhabib; Carr & Kemmis; Habermas; Young	Practice invites *technical reasoning* about the efficient use of means for given ends in particular contexts, and *functional reasoning* about organisational capacities to achieve goals – guided by a *technical* knowledge-constitutive interest in achieving particular ends using appropriate means (Carr & Kemmis; Habermas;

Fig 8.3 (continued)

not merely "objects" operated on or influenced by practitioners, but persons-in-themselves who are, to a greater or lesser degree, knowing subjects who are co-participants in practice. Thus, for example, learners are not merely "objects" on which teachers "operate", but persons-in-themselves who are co-participants in the joint activity better described as "learning and teaching" than merely "teaching" (which directs our attention to just one of the players in the game of learning and teaching).

To a greater or lesser degree, "clients" of different practices – patients or students for example – are knowledgeable about the relevant practices and know something about how they are to participate in them. Even an acute hospital patient meeting, say, an occupational therapist for the first time knows something about how to interact with this person – for example, that they are to get some kind of help through some kind of "therapy", that the conversation between them will probably be conducted in a "professional" manner, and that this is a service somehow linked to an institution (like a hospital) and a profession with relevant professional bodies and a distinctive specialist discourse (sometimes perceived as jargon). The acute patient meeting the occupational therapist for the first time thus begins learning how the particular "game" of occupational therapy is played, in terms of the languages and discourses appropriate to it, the kind of activities and work processes involved, and the social relations and organisational and institutional goals, roles and rules that apply to their interactions.

I want to suggest that one might explore the client's perspective on practice using the table of key features of practice as presented in Fig. 8.3. Indeed, I would like to suggest that "learning the game" of the practice involves the client (patient, student) in aligning their perspective on the practice with the perspective implied in the words and actions and social relationship offered by the practitioner. Sometimes practitioners must re-align their presuppositions about the conduct of their practice to connect with those of their clients, and almost assuredly clients will need to re-align their presuppositions to connect with those of the practitioner.

Without the detail of Fig. 8.3, Fig. 8.4 below is intended to portray the juxtaposition of practitioners' and clients' perspectives, though inadequately demonstrating that both have some ideas and experience related to all or most of the cells in the matrix.

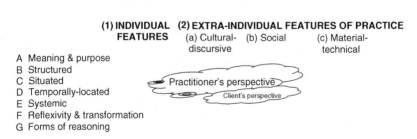

Fig. 8.4 Clients' and practitioners' perspectives on practice in relation to the key features of practice

Of course neither practitioners nor clients exist in a social vacuum. On the one side, from the perspective of a professional practice, we might readily point to the community of practice of the practitioner – the professional bodies and institutions, frequently including universities, carrying the knowledge and traditions of the practice of that profession, and perhaps responsible for accreditation and regulation of members of profession. On the other side, from the perspective of the client, we may also point to those social groups, including family, community and other kinds of affiliations and connections that furnish a background of meanings, purposes, values and the rest brought by the client to the practice situation. And it should be noted that the practitioner also has a background of family, community and other connections that she or he brings to the situation. These backgrounds are roughly portrayed in Fig. 8.5.

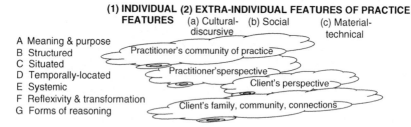

(1) INDIVIDUAL (2) EXTRA-INDIVIDUAL FEATURES OF PRACTICE
FEATURES   (a) Cultural-   (b) Social   (c) Material-
                      discursive   technical

A Meaning & purpose
B Structured   Practitioner's community of practice
C Situated
D Temporally-located   Practitioner'sperspective
E Systemic   Client's perspective
F Reflexivity & transformation
G Forms of reasoning   Client's family, community, connections

Fig. 8.5 The widening social context of clients' and practitioners' perspectives on practice

As suggested in relation to practitioners' and clients' perspectives, the presuppositions and perspectives of communities of practice and the social groups to which clients belong may also be considered against the framework of key features of practice listed in Figs. 8.3 and 8.5. Here, this is simply at the level of a thought-experiment. Perhaps the example of successful professional practice you considered earlier allows you to speculate about the relationships between practitioners' and clients' perspectives in that case (cf. Fig. 8.4); the task becomes far more demanding in relation to the variety of perspectives depicted in Fig. 8.5.

In my view, pursuing an analysis of the kind suggested by Fig. 8.5 takes us, reflexively, back into the key features of practice presented in Fig. 8.3. It begins to show, at greater depth, what the columns referring to the social and cultural features of practice refer to, and what the rows referring to forms of reasoning and reflexivity refer to. Perhaps it is to suggest something about the "forms of life" practices represent, as a Wittgensteinian analysis of practice might begin to show (cf. Wittgenstein, 1974). Some steps towards such analyses have been taken in some recent writing on practice (e.g., Schatzki, 1996, 2002; Shotter, 1996, 1999, 2000; Katz & Shotter, 1996).

Applied to the case of mathematics education, we might think of the relationships depicted in Fig. 8.5 in terms of the perspectives of a mathematics teacher, her or his students, any community or communities of practice with which the teacher is involved, and the families, communities and other connections of the students.

Clearly, the social networks brought into contact at the point of learning and teaching stretch far beyond the teacher and students in physical and social space, in time, and in terms of discursive resources and relationships. As Shotter suggests, in the *poetics* of conversations like those between students and teachers, *worlds* of meaning connect or collide, occasionally re-orienting both students and teachers as they glimpse aspects of each others' realities through the windows of their worlds in the here and now, sometimes yielding surprising insights into how each construes his or her apparently shared world. Of course, this refers in one way to the "aha!" experience that teachers revel in whenever they see it, and to the idea of "the teachable moment" that teachers aim to construct or respond to when they find it. But it also refers to the "aha!" of the teacher who makes sense of the nature of a student's misunderstanding, or is surprised by facts about a student's family life or background that explain why there have been difficulties "connecting" with John or Jane.

What I hope to do by juxtaposing the practitioner's and client's perspectives on practice with the framework of features of practice as sketched in Fig. 8.3, however, is to say more than that the worlds of the mathematics teacher and student are *different* – I hope also to suggest some of the *ways* they differ.

I invite you to think about a particular case of practice you know well, or a particular case of research on practice, using the framework provided in Fig. 8.3. I hope that using the table will illuminate the richness of the space of practice. I think the exercise will also show, in practice, how practice richly understood is illimitable.

Recognising and Respecting Diversity in Understandings of Practice

As Theodore Schatzki (2002) eloquently argues, practices pre-figure individual actions. I agree – practices have shapes that precede particular actors and actions, and that envelop them (like gloves, perhaps) as they perform a practice, giving what they do meaning and significance in the cultural-discursive dimension; solidarity, legitimacy and belongingness in relation to others in the social dimension; and practical efficacy and various kinds of satisfaction in the material-economic dimension. Human coexistence – as Schatzki (1996, 1997, 2001, 2002) describes the social – is ordered and pre-figured by the shapes of practices that, as modes of performance, "speak" to us as actors, organising our thoughts and actions, and our relationships with the others who are involved in and affected by our actions. In Schatzki's view, the practices themselves carry these meanings, significances and connections, and the varied and locally adapted performance of practices acts as a kind of living social tissue that connects us to one another.

In the sections that follow, I will explore some of the key individual and extra-individual features of practices, to show some of the dimensions in which they envelop individual actors or practitioners. The sections refer to the rows in Fig. 8.3, and the brief comments on each are intended to show how the individual "side" or aspect of practice is set in a context of extra-individual conditions that shape or envelop it.

Intention and Meaning

One of the things that makes some behaviour or action a practice is that it is
guided by *intentions*. Looking at practices entirely from the "outside", as behaviour,
may make the practice uninterpretable or even incomprehensible. What seem to
be the same behaviours may be and mean very different things (e.g., typing a letter to a lover versus typing a chapter on practice). And practices are "bigger than"
actions, though both share the characteristic of being guided by intentions. Michael
Oakeshott (1962), Charles Taylor (1985) and Anthony Giddens (1979, 1984) are
among the philosophers who have written about the distinction between behaviour
and intentional action; few theorists of practice do without the notion of intentions
altogether, though some, like Barry Hindess (1977), have also pointed out the fal-
lacy of Max Weber's (1946) rationalist conception of action (assuming that action
is "oriented in its course" by meaning) that people's actions are and mean what they
intend them to be and mean.

Different participants in a professional practice may have different *intentions*
from one another (to heal or be healed, in the case of a medical practice, for example). In understanding the situation in which they find themselves, the different
people involved draw on different resources of *meaning* – different *cultural* and
discursive resources (in the case of a patient, for instance, a language about pain
or suffering, grounded in personal experience and experience of the suffering of
others; and, in the case of a doctor, different kinds of medical and therapeutic discourses). These people encounter each other not just as persons, but also as the
bearers of roles (the roles of patient and doctor), to which different values and
norms are attached, giving their interaction different *social* meanings and significances for each. One is anxious to be cared for and cured; the other aims to give care
or effect a cure. The actions of each fit into different parts of a *material-economic*
world of goals, functions and actions (those of a health provider, for instance), and
a world of economic relations (the one may pay for the other's services, the other
may be paid to provide the service, but perhaps not be paid directly by the client or
patient).

These cultural-discursive, social and material-economic frameworks existed
prior to the arrival of these particular people in *this* encounter, in *this* setting. To
change what is meant and intended by *this* social practice in *this* setting may thus
require changing not just what the actors themselves think or do, or how they relate,
it may also require changes in the language and discourse they use (e.g., new developments in the theory of how burns should be treated); changes in the relationships
between people around the particular practice (e.g., changing the ways different
people in different roles relate to each other in the burns unit of a hospital, or the
values and norms of care and respect that guide their work); and changes in the
material-economic arrangements of what people do, with what resources, in return
for what rewards (e.g., new ways of treating burns, new technologies like new
dressings for burns, or new pay scales for specialist staff working in burns units).

As already intimated, different theorists of practice draw attention to different
aspects of practice relating to meaning and intention. Oakeshott, Taylor and Giddens

have already been mentioned in relation to practice as seen from the side of the individual actor. Many others, like Bourdieu (1977, 1984, 1990, 1998); Bourdieu and Wacquant (1992) and especially Foucault (1970, 1972, 1977, 1979, 1985, 1990a, 1990b, 2001) refer to the cultural-discursive framing of actors' meanings and intentions. Carr and Kemmis (1986) also regard professional practice as implying a theory or theories that make it a practice of that kind – in the sense that to be an educational practice, or a medical practice, or a practice of doing history, the relevant practitioners rely on discourses framed in traditions that give the practice its character, meaning and significance.

Many theorists refer, too, to the *social* framing of intentions and meanings that form and inform practice – through *values* and *norms*, for example, in the case of theorists like MacIntyre (1982), Charles Taylor (1991), Stephen Toulmin (1972) and Giddens (1979, 1984). MacIntyre also insists on the importance of virtues in understanding practices of any significant kind – virtues that are partly definitive of the practice.

And, in the Marxian tradition, many theorists of practice have drawn particular attention to the *material* and *economic* framing of practice, including, for example, Louis Althusser (1971). Following Marx himself, such theorists see the intentions and meanings of participants in social life as culturally, socially and politically shaped by material conditions and the goals and ends of economic relationships – indeed, they see even participants' perceived *needs* and *problems* as frequently pre-structured by economic relations.

Structure

Although there have been spirited debates about "structure", "structuralism" and "post-structuralism", it is doubtful whether it is possible to understand a practice without having some sense of its structure – both for the individual participant in the practice and in terms of the cultural-discursive, social and material-economic dimensions of practices – each differentially emphasised in different kinds of theorising about practice, with the relative significance of each dimension being contested between theories of practice. Without resolving the question of what structure is, or in what structure is constituted, let us merely assert for the time being that practices have "shapes".

Practices have distinctive "shapes", and sometimes, as the example of the doctor and patient shows, these shapes may be different for different participants (e.g., they may be complementary or reciprocal). The shape of a general practitioner's day may involve getting to work from home, seeing many patients with different complaints in a surgery and office, working with each patient differently (drawing on different kinds of knowledge; employing different interpretive and therapeutic techniques; using relevant technologies; referring patients to other specialists for tests or treatments), working with related professionals, managing support staff, overseeing finances, and going home. The patient also comes from home to see the doctor in the surgery, but might only be in the surgery for 15 min, having waited in a waiting room for half an hour. After the consultation, the patient might go to a pharmacy, to be dealt with by different people (e.g., the person at the counter and the pharmacist in the back room who prepares the prescription), and then go on to her or his own place of work to be involved in a completely different practice involving still different discourses, social relationships and material-economic relationships and exchanges.

From the point of view of a professional practitioner, his or her practice draws on a particular history of personal experience; it involves a particular view of what an appropriate professional identity is, and a particular way of being a "subject" (a knowing and knowledgeable person); a particular kind of agency about how he or she can act on the world, and with what likely effect (and what likely resistances); and it involves the exercise of learned skills and capacities (some learned, perhaps, over several years of formal professional preparation).

The shape of the practitioner's practice is not only "given" by the people actually performing the practice, it is also pre-structured and pre-figured in *discourses* (e.g., how knowledge of the practice is represented in texts and curricula), in social relationships (e.g., through learning to be a doctor from teachers of medicine, and through experiencing the *social relationships* of medical work – with nurses, patients and relationships with professional accrediting bodies) and in *material-economic* arrangements (e.g., buying and using equipment, being paid for services and paying taxes for the business from which the practice is offered). These more general structures impress themselves upon the particular structure of this particular practitioner's identity and capacities, and the way she or he performs the practice on this occasion, with this client. The same may also be true for the client of the practice, even if they encounter the practice only occasionally (e.g., only occasionally being in the role of patient and seeing a doctor). The structures that pre-figure the shape of the doctor's practice are indirectly impressed into the experience of the patient by the doctor's performance of the practice and the patient's particular personal reactions to it, expressed in the patient's performance of the role of patient. But the patient's experience as a patient is also pre-structured – by past encounters with doctors or illness (or this particular doctor and illness), and by the way illness and doctors and such things as following through with treatment regimes are regarded by this patient, and her or his family and friends. Such background structures shape the practice of being a patient for this person – and project themselves into the way *this* patient will be perceived by and then acted with or on by *this* doctor in *this* case of *this* illness.

A variety of theorists of practice have chafed at apparently deterministic implications implied by the notion of "structure" – for example Foucault (famously in *The Archaeology of Knowledge*, 1972). Other thinkers like Bakhtin (1984), Derrida (1974, 1978) and Lyotard (1984) are interested in shapes within *language* and *discourses*, and their consequences for social ordering in a variety of dimensions, in contrast to Marx and various post-Marxians like Antonio Gramsci (1977) and especially Louis Althusser (1971) for whom *social-political* and *material-economic* structures are of paramount importance, even in the context of the reproduction of the material-economic base and material-economic conditions through the cultural "superstructure"[1]. For cultural theorists of practice, it seems to me that structure reasserts itself in the forms of discourses, in the language and representations people use and, beyond that, in what Shotter (1996), following Wittgenstein and Bakhtin, calls the *poetics* of practice.

Across the cultural-discursive, social and material-economic dimensions of practice, Pierre Bourdieu's (1977, 1984, 1990, 1998; Bourdieu & Wacquant, 1992) theory of practice finds the structure of practices in cultural, symbolic, social and economic fields, each with associated "capitals" (the others by analogy with economic capital). The capitals are what can be accumulated through participating in the practice when practitioners are in the fields in which a practice takes place, and capitals and fields impress themselves into the dispositions of actors to form a "habitus" or learned capacity to participate appropriately in this or that practice as a "player" (as a journalist, an academic or a football player, for example). Bourdieu's careful analyses of practices aim to show how practices are characteristically structured in terms of habitus, fields and capitals in play.

Situatedness

In terms of the *situatedness* of practice, clearly different participants in a practice enact it in different ways, using their bodies in different ways. Clearly, not only the physiotherapist or the baseball player, for example, depend on using their bodies with particular and elite skill, so do practitioners of almost all practices – including the person sitting at the computer screen. This embodiment has profound effects on practices and their performance – indeed, the physical performance of a practice powerfully shapes the identity of the practitioner. Especially from the perspective of the identity and subjectivity of the practitioner, the performance of a practice has much more significance than might be suggested by what the practitioner has learned in order to perform the practice – competences and capacities whose significance is that they are elements that come into play in the performance, that are brought into play as needed, with judgement and discretion as part of the "orchestration" of the professional practitioner's practice with *this* client, in *this* setting, under *these* particular circumstances. Seyla Benhabib (1992) speaks of "situating

---

[1]Following Marx, for the first half of the twentieth century at least, many questions about the relationship between culture and social and economic structures was conceived in Marxian terms, as the problem of the relationship between the economic base and the cultural superstructure – a problem addressed through the concept of *ideology* (for example, in Gramsci and Althusser, already cited, and Giddens, 1979, 1984). Reviewing a range of usages of the term, Jacques Larrain (1979) concluded that ideology is to be found in and as *practice*. Post-structuralists like Derrida and (perhaps) Foucault took the debate about the discursive formation of society out of the Marxian frame of base and superstructure, discovering a variety of kinds of discursive ordering beyond the 'traditional' concerns of Marxian theory. It is against the backdrop of those concerns that they are to be considered *post*-structuralist. One might wonder, however, whether or not some concept of ideology is reasserting itself in contemporary post-Marxian theory through the extended concepts of practice that emerged in the closing decades of the century.

the self" not just spatially or temporally but also in relation to values and norms which imply universals (like justice and truth). And the physicality of the performance of the practice also calls forth characteristic emotions (perhaps elation or fatigue in the case of the baseball player), although some personally relevant emotions are characteristically suppressed in the performance of a professional practice (e.g., the doctor's anxiety about causing pain, or the teacher's anger). Thus some professions, like teaching, are described as involving "emotional work" (e.g., see Hargreaves & Earl, 2001).

On the side of the extra-individual features of practice, practices are situated in the sense that they are clearly located in space and time (described later in the chapter). The practitioner and others involved in the practice operate in a cultural and discursive context, under particular *cultural* and *discursive* conditions that may conform to general or even universal theories, rules or principles, but they are enacted and applied under immediate local cultural and discursive conditions (with these particular people, in their particular community, and their particular backgrounds and experiences). Similarly, the practice is enacted in local social conditions, involving specific kinds of social connections and relationships, with these particular people, here, building or changing local and particular solidarities with particular others and building different kinds of relationships with different groups. (Thus, as she proves her worth to a community, the community development practitioner helping women establish micro-economic enterprises may find herself becoming a key person in the village, at the nexus of particular social connections and arrangements.) And similarly, the practice occurs in a local *material* and *economic* context or environment, involving interactions and exchanges with particular aspects of the physical and natural world of objects, and with particular others encountered as subjects worthy of respect (as well as in some cases, being the "objects" worked on in the practice).

Location matters. Rural practice may differ from urban; practice with indigenous people may differ from practice with non-indigenous people; practice in *this* setting may differ depending whether the others involved are men or women; practice in communally oriented Asia may be different from practice in the individualist West. In practice, practice is inevitably *situated*.

The situatedness of practice is recognised in different ways in different theories of practice. On the side of the individual participating in the practice, Bourdieu's notion of *habitus* has already been mentioned. Giddens's (1984) notion of *agency* is similarly situated, mutually constituted with social structure in his dialectical pairing of agency and structure. There is also a wide range of theorists who emphasise the situatedness of identity and subjectivity in terms of the *standpoints* of different participants in different kinds of groups.

On the side of the extra-individual, Foucault and others emphasise the situatedness of practices in *cultural-discursive* orders – for example, through the concepts of "disciplines" and "regimes of truth" by Foucault (1979). From a very different perspective, Habermas (1984, 1987a) sees persons and practices as located in *lifeworlds* which give them the cultural-discursive resources for understanding themselves and the world, as well as the social resources (of norms and legitimacy, belonging and connectedness) that find expression in the sense of identity, the personality and the learned capacities of each participant. He distinguishes these lifeworlds, with their characteristic processes of cultural reproduction and transformation, social reproduction and transformation, and the formation and transformation of individual identities and capabilities, from the social *systems* in which participants characteristically play particular roles according to relevant rules, performing particular functions in pursuit of system goals. But both lifeworlds, in which people relate in a person-to-person sense, and systems, in which they relate in an organisational sense, situate practices and participants and form multiple extra-individual matrices within which their lives and work are conducted.

Other theorists of practice emphasise situatedness in *social* terms, in terms of the social formation of practices and practitioners. For example, Lave and Wenger (1991) and Wenger (1998) draw attention to the role played by *communities of practice* in the formation of practices and practitioners.

Still other theorists of practice emphasise situatedness in terms of the *materiality* of the interactions that form practices – like activity theorists Vygotsky (1978, 1986), Leontiev (1974, 1981), Engeström (1987, 2000) and, arguably, action science advocates Argyris (1990), Argyris and Schön (1974, 1978) and Argyris, Putnam and McLain Smith (1985). Similarly, many Marxian theorists focus on situatedness in terms of the materiality of practices, especially in relation to *economic* interactions and their social and cultural effects.

From a social geographer's perspective, David Harvey (1996) draws cultural-discursive, social and material-economic threads together in his exploration of the *positionality* of people, groups and practices. From a philosophical perspective, Theodore Schatzki (1996, 2001, 2002) also emphasises the situatedness of practices through his concept of the *social* ("human coexistence") and the "hanging together" of people and practices in social space (*elaborated* in conceptual detail in Schatzki, 2002).

Temporally Located

Practice is also located in time. The performance of a practice occurs through or over time: it has duration. Social practices, professional practice included, takes place at particular times, at particular moments in the lives of the people involved, against the wider background of the narratives of their lives [cf. MacIntyre's (1982) notion of "the narrative unity of a human life"]. Moreover, the conduct of the practice may occupy a special place in the life and identity of the practitioner, especially a professional practitioner. For such reasons, Habermas (1984, 1987a), for example, refers to the *dramaturgical* character of practices (i.e., the quality of being like a dramatic performance, especially one performed by its author).

On the side of the extra-individual, in the cultural-discursive dimension, practice also occurs in the temporal context of evolving traditions of thought in particular communities of practice (Lave & Wenger, 1991; Wenger, 1998). A stream in the philosophy and sociology of science continues to explore the nature of scientific traditions, brought into sharp relief by the publication of Thomas Kuhn's (1970) *The Structure of Scientific Revolutions* and various commentators and critics (e.g., in Lakatos & Musgrave, 1970; Feyerabend, 1970; and Toulmin, 1972) of Kuhn's views about evolutionary and revolutionary developments in science. MacIntyre (1982, 1988, 1990), too, has emphasised the role of tradition in shaping practices, evident in continuities and developments, over longer historical periods. A significant contribution to understanding traditions in relation to practices, especially the practice of interpretation in history and art, is Hans-Georg Gadamer's (1975) notion of "effective-historical consciousness" (the historian's consciousness of the historicality of her or his own interpretive categories as well as of the historicality of the tradition being interpreted) – a notion that generalises to the "double hermeneutic" of interpretation of the subject as well as the object, crucial to the notion of understanding a practice.

In the *social* dimension, practices are historically formed and structured, involves different connections and relationships among particular people (who are also at particular moments in their lives), building or undermining particular kinds of solidarities among people, and contributing to or diminishing social integration among those involved and affected (e.g., in communities of practice; Lave & Wenger, 1991; Wenger, 1998).

In the *material-economic* dimension, practices are also located in time. The continuity and change in practices over time in relation to material-economic contexts and conditions has been a particular focus in reproduction theory – which has explored cultural-discursive and social reproduction and transformation as well as the reproduction and transformation of the material conditions of different groups over time – especially in relation to education and social class, for example (Bourdieu & Passeron, 1977; Bernstein, 1977, 1996; Connell, et al., 1982; Giroux, 1983; Kemmis & Fitzclarence, 1986; Willis, 1977).

As an example of the temporal location of the practice of education, teachers and students have characteristically different perspectives on the unfolding drama of education offered and received, through all its episodes, and at the different stages in their lives and careers. It is composed on multiple timescales – the "period", the unit of work, the term or semester, the year, the stage or level, and so on. The teacher teaches students with their own narrative understandings of the unity of their lives and prospective careers, and their own personal goals and ideas of the good for humankind. And the student experiences not *only* Mr Jones the mathematics teacher, but *also* Mr Jones the person, with his own character, background and view of life. Student and teacher also have very different views of how the present class, the present episode of practice can be viewed against the background of history. Is Mr Jones merely old fashioned, or does he believe that his social constructivist view of mathematics education has roots reaching back as far as, and perhaps beyond John Dewey, and so he teaches in a way some regard as "progressive" but that he regards as justified because it is necessary to draw on students' experience to make explicit the relationship between the students' knowledge and experiences and the topic now before them? Of course the students also bring a history to the class – a history of success and failures in schooling, of interests inflamed and extinguished, of expectations raised or lowered in a history of attainments in schooling and outside it. Some, of course, experience their greatest educational successes in educational episodes outside the school – in workplaces, social clubs, family life and the adventures of adolescent peer group activities that raise the ire or eyebrows of adults. And each draws in different ways on the historically given store of meanings in words, discourses and theories available to them, and each draws on these resources in different ways, for different purposes which may, in the end, converge in something like the practice of mathematics or ideas about the good life or the good society – but which may not converge, and will probably diverge as students go on to live their lives by other lights than the ones that guide their teachers.

Systemic

In terms of the *systemic* character of the relationships between participants in a setting like education, clearly teacher and students occupy different and reputedly reciprocal *roles*.

From the extra-individual perspective, these roles are discursively framed and interpreted in traditions and theories internal to the field and profession of education. But these are not the only ways teachers and students are discursively framed. Alongside educational theories, many people involved in or affected by the education of rising generations – parents, potential employers and administrators and legislators responsible for education systems, for example – have ideas and expectations about what education is meant to achieve that are very different from the ideas and expectations internal to education as a field. External to the practice of education, students and their families are construed in some discourses as clients receiving services, or as consumers exchanging money for educational services. These ways of framing learners and correspondingly framing teachers (e.g., as service providers) have become increasingly prevalent in the discourses of educational policy in recent decades.

Such educational and extra-educational administrative and market discourses shape not only how education is understood, but also have an impact on the ways participants in education relate to one another *in social space.* Once upon a time, schools stood *in loco parentis* (in the relationship of parents) to their pupils, especially younger pupils. Nowadays, the roles are more "professionalised" in the particular sense that the rights and responsibilities of schools, teachers and whole state school systems are differentiated from the rights and duties of parents, with the former increasingly regarded as providers of professional services, and therefore as subject to professional accreditation and regulation.

This transformation is marked by the rise of corresponding system structures in education, beyond the level of the particular classroom or school or state education system. As Habermas (especially 1984, 1987a, 1987b; see also Kemmis, 2000, 2001) shows in his theory of lifeworld and system, these administrative systems, like economic systems, become increasingly "autonomous" in the sense that they operate according to their own principles and procedures, with the individual people in the system being decreasingly treated as subjects in the philosophical sense – as persons worthy of respect in their own right – and increasingly being treated as objects to be regulated. This shift from a *lifeworld* perspective on the educational encounter – the perspective in which subjects encounter one another as "persons" – to a *system* perspective – in which persons encounter one another as *incumbents of roles* – is characteristic of modern administrative and administrative relations, Habermas argues, and has led to a further development: the colonisation of lifeworlds by the imperatives of economic and administrative systems. This colonisation occurs, in particular, through the operation of the "steering media" of money and administrative power that penetrate the lifeworld as stand-ins for intersubjective understanding, mutual agreement and consensus about what to do. As a consequence of this colonisation, intersubjective understanding, agreement and consensus become contractualised, on the one hand in terms of a fair trade between the buyer and seller of services, or on the other through state regulation and surveillance. But it remains true that education itself still requires the particular achievements that can only be attained through lifeworld processes – processes of cultural-discursive reproduction and transformation by which intersubjective agreement and understanding can be achieved between people; processes of social reproduction and transformation by which consensus, social integration and legitimacy can be achieved; and processes of socialisation and identity formation and transformation by which personal identities can be secured and validated in capabilities necessary for people to lead satisfactory lives.

In the *material-economic* dimension, teachers and students are also recipro- cally enmeshed in material exchanges of work for grades, for example, as part of larger institutional-administrative systems of schooling, educational administra- tion, teacher professional development and educational research and evaluation. Both students and teachers find themselves enmeshed in institutional processes of evaluation, assessment, accreditation and regulation as part of the social system they jointly inhabit, with characteristically different, sometimes cooperative and sometimes mutually resistant, perspectives on what it means to be enmeshed (or entrapped) together in these systems.

Different theorists of practice emphasise different elements of the spectrum of individual and extra-individual features of practice in relation to the systemic char- acter of practice. For example, on the side of the individual, psychological role theory and organisational theory have offered one way into understanding the roles of people involved in practice. And theories like Habermas's theory of lifeworld and system explore the boundary crises between lifeworlds and systems which leave their marks on persons obliged to interpret themselves in the different terms provided by the systems to which they must relate as well as in terms of the diverse lifeworlds they inhabit as persons coexisting with other persons in families, workplaces and a variety of social groups in civil society.

On the extra-individual side, the systemic character of practices has been explored in the *cultural-discursive* dimension by theorists such as Foucault (on regimes of truth, performativity); in the social dimension by researchers in the sociology of the professions, for example; and in the material-economic dimension by researchers in such fields as activity theory and systems theory including "soft systems theory" (Checkland & Scholes, 1990; Flood & Jackson, 1991; Jackson, 1991).

Reflexivity and Transformation

Practices are always reflexive – people involved in practices "observe themselves" in the conduct of their practice and can modify their performance as they do so, or on future occasions. Professional practice, moreover, always invites historical self-consciousness of oneself as a practitioner in relation to other practitioners previously encountered (through experience or texts). In modifying her or his professional practice to a lesser or greater extent in the light of experience, practitioners (e.g., social workers, builders and farmers) not only reproduce and transform different elements of the form or "shape" of their practice, they also reproduce and transform aspects of their identities as practitioners, sometimes becoming more specialised (and seeing themselves increasingly as specialists) in particular areas of practice as they do so.

Many theorists have explored reflexivity on the side of the individual in theorising practice – including Bourdieu, Giddens, and Gouldner (1976), Schatzki and Toulmin, to name just a few.

On the extra-individual "side", the performance of a practice understood through particular *discourses*, particular interpretations of events, and particular communications with others in and around the field of practice also leads to the reproduction and transformation of the cultural-discursive contents and conditions that give the practice meaning and significance – potentially contributing to the evolution of the cultural-discursive dimension of the practice (e.g., the ways these symptoms will now be understood, as indications of the possible presence of a newly identified virus). Similarly, the *social* connections and relationships involved in particular instances of practice can contribute to reproduction and transformation of the social content and conditions of the practice, and the ways people involved relate to one another, potentially contributing to the evolution of the social dimension of the practice (e.g., the ways doctors will relate to nurses in the future). And, likewise, the performance of the practice can contribute to the reproduction and transformation of the *material-economic* arrangements supporting the practice – potentially contributing to the evolution of the practice as materially and economically constituted (e.g., the development of new pharmaceuticals to combat the newly identified virus).

Theorists focusing on *cultural-discursive* features of reflexivity and transformation include Shotter and Lyotard, for example; some of those focusing on *social* features include Benhabib, Habermas and Young (1990); some focusing on *material-economic* features include the Marxians (Althusser, Gramsci), reproduction theorists (like Bourdieu and Passeron) and activity theorists (like Vygotsky, Leontiev and Engeström).

Forms of Reasoning

Different theorists and theories of practice have different ways of understanding practice and contribute to different forms of reasoning about it. Since Aristotle (especially in his *Ethics*, 2003), distinctions have been drawn between forms of knowledge and reasoning that relate to action or practice in different ways – a set of distinctions employed by Habermas (1972) in his *Knowledge and Human Interests* to describe the different kinds of "knowledge-constitutive interests" that impelled scientists to produce different kinds of knowledge to serve different kinds of purposes. (For a revised and updated view, see Habermas, 2003, especially Ch.7 "The Relationship between Theory and Practice Revisited".) Using the example of teacher education, Fig. 8.6 gives an overview of these different perspectives on how, for the individual, knowledge relates to action, and how, in the realm of public knowledge, theory relates to practice. These or similar distinctions were discussed in Carr and Kemmis (1986).

A similar table to Fig. 8.6 could be produced, for other professions and practices, to disentangle the forms of reasoning characteristically employed at particular

	Theoretical perspective	Technical perspective	Practical perspective	Critical-emancipatory perspective
Telos (Aim)	The attainment of knowledge or truth	The production of something	Wise and prudent judgement; acting rightly in the world	Overcoming irrationality, injustice, suffering, felt dissatisfactions
Disposition	Episteme A disposition to seek the truth for its own sake	Techné A disposition to act in a true and reasoned way according to the rules of a craft	Phronesis A moral disposition to act wisely, truly and justly; goals and means are both always open to review	Critical A disposition towards emancipation from irrationality, injustice, suffering, felt dissatisfactions
Example in teacher education	Studying philosophy of education with the aim of developing a personal theory of education	Learning knowledge (like theories of learning, individual differences, motivation) and skills to teach a lesson, manage a class, assess learning	Learning about the nature, traditions and purposes of education as a moral activity intrinsically involved with the formation of good persons and the good for humankind	Community projects aimed at developing understanding of historical, discursive, social and material-economic circumstances which constrain capacities for self-expression, self-development and self-determination
Action	Theoria Contemplation, involving theoretical reasoning about the nature of things	Poietike 'Making' action, involving means-ends or instrumental reasoning to achieve a known objective or outcome	Praxis 'Doing' action, morally-informed action oriented by tradition, involving practical reasoning about what it is wise, right and proper to do in a given situation	Emancipatory Collective reflection and action aimed at historical self-understanding and collective consensus about what to do to overcome constraints on rationality, justice, well-being
Example in teacher education	Development of logical thinking using and building on the theoretical resources of educational traditions	Development of lesson preparation skills, skills to teach state curriculum, skills to assess students according to policy or rules	Development of reflexive capacity to adapt immediate goals and means to changing circumstances in a class or school in light of educational values about the good for students and the good for humankind	Community action and education projects (and action research projects) taking emancipatory action on educational and social issues confronted by a community

Fig. 8.6 Different perspectives on the relationship between knowledge and action, theory and practice

moments in the practice of those professions (e.g., the occupational therapist acting in a theoretical way to elucidate the concept of "therapy"; the social worker acting in a technical way in following state procedures for removal of a child as the subject of domestic abuse; the historian acting in a practical way to inform debate about contemporary immigration policy; and the doctor acting in a critical-emancipatory way on a public health issue like the effects of herbicides and pesticides on a rural community).

Returning to the question of forms of reasoning about practice as outlined in Fig. 8.3, however, on the side of the individual much reasoning about practice is based on taking the *practical* perspective, taking into account current circumstances and theories and traditions of thought relevant to a practical situation so the person will act wisely and prudently in the situation (*praxis*; see also Aristotle, 2003; Gauthier, 1963; Grundy, 1987; Schwab, 1969).

On the side of the extra-individual, however, different forms of reasoning may be brought into play. Some theorists (and some participants in a practice) explore the *cultural-discursive* dimension of practice – the discourses that shape it (e.g., following Wittgenstein, Shotter, and Schatzki). A theorist like Shotter has a particular interest in *expressive-aesthetic* understandings of practice. In some ways, Gadamer (1975, 1977) takes a similar line, arguing that a positivistic-scientific view of "method" cannot replace, and indeed distorts, proper understanding of practices which can only occur through interpretation.

Other theorists, linking the cultural-discursive and *social* dimensions, explore practice through *critical reasoning* (e.g., Habermas, 1972, 1974; Benhabib, 1992; Carr & Kemmis, 1986). And still other theorists and practitioners approach practice in terms of its *material-economic* dimension, in terms of *technical reasoning* – that is, with a primary interest in controlling practice as a means to produce particular ends or effects. This technical understanding of practice dominates some literatures of practice, especially in the Anglo-American literature, where practice is understood almost entirely in instrumental or functional terms – a position criticised by many in the literature (e.g., Habermas, 1984, 1987b, in his *Theory of Communicative Action*). I will conclude with a few remarks about the inadequacy of the technical view of practice when it becomes so dominant as to obscure the other proper ways in which practice must also be understood and enacted.

Conclusion

The technicist view of practice has become prevalent in public administration in recent decades. This view is particularly apparent in the recent "evidence-based practice" movement, which, in my view, demeans practice by its resolute focus on measurable outcomes or outputs at the expense of many of the other features of practices outlined in my "practice table". In its zeal for measuring practice, the evidence-based view makes practice almost unrecognisable from the perspective of professional practitioners whose intentions, values and commitments are crucial in the conduct of their work. It also makes practice almost unrecognisable from the perspective of anyone who understands that practice is constructed in cultural-discursive, social and material-economic dimensions, through history and the living traditions of communities of practice – anyone, that is, who understands that practices have historical and social consequences, meaning and significance for communities and societies which are beyond the particular measurable effects (and effectiveness) of particular acts of particular practitioners at particular times. In particular, and based on a long tradition of splitting facts and values in positivistic science and pseudo-science, the technicist view threatens to empty practice of its *moral* dimension. This is a price professional practitioners should not be prepared to pay for the "certainties" allegedly given by the particularly restricted range of "evidence" that "counts" in the evidence-based approach to practice. Practice is just not that simple.

Using the framework presented in my "practice table" may yield a richer under-standing of the ends and goods of education and can give a more profound reading of practice than can be gained by assessing the "quality" of practices against techni-cal, instrumental performance measures. We may hope such measures point towards the unmeasurable aspects of quality, but they do not adequately capture the quality of practice in the more encompassing sense as outlined in Fig. 8.3 – *nor can they be expected to do so*. For example, making some assessment of the outcomes of learn-ing and the conduct of teaching is technically necessary for a teacher to have an idea of whether she is achieving her aims as a teacher, but it is not sufficient. The quality of learning and teaching in the richer sense of participation in the practice of *educa-tion* (aimed at the development and continuing self-development of individuals and the development and continuing self-development of societies in which they live) is not measurable by tests or assessments, no matter how allegedly valid or reliable. In addition to and instead of these measures, educators do, however, make assess-ments, evaluations, interpretations and judgements of their work as *education* – as do professional practitioners in every other field, in interpreting and judging the quality of their practice and the quality of their lives as practitioners of that practice. In my view, they do so not so much by measuring as by *reading* practice.

One can make a reading of an act, an episode, or a life of professional practice, against a framework of features of practice like the one I have offered here, and make one's own judgement – which may disagree with the judgements of others – of the quality of the practice on this or that occasion or over that whole life. Such a reading is not a measure or an assessment, it is an elucidation of the way in which the act or episode or life holds up as a consistent, developing effort to realise the distinctive ends and goods of the practice (MacIntyre, 1982) in one's own life, in the lives of others with whom one works, and in a society. And it is *one's own* elucidation of the "facts" of the act or episode or life with which one is presented – a judgement that is informed, to a greater or lesser degree, by relevant theory and traditions, and by a community of practice whose interest is in the maintenance and continuing development of the tradition. As Gadamer's notion of "effective-historical consciousness" (understanding the historicality of the interpreter as well as the thing being interpreted) reminds us, the judgement tells as much about the judge as about what is judged.

In this chapter, I have attempted to show that different theorists of practice, and different traditions in the study of practice, have very different views about what the key features of practice are. The "practice table" presented in Fig. 8.3 is one "map" of a conversation-space between some of these different theories and traditions.

My central purpose in characterising the individual and extra-individual features in a "map" like Fig. 8.3 is to suggest how complex and manifold "practice" is, and to emphasise that changing a practice requires not only changing the knowledge and actions of individual practitioners but also changing extra-individual features and elements of situations that are necessarily implicated in practices. In short, changing practice requires changing more than people – it requires changing (at least) the cultural and discursive fields in which practices are understood locally and more generally, the social fields in which practices connect people with one another locally and more generally, and the material-economic fields in which they act in and on the material world – in particular in relation to the acts of production and consumption that locate them in local and wider economies.

If my "practice table", Fig. 8.3, does provide a provisional framework for understanding and researching practice, it shows how rich and complex practice is, stretching out from the here-and-now of particular episodes of behaviour and action in time and physical, material, cultural, semantic and social space. It suggests what *lies behind* or *may* lie behind particular acts, in the minds of those participating in them. It suggests what cannot be "seen" by research that limits its purview just to the actions of a practitioner as seen by an observer, or to exploring the perspectives of particular participants. It suggests a kind of *illimitability* of practice, for example in the dimension of history and tradition, even though it points towards a genealogy of connections between these people and acts and others long gone and far distant. And this illimitability of practice itself makes a mockery of most "measures" of practice that observe only particular behaviours or acts without attention to the wider conditions which form and inform them.

On the other hand, using Fig. 8.3 as a framework for critique of practice makes it possible to explore at least the nearby regions of the illimitable space occupied by a practice in particular cases. This is a task I have begun to pursue using the "practice table" as a guide or "table of invention" – as a schedule or set of prompts to guide interviews, observations and document analysis – in a new program of research to explore the manifold character and richness of practice through case studies of particular initiatives in teacher education and education for sustainability.

References

Althusser, L. (1971). *Lenin and philosophy and other essays*. London: New Left Books.

Argyris, C. (1990). *Overcoming organisational defenses: Facilitating organisational learning*. Boston: Allyn and Bacon.

Argyris, C., & Schön, D. A. (1974). *Theory in practice: Increasing professional effectiveness*. San Francisco: Jossey-Bass Publishers.

Argyris, C., & Schön, D. A. (1978). *Organisational learning: A theory of action perspective*. Reading, MA: Addison-Wesley.

Argyris, C., Putnam, R., & McLain Smith, D. (1985). *Action science*. San Francisco: Jossey-Bass.

Aristotle (2003). *Ethics* (Trans. J. A. K. Thompson (1953), revised with notes and appendices H. Tredennick (1976), with an introduction J. Barnes (1976, 2003), and preface A. C. Grayling (2003)). London: The Folio Society.

Bakhtin, M. (1984). *Problems of Dostoevsky's poetics* (C. Emerson, Trans. and Ed.). Minneapolis, Minnesota: University of Minnesota Press.

Benhabib, S. (1992). *Situating the self: Gender, community and postmodernism in contemporary ethics*. Cambridge: Polity Press.

Bernstein, B. (1977). *Class, codes and control, volume. 3: Towards a theory of educational transmissions*. London: Routledge and Kegan Paul.

Bernstein, B. (1996). Pedagogy, symbolic control and identity: Theory, research, critique. London: Taylor & Francis.

Bourdieu, P. (1977). *Outline of a theory of practice* (R. Nice, Trans.). Cambridge: Cambridge University Press.

Bourdieu, P. (1984). *Homo academicus*. Cambridge: Polity Press.

Bourdieu, P. (1990). *The logic of practice* (R. Nice, Trans.). Cambridge: Polity Press.

Bourdieu, P. (1998). *Practical reason: On the theory of action*. Cambridge: Polity Press.

Bourdieu, P., & Passeron, J-C. (1977). *Reproduction in education, society and culture* (R. Nice, Trans.), (2nd ed.). London: Sage.

Bourdieu, P., & Wacquant, L. (1992). *An invitation to reflexive sociology*. Chicago: The University of Chicago Press.

Carr, W. (2005). The role of theory in the professional development of an educational theorist. *Pedagogy, Culture & Society, 13*(3), 333–346.

Carr, W., & Kemmis, S. (1986). *Becoming critical: Education, knowledge and action research*. London: Falmer.

Checkland, P., & Scholes, J. (1990). *Soft systems methodology in action*. Chichester, UK: Wiley.

Connell, R. W., Ashenden, D., Kessler, S., & Dowsett, G. (1982). *Making the difference: Schools, families and social division*. Sydney: George Allen and Unwin.

Derrida, J. (1974). *On grammatology* (G. Spivak, Trans.). Baltimore: Johns Hopkins University Press.

Derrida, J. (1978). *Writing and difference* (A. Bass, Trans.). Chicago: University of Chicago Press.

Dunne, J. (2005). An intricate fabric: Understanding the rationality of practice. *Pedagogy, Culture & Society, 13*(3), 367–390.

Engeström, Y. (1987). *Learning by expanding: An activity-theoretical approach to developmental research*. Helsinki: Orientat-Konsultit.

Engeström, Y. (2000). Activity theory as a framework for analysing and redesigning work. *Ergonomics, 43*(7), 960–974.

Eraut, Michael (1994). *Developing professional knowledge and competence*. London: Falmer.

Feyerabend, P. (1970). Against method: Outline of an anarchistic theory of knowledge. In M. Radner & S. Winokur (Eds.), *Minnesota Studies in the Philosophy of Science* (Vol. 4). Minneapolis: University of Minnesota Press.

Flood, R.L., & Jackson, M.C. (1991). *Creative problem solving: Total systems intervention*. Chichester, UK: Wiley.

Foucault, M. (1970). *The order of things: An archaeology of the human sciences*. London: Tavistock.

Foucault, M. (1972). *The archaeology of knowledge* (A.M.S. Smith, Trans.). London: Tavistock.

Foucault, M. (1977). *Language, counter-memory, practice* (D.F. Bouchard, Ed., D.F. Bouchard and S. Simon, Trans.). Ithaca, NY: Cornell University Press.

Foucault, M. (1979). *Discipline and punish: The birth of the prison* (A. Sheridan, Trans.). New York: Vintage.

Foucault, M. (1985). *Discourse and truth: The problematisation of parrhesia* (Ed. J. Pearson). Evanston, Illinois: Northwestern University. Retrieved October 10, 2005 from http://foucault.info/documents/parrhesia.

Foucault, M. (1990a). *The history of sexuality, volume 1: Introduction* (R. Hurley, Trans.). New York: Vintage.

Foucault, M. (1990b). *The use of pleasure: Volume 2 of the history of sexuality* (R. Hurley, Trans.). New York: Vintage.

Foucault, M. (2001). *Fearless speech* (Ed. J. Pearson). Los Angeles, California: Semiotext(e).

Gadamer, H-G. (1975). *Truth and method*. London: Sheed and Ward.

Gadamer, H-G. (1977). Theory, science, technology: The task of a science of man. *Social Research*, 44, 529–561.

Gauthier, D. P. (1963). *Practical reasoning: The structure and foundations of moral arguments and their exemplification in discourse*. London: Oxford University Press.

Giddens, A. (1979). *Central problems in social theory: Action, structure and contradiction in social analysis*. London: Macmillan.

Giddens, A. (1984). *The constitution of society*. Cambridge: Polity Press.

Giroux, H. (1983). *Theory and resistance in* education. South Hadley, MA: Bergin and Garvey.

Gouldner, A. (1976). *The dialectic of ideology and technology*. London: Macmillan.

Gramsci, A. (1977). *Selections from political writings 1910–1920* (J. Matthews, Trans. And Q. Hoare, Ed.). London: Lawrence and Wishart.

Grundy, S. (1987). *Curriculum: product or praxis?* London: The Falmer.

Habermas, J. (1972). *Knowledge and human interests* (J. J. Shapiro, Trans.). London: Heinemann.

Habermas, J. (1974). *Theory and practice* (J. Viertel, Trans.). London: Heinemann.

Habermas, J. (1984). *Theory of communicative action, Volume 1: Reason and the rationalisation of society* (T. McCarthy, Trans.). Boston: Beacon.

Habermas, J. (1987a). *The theory of communicative action, volume 2: Lifeworld and system: A critique of functionalist reason* (T. McCarthy, Trans.). Boston: Beacon.

Habermas, J. (1987b). *The philosophical discourse of modernity: Twelve lectures* (F. G. Lawrence, Trans.). Cambridge, MA: MIT.

Habermas, J. (1996). *Between facts and norms: Contributions to a discourse theory of law and democracy* (W. Rehg, Trans.). Cambridge, MA: MIT.

Habermas, J. (2003). *Truth and justification* (B. Fultner, Trans. and Ed.). Cambridge, MA: MIT.

Hargreaves, A. and Earl, L. (2001). *Learning to change: Teaching beyond subjects and standards*. San Francisco: Jossey Bass.

Harvey, D. (1996). *Justice, nature and the geography of difference*. Oxford: Blackwell.

Higgs, J., Titchen, A., & Neville, V. (2001). Professional practice and knowledge. In J. Higgs & A. Titchen (Eds.), *Practice knowledge and expertise in the health professions* (Chapter 1). Oxford: Butterworth-Heinemann.

Hindess, B. (1977). *Philosophy and methodology in the social sciences*. Hassocks, Sussex: Harvester Press.

Jackson, M.C. (1991). *Systems methodology for the management sciences*. New York: Plenum.

Katz, A.M., & Shotter, J. (1996). Resonances from within the practice: Social poetics in a mentorship program. *Concepts and Transformation*, 1(2/3), 239–247.

Kemmis, S. (2000). System and lifeworld and the conditions of learning in late modernity. *Curriculum Studies*, 6(3), 269–305.

Kemmis, S (2001). Educational research and evaluation: Opening communicative space. *Australian Educational Researcher*, 28(1), 1–30.

Kemmis, S. (2005a). Knowing practice: Searching for saliences. *Pedagogy, Culture & Society*, 13(3), 391–426.

Kemmis, S. (2005b). Is mathematics education a practice? Mathematics teaching? In M. Goos et al. (Eds.), *Proceedings of the Mathematics Education and Society 4 Conference*. Brisbane: Centre for Learning Research, Griffith University. Retrieved October 27, 2005 from http://www.griffith.edu.au/conference/mes2005/pdfs/Kemmis.pdf.

Kemmis, S. & McTaggart, R. (2000). Participatory action research. In N. Denzin & Y. Lincoln (Eds.), *Handbook of qualitative research* (2nd ed.). Thousand Oaks, CA: Sage.

Kemmis, S. & McTaggart, R. (2005). Participatory action research: Communicative action and the public sphere. In N. Denzin & Y. Lincoln (Eds.), *The Sage handbook of qualitative research* (3rd ed.). Thousand Oaks, California: Sage.

Kemmis, S., & Fitzclarence, L. (1986). *Curriculum theorizing: beyond reproduction theory*. Geelong, VIC: Deakin University Press.

Kuhn, T. (1970). *The structure of scientific revolutions* (2nd ed.). Chicago: University of Chicago Press.

Lakatos, I., & Musgrave, A. (1970). *Criticism and the growth of knowledge*. London: Cambridge University Press.

Larrain, J. (1979). *The Concept of Ideology*. London: Hutchinson.

Lave, J., & Wenger, E. (1991). *Situated Learning: Legitimate peripheral participation*. Cambridge: Cambridge University Press.

Leontiev, A. N. (1974). On the importance of the notion of object-activity for psychology. *Proceedings of the XXth International Congress of Psychology* (Tokyo, August 13–19). Japan: University of Tokyo Press.

Leontiev, A. N. (1981). *Problems of the development of the mind*. Moscow: Progress.

Lyotard, J-F. (1984). *The postmodern condition: A report on knowledge* (G. Bennington and B. Massumi, Trans.). Manchester: Manchester University Press.

MacIntyre, A. (1982). *After virtue*. London: Duckworth.

MacIntyre, A. (1988). *Whose justice? Which rationality?* London: Duckworth.

MacIntyre, A (1990). *Three rival versions of moral theory: Encyclopaedia, genealogy and tradition*. London: Duckworth.

Noddings, N. (2003). Is teaching a practice? *Journal of Philosophy of Education, 37*(2), 241–251.

Oakeshott, M. (1962). *On human conduct*. Oxford: Clarendon Press.

Rönnerman, K. (2005). Participant knowledge and the meeting of practitioners and researchers, *Pedagogy, Culture & Society, 13*(3), 291–312.

Saugstad, T. (2005). Aristotle's contribution to scholastic and non-scholastic learning theories, *Pedagogy, Culture & Society, 13*(3), 347–366.

Schatzki, T. R. (1996). *Social Practices: A Wittgensteinian approach to human activity and the social*. Cambridge: Cambridge University Press.

Schatzki, T. R. (1997). Practices and actions: A Wittgensteinian critique of Bourdieu and Giddens. *Philosophy of the Social Sciences, 27*(3), 283–308.

Schatzki, T. R. (2001). Introduction: practice theory. In T. R. Schatzki, K. Knorr Cetina & E. von Savigny (Eds.), *The Practice turn in contemporary theory*. London: Routledge.

Schatzki, T. R. (2002). *The site of the social: A philosophical account of the constitution of social life and change*. Pennsylvania: University of Pennsylvania Press.

Schön, D. A. (1987). *The reflective practitioner: How professionals think in action*. New York: Basic Books.

Schwab, J. (1969). The practical: a language for curriculum. *School Review, 78*, 1–24.

Schwandt, T. A. (2005). On modelling our understanding of the practice fields. *Pedagogy, Culture & Society, 13*(3), 313–332.

Shotter, J. (1996). Living in a Wittgensteinian world: Beyond theory to a poetics of practices. *Journal for the theory of social behaviour, 26*(3), 293–311.

Shotter, J. (1999). 'Living moments' in dialogical exchanges. *Human Systems, 9*, 81–93.

Shotter, J. (2000). From within our lives together: Wittgenstein, Bakhtin, Voloshinov and the shift to a participatory stance in understanding understanding. In L. Holzman & J. Morss (Eds.), *Postmodern psychologies, societal practice and political Life*. New York: Routledge.

Taylor, C. (1985). *Interpretation and the human sciences. Philosophy and the Human Sciences: Philosophical Papers 2*. Cambridge: Cambridge University Press.

Taylor, C. (1991). *The malaise of modernity*. Concord, ONo: House of Anansi Press.

Toulmin, S. (1972). *Human understanding, volume 1: The collective use and evolution of concepts*. Princeton, NJ: Princeton University Press.

Vygotsky, L. S. (1978). *Mind in society: The development of higher psychological processes* (M. Cole, V. John-Steiner, S. Scribner and E. Souberman, Trans. and Eds.). Cambridge, MA: Harvard University Press.

Vygotsky, L. S. (1986). *Thought and language* (A. Kozulin, Trans.). Cambridge, MA: Harvard University Press.

Weber, M. (1946). *From Max Weber: Essays in sociology* (H.H. Gerth and C. Wright Mills, Trans. and Eds.). New York: Oxford University Press.

Wenger, E. (1998). *Communities of practice: Learning, meaning and identity.* Cambridge: Cambridge University Press.

Willis, P. (1977). *Learning to labour.* Aldershot: Saxon House.

Wittgenstein, L. (1974). *Philosophical investigations* (G.E.M. Anscombe, Trans.). Oxford: Basil Blackwell.

Young, I. M. (1990). *Justice and the politics of difference.* Princeton: Princeton University Press.

Chapter 9
An Approach to Notions of Subject Position and Discourse in Activity Theory

Harry Daniels

This chapter is concerned with the learning of professionals in new forms of practice that require joined-up solutions in order to meet complex and diverse client needs. This form of work is neither that of a stable team or network. It demands changes in inter-professional practice and relationships with clients. Such demands confront all services that are engaged in joined-up responses to clients' complex needs. Current policy on social inclusion is running ahead of conceptualisations of inter-professional collaboration and the learning it requires in a number of fields. These include nursing (Freeman, Miller, & Ross, 2000); mental health (Secker & Hill, 2001); child protection (Morrison, 2000); abuse (Slater, 2002); family based intervention (Sturge, 2001); and local regeneration (Diamond, 2001). Responsive inter-agency work in these contexts requires a new way of conceptualising collaboration that recognises the construction of constantly changing combinations of people and resources across services, and their distribution over space and time. The creation of such professional contexts is central to current UK government policy (e.g. DfES, 2002a, 2002b), and matches similar developments in other constituencies.

"Joined up" responses need to be flexible and require practitioners to be able work together to support clients. This kind of fluid collaboration of practitioners from different professional backgrounds is not simply a matter of creating new inter-professional teams. Rather, it is a question of learning to identify the broad needs of clients, recognise how the expertise of other professionals can meet those needs and be able to work across a number of professional boundaries in responding to them. This process cannot be reduced to formulaic ideas of partnership. Rather, it requires practitioners to learn how to see and use the potential to be found in working with a wide range of possible collaborators when enhancing the life chances of clients. The central concern of Daniels et al. (2005a) is how these professionals learn to collaborate to provide responsive support to these young people. There has been much discussion of the notion of professional hybridisation that is taken as

H. Daniels (✉)
University of Bath, Bath, UK
e-mail: h.r.j.daniels@bath.ac.uk

C. Kanes (ed.), *Elaborating Professionalism*, Innovation and Change in Professional Education 5, DOI 10.1007/978-90-481-2605-7_9,
© Springer Science+Business Media B.V. 2010

an indicator of the erosion of professional boundaries and the silos, which they constitute. In this chapter I will provide a discussion of a way of theorising this notion of hybridity in a way that relates the emergence of new formations to the structural antecedents from which it arises.

In the course of an inter-professional development workshop conducted as part of this research, a community paediatrician remarked that her biggest learning challenge was "to learn to *be and talk* like a inter-agency person when I am not in inter-agency meetings" (emphasis in the original). The theoretical challenge implicit in this short statement is how we can understand the relations between the social organisation of work, discursive practice (all the ways in which discourse is produced, distributed, and consumed) and social position.

This extract was collected in the course of project in which we are studying how professionals learn to discursively create new forms of activity (see Daniels et al., 2005a, 2005b). One of the significant methodological challenges is to capture the ways in which historical and contemporary processes of discursive construction are mutually constitutive in talk and action about the object of the activity. This involves the tracing of the objects of professional work as they move in space and time across various situations and professional practices.

The history of the interlinking of situations and events is to be seen through the object of the activity. Methodologically this calls on us to involve the client or service user (in this case the young person) in the study of the discursive construction of new forms of object related action. This involves both the study of formal case conferences and planning meetings (which are both reflective and practical) as well as informal small talk and incidental and spontaneous negotiation. These events embody different forms of relation between practical activity and discourse. An understanding of discursive hybridity (Sarangi & Roberts, 1999) requires us to study multi-sited and temporally distributed professional discourse. In this study discourse is viewed as linguistic and other semiotic meaning making activities between and among professionals in their work contexts.

We aim to understand how language used by various participants expands the object of work resulting in the object itself becoming a genre with its own distinctive discourse. We consider how these genres are maintained and expanded by professionals as members of overlapping communities brought together in various combinations in their discursive construction of the object. Our original focus on the object moved us away from a concern with the subject identity formation of professionals to a concern with how participants construct and sustain the object as genre. In particular, we analysed how language by different participants is used to interpret and expand the object. I will now outline our theoretical point of departure and then move to suggest that new forms of theoretical development are required as we reflect on the theoretical demands of data such as the statement "to learn to *be* and *talk* like a inter-agency person when I am not in inter-agency meetings".

I will now discuss the way in which the concept of social position can be used to promote theoretical development in activity theory and enhance the explanatory power of the theoretical tools that are deployed in the project described above. Throughout the initial data collection phases of this project the concept of professional identity has as a key construct for many of the practitioners we have interviewed and observed. In so doing I will consider the way in which the cultural artefact, discourse, is deployed in relation to the social position of the subject. Thus the chapter is primarily concerned with the analysis of subject positioning and discursive practice within activity systems. My key points of departure are to be found in three areas of academic endeavour:

- Post Vygotskian and activity theory based approaches to the study of artefact mediated, object-oriented human activity as exemplified by the work of Yrjö Engeström (1999) and Michael Cole (1996);
- Recent attempts by Holland, Lachiotte, Skinner, and Cain (1998) to synthesise the work of the Russian linguist, M. M. Bakhtin, Vygotsky and the French social theorist Pierre Bourdieu in an account of identity and agency in cultural worlds; and
- The theory of the social structuring of discourse in society developed by Basil Bernstein (2000) and discussed in relation to the work of Halliday (1973, 1975, 1978) and Vygotsky by the linguist Ruqaiya Hasan (2001).

Activity Theory

The development and principles of activity theory have been discussed at length (e.g., Engeström & Miettinen, 1999). I will not revisit such an account in this chapter. I wish to direct attention to what Engeström terms the third generation of activity theory.

Engeström (1999) sees joint activity as the unit of analysis for activity theory, not individual activity. He is interested in the processes of social transformation and includes the structure of the social world in his analysis whilst taking into account the conflictual nature of social practice. He sees instability (internal tensions) and contradiction as the "motive force of change and development" (Engeström, 1999, p. 9) and the transitions and reorganisations within and between activity systems as part of development. In activity theory the subject is taken as the individual or subgroup whose agency is chosen as the point of view in the analysis (Engeström et al., 1999). It is not only the subject, but also the environment, that is modified through mediated activity. He views the "reflective appropriation of advanced models and tools" as "ways out of internal contradictions" that result in new activity systems (Cole and Engeström, 1993, p. 40).

The third generation of activity theory (Fig. 9.1), as proposed by Engeström, intends to develop conceptual tools to understand dialogues, multiple perspectives and networks of interacting activity systems. The idea of networks of activity within which contradictions and struggles take place in the definition of the motives and object of the activity calls for an analysis of power and control within developing activity systems. The minimal representation that Fig. 9.1 provides shows but two of what may be a myriad of systems which may exhibit patterns of contradiction

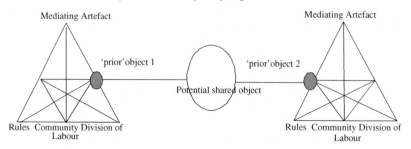

Fig. 9.1 Third-generation activity theory model

and tension and conflict within and between their component parts. As two or more activity systems come into play at one moment they do so with objects which are prior to the new formation (see Fig. 9.1). The formation of a new shared object involves transformations of both legacy activity systems. In our study of learning for and in inter-agency working we are drawing on this third generation of activity theory as we model networks of interacting activity (Daniels et al., 2005a). As noted above we are studying professional learning in services that aim to promote social inclusion through inter-agency working. Working with other professionals involves engaging with configurations of several, diverse social practices and the development of new forms of hybrid practice. The implications for notions of expertise have been explored by Hakkarainen et al. (2004):

> Expertise in a certain domain may also be represented in a hybrid expert who is able to translate one expert culture's knowledge into form that participants of another expert culture can understand . . . . . . innovation emerges in networks of these kinds of communities. Creation of innovations supports gradually developing division of labour and increased specialisation as well as combination of existing dispersed resources for novel purposes. (Hakkarainen et al., 2004, p.17)

Agency is typically left in the background in activity theory. References are made to notions of "subject" and "division of labour" that are suggestive of agency rather than direct articulations. Pirkkalainen et al. (2005) have argued that such hybrid practice is different from collaboration, cooperation or networking in which the constituent activities remain distinct. They suggest that hybridisation involves change in positional relations *between* the agents of different activity systems and positional change of agents *within* one activity system. Such changes involve shifts in relations of power (in the division of labour) and control (within the categories established by the division of labour) within and between activity systems. These theoretical speculations deploy the term *agency* to refer to human collective or individual action to affirm the argument that activity can be realised in terms of collective activity systems as well as in individual activity

This means that in new hybrid functions the activity systems themselves and their positional relations to other activity systems change. Nominations and contracts, plans and commissions could be examples of indicators or mediators of such hybrid agency. These mediators combine two activity systems together in a way that can be expected to create new activity and therefore new activity systems. By this we mean that by changing the boundaries related to the division of labour these new hybrids create spheres for activity to emerge from new – or at least changed – positions. This we argue differentiates the concept of hybrid agency from other concepts of collaboration or cooperation e.g. networking. (Pirkkalainen et al., 2005, p. 2)

It is here that a present theoretical weakness is revealed by the introduction of the notion of hybridisation and the focus on positional relations instead of object formation, and historically generated forms of social relations instead of historical forms of work and organisations (Pirkkalainen et al. 2005). This focus on positional relations raises the question as to how do we develop a theoretical account of the discursive regulation of interpersonal relations that is compatible with the assumptions of activity theory.

Hasan (1992a, 1992b, 1995) and Wertsch (1985, 1991) note the irony that whilst Vygotsky developed a theory of semiotic mediation in which the mediational means of language was privileged, he provides very little, if anything, by way of a theory of language use. In an account of the social formation of mind there is a requirement for theory that relates meanings to interpersonal relations. The absence of an account of the ways language both serves to regulate interpersonal relations and how its specificity is in turn produced through specific patterns of interpersonal relation and thus social regulation constitutes a serious weakness. That is that language both shapes and is shaped by specific patterns of interpersonal relation and thus social regulation. This absence has carried through in the development of activity theory. As Engeström and Miettinen (1999) note, it has yet to develop a sophisticated account of discursive practice that is fully commensurate with the assumptions of activity theory itself. At the same time, Engeström acknowledges the methodological difficulty of capturing evidence about community, rules and division of labour in the practice of studying an activity system (Engeström, 1999).

A theoretically powerful move would be to understand the discursive regulation of interpersonal relations in terms of processes of social, cultural and historical regulation as witnessed in activity theory by the notions of rules and division of labour. I have used the term *witnessed* because I argue that there is theoretical work to be done here. As Pirkkalainen et al. (2005) note at the end of their paper, the study of hybridisation raises key questions such as "how do we understand division of labour – how do we understand rule in any given activity system" (p. 7). They also suggest that there is a need to differentiate/unify concepts of agency, subject and actor. In the rest of this paper I will attempt to address some aspects of these questions along with questions about the place of the construct identity in this theoretical framework.

Engeström (1999) offers the suggestion that the division of labour in an activity creates different positions for the participants and that the participants carry their own diverse histories with them into the activity. This echoes the earlier assertion from Leontiev:

> Activity is the minimal meaningful context for understanding individual actions. . .. In all
> its varied forms, the activity of the human individual is a system set within a system of
> social relations. . ... The activity of individual people thus *depends on their social position*,
> the conditions that fall to their lot, and an accumulation of idiosyncratic, individual factors.
> Human activity is not a relation between a person and a society that confronts him. . .in a
> society a person does not simply find external conditions to which he must adapt his activity,
> but, rather, these very social conditions bear within themselves the motives and goals of his
> activity, its means and modes. (Leontiev, 1978, p.10)

In activity the possibilities for the use of artefacts depends on the social position occupied by an individual. Sociologists and sociolinguists have produced theoretical and empirical verification of this suggestion (e.g., Bernstein 2000, Hasan 2001, Hasan & Cloran 1990). However, as indicated above, the notion of "subject" within activity theory requires expansion and clarification. In many studies the term *subject perspective* is used, which arguably infers subject position, but this does little to illuminate the roots or formative processes, the trajectory, that gave rise to the perspective in question. I will now explore some aspects of the ways in which it is possible to consider the position that a subject takes up in the spaces afforded by the social practices in which they participate.

Identity and Agency in Cultural Worlds

Holland et al. (1998) have studied the development of identities and agency specific to historically situated, socially enacted and culturally constructed worlds. They draw on Bakhtin and Vygotsky to develop a theory of identity as constantly forming and person as a composite of many, often contradictory, self-understandings and identities which are themselves rarely durable, but distributed across the material and social environment (p. 8). They draw on Leontiev in the development of the concept of socially organised and reproduced "figured worlds" which shape and are shaped by participants and in which social position establishes possibilities for engagement. They also argue that figured worlds:

> Distribute 'us' not only by relating actors to landscapes of action (as personae) and spread-
> ing our senses of self across many different field s of activity, but also by giving the
> landscape human voice and tone. – Cultural worlds are populated by familiar social types
> and even identifiable persons, not simply differentiated by some abstract division of labour.
> The identities we gain within figured worlds are thus specifically historical developments,
> grown through continued participation in the positions defined by the social organisation of
> those world's activity. (Holland et al., 1998, p. 41)

Thus this approach to a theory of identity in practice is grounded in the notion of a figured world in which positions are taken up, constructed and resisted. The Bakhtinian concept of the "space of authoring" is deployed to capture an understanding of the mutual shaping of figured worlds *and* identities in social practice. They refer to Bourdieu (c.f. 1977) in their attempt to show how social position becomes disposition. They argue for a theory of the development of social position into a positional identity into disposition and the formation of what Bourdieu refers to as "habitus". It is here that I feel that this argument could be strengthened through reference to a theoretical account that provides greater descriptive and analytical purchase on the principles of regulation of the social figured world, the possibilities for social position and individual and collective agency.

The concept of habitus has itself been subject to strident critique in respect of the way in which its social origins are theorised. Bernstein (2000) is one of those who appreciate the concept's theoretical heuristic value but is doubtful of its empirical utility. He suggests that when faced with the empirical task of distinguishing between one habitus and another, a researcher is left without any analytical or descriptive research tools.

> [I]f we take a popular concept *habitus*, whilst it may solve certain epistemological problems of agency and structure, it is only known or recognised by its apparent outcomes. Habitus is described in terms of what it gives rise to, and brings, or does not bring about ... But it is not described with reference with reference to the particular ordering principles or strategies, which give rise to the formation of a particular habitus. The formation of the internal structure of the particular habitus, the mode of its specific acquisition, which gives it its specificity, is not described. How it comes to be is not part of the description, only what it does. There is no description of its specific formation. ... Habitus is known by its output not its input. (Bernstein, 2000, p.133)

Similarly, the study of processes of hybridisation would be left without a means of distinguishing between key aspects of the activity systems in play. Hasan (1992a) also contends that the same problem is to be found with attempts that refer to Bakhtin's concept of speech genre:

> Though Bakhtin's views concerning speech genres are rhetorically attractive and impressive, the approach lacks -- both a developed conceptual syntax and an adequate language of description. Terms and units at both these levels in Bakhtin's writings require clarification; further, the principles that underlie the calibration of the elements of context with the generic shape of the text are underdeveloped, as is the general schema for the description of contexts for interaction.

Linehan and McCarthy (2000) develop a strong argument in favour of the deployment of a notion of positioning in communities of practice as an approach to studying participation in social settings. They outline a problem space which echoes some of the concerns raised by Holland et al. (1998) but the problem of theorising social and cultural position in such a way that the analytical and empirical engagement with the figured world becomes visible remains elusive.

The Social Regulation of Subject Position

Bernstein (1990, p. 13) used the concept of social positioning to refer to the establishing of a specific relation to other subjects and to the creating of specific relationships within subjects. This seems to me to concur with the analysis outlined by Holland et al. (1998). He relates social positioning to the formation of mental dispositions in terms of the identity's relation to the distribution of labour in society. It is through the deployment of his concepts of voice and message that Bernstein forges the link between division of labour, social position and discourse and opens up the possibilities for a language of description that will serve empirical as well analytical purposes. In what follows I will provide a very brief presentation of the essence of this argument. Full details may be found in Bernstein (2000).

Bernstein's work is concerned with inter-relations between changes in organisational form, changes in modes of control and changes in principles of communication. His language of description is generated from an analysis of power (which creates and maintains boundaries in organisational form) and control that regulates communication within specific forms of interaction. Initially he focuses upon two levels: a structural level and an interactional level. The structural level is analysed in terms of the social division of labour it creates ("classification") and the interactional level with the form of social relation it creates ("framing"). The social division of labour is analysed in terms of strength of the boundary of its divisions, that is, with respect to the degree of specialisation. Thus within an organisation the social division of labour is complex where there is an array of specialised actors and categories of work, and it is relatively simple where there is a reduction in the degree of specialisation. Thus the key concept at the structural level is the concept of boundary, and structures are distinguished in terms of their boundary arrangements and their power supports and legitimations (Bernstein, 1996). The interactional level emerges as the regulation of the transmission–acquisition relation, for example, between teacher and taught or manager and worker: that is, the interactional level comes to refer to the context and the social relations of the classroom or its work setting. The interactional level then gives the principle of the context through which the social division of labour, in Bernstein's terms, speaks.

Bernstein (1996) refined the discussion of his distinction between instructional and regulative discourse. The former refers to the transmission of skills and their relation to each other, and the latter refers to the principles of social order, relation and identity. Whereas the principles and distinctive features of instructional discourse and its practice are relatively clear (the what and how of the specific skills/competences to be acquired and their relation to each other), the principles and distinctive features of the transmission of the regulative are less clear as this discourse is transmitted through various media and may indeed be characterised as a diffuse transmission. Regulative discourse communicates the school's (or any institution's) public moral practice, values beliefs and attitudes, principles of conduct, character and manner. It also transmits features of the school's local history, local tradition and community relations. Pedagogic discourse is modelled as one discourse created by the embedding of instructional and regulative discourse. This model of pedagogic discourse provides a response to one of the many theoretical demands that have remained unfulfilled in the post-Vygotskian framework. A model within which a unitary conception of thinking and feeling could be discussed and implemented within empirical research did not follow the rejection of the cognitive–affective dualism which Vygotsky announced.

The language that Bernstein has developed allows researchers to take measures of school modality. That is to describe and position the discursive, organisational and interactional practice of the institution. Research may then seek to investigate the connections between the rules the children use to make sense of their pedagogic world and the modality of that world. Bernstein provides an account of cultural transmission that is avowedly sociological in its conception. In turn the psychological account that has developed in the wake of Vygotsky's writing offers a model of aspects of the social formation of mind that is underdeveloped in Bernstein's work.

He defines modalities of pedagogic practice in terms of principles for distinguishing between contexts ("recognition rules") *and* for the creation and production of specialised communication within contexts ("realisation rules"). Pedagogic practice refers to the instructional context, the instructional practice and the regulative practice. Modalities of pedagogic practice and their discourses may then be described in terms directly referenced to the theory. Features of cultural artefacts may be described in terms of the cultural context of their production. Bernstein argues that much of the work that has followed in the wake of Vygotsky "does not include in its description how the discourse itself is constituted and recontextualised".

Thus for Bernstein power relations regulate the degree of insulation between categories. Boundaries are established and challenged in relationships of power. For him power establishes "voice" in that it demarcates that which is legitimate within categories and thus establishes the rules by which voice may be recognised. The distinction between what can be recognised as belonging to a voice and a particular message is formulated in terms of distinction between relations of power and relations of control. Bernstein (1990) adapted the concept of voice from his reading of *The Material Word* by Silverman and Torode (1980). He grounds the concept in the material division of labour. Thus allowing for the move between the analysis and description of the social order and that of the practices of communication.

> From this perspective classificatory relations establish "voice". "Voice" is regarded somewhat like a cultural larynx which sets the limits on what can be legitimately put together (communicated). Framing relations regulate the acquisition of this voice and create the 'message' (what is made manifest, what can be realised) (Bernstein, 1990, p. 260)

In his last book he continues

> Voice refers to the limits on what could be realised if the identity was to be recognised as legitimate. The classificatory relation established the voice. In this way power relations, through the classificatory relation, regulated voice. However voice, although a necessary condition for establishing what could and could not be said and its context, could not determine what was said and the form of its contextual realisation; the message. The message was a function of framing. The stronger the framing the smaller the space accorded for potential variation in the message. (Bernstein, 2000, p. 204)

Thus social categories constitute voices and control over practices constitutes message. Identity becomes the outcome of the voice – message relation. Production and reproduction have their social basis in categories and practices; that categories are constituted by the social division of labour and that practices are constituted by social relations within production/reproduction; that categories constitute "voices" and that practices constitute their "messages"; message is dependent upon "voice", and the subject is a dialectical relation between "voice" and message (Bernstein, 1990, p. 27).

One may speak with the "voice" of the psychology but the particular identity as a psychologist is revealed in the actual messages produced/spoken. Change occurs when "new" messages are produced and give rise to changes in voice/classification/power relations. Identity may be studied in terms of utterance and the principles of social regulation through which it is generated and transformed. The rules of activity theory include what Bernstein refers to as framing and the division of labour (hierarchical and vertical) refers to classification. Hasan (2002a) argues that Bernstein paid very close attention to invisible semiotic mediation – how the unself-conscious everyday discourse mediates mental dispositions, tendencies to respond to situations in certain ways and how it puts in place beliefs about the world one lives in, including both about phenomena that are supposedly in nature and those which are said to be in our culture. She asserts that discourse is not treated as simply the regulator of cognitive functions; it is as Bernstein (1990, p. 3) states also central to the shaping of "identities and practices".

Hasan (2001, p. 8) suggests that Bernstein's analysis of how subjects are positioned and how they position themselves in relation to the social context of their discourse, offers an explanation of hybridity, in terms of the classification and framing practices of the speaking subjects. The invisible semiotic mediation is to be found in the relations of power and control that give rise to the voice message relation in which identities are formed and social positions are bequeathed, taken up and transformed. In Hasan's empirical work she has evidenced this effect: "What the mothers speak, their selection and organisation of meanings is a realisation of their social positioning" (Hasan, 2002, p. 546).

Conclusion

Subject-subject and within subject relations are under-theorised in activity theory. Such a theorisation would require a theoretical account of social relations and positioning. Holland et al. bring Bakhtin's notion of the "space of authoring" into play as they outline the processes of mutual shaping of figured worlds *and* identities in social practice. They also argue that multiple identities are developed within figured worlds and that these are "historical developments, grown through continued participation in the positions defined by the social organisation of those world's activity" (Holland et al., 1998, p. 41). This body of work represents a significant development in our understanding of the concept of the "subject" in activity theory. From my point of view there remains a need to develop the notion of "figured world" in such a way that we can theorise, analyse and describe the processes by which that world is "figured". However the theoretical move which Bernstein makes in relating positioning to the distribution of power and principles of control opens up the possibility of grounding the analysis of social positioning and mental dispositions in relation to the distribution of labour in an activity. Through the notions of "voice" and "message" he brings the division of labour and principles of control (rules) into relation with social position in practice. This theoretical stance suggests that activity theory should also develop a language of description which allows for the parameters of power and control to be considered at structural and interactional levels of analysis. A systematic approach to the analysis and description of the formation of categories through the maintenance and shifting of boundaries and principles of control as exercised within categories would bring a powerful tool to the undoubted strengths of activity theory. This would then allow the analysis to move from one level to another in the same terms rather than treat division of labour and discourse as analytically independent items. Given that in Bernstein's terms, positioning is in a systematic relation to the distribution of power and principles of control, it is argued that this approach to our understanding the notion of social positioning affords the underlying, invisible component which "figures" practices of communication.

> [A] specific text is but a transformation of the specialised transactional practice; the text is the form of the social relationship made visible, palpable, material . . . Further the selection, creation, production, and changing of texts are the means whereby the positioning of the subjects is revealed, reproduced and changed. (Bernstein 1990, p. 17)

In his last paper, Bernstein (1999b) moved his analysis to the internal principles of the construction and social base of pedagogic discourses. Having provided a theory of the construction of pedagogic discourse he moved to an analysis of the discourses subject to pedagogic transformation. This move will be of particular significance when this body of theory and its language of description are brought to bear on the discussion of the relationship between everyday and scientific concepts as outlined in "Thinking and Speech". The analysis outlined by Bernstein (1999b) allows for greater differentiation within and between the forms identified by Vygotsky. The analytical power of the distinctions made between vertical and horizontal discourses and hierarchical and horizontal knowledge structures provides research with an enhanced capacity to provide descriptions that capture the delicacy of the forms and their interrelation. This move would bring a more discriminating form of analysis to bear on the notion of tool in activity theory.

Horizontal discourse that arises out of everyday activity is usually oral, local, context dependent and specific, tacit, multilayered and contradictory across but not within contexts. Its structure reflects the way a particular culture is segmented and its activities are specialised. Horizontal discourse is thus segmentally organised. In contrast, vertical discourse has a coherent, explicit and systematically principled structure that is hierarchically organised or takes the form of a series of specialised languages with specialised criteria for the production and circulation of texts (Bernstein, 1999b, p. 159). Bernstein suggests that Bourdieu's notion of discursive forms which give rise to symbolic and practical mastery and Habermas's reference to the discursive construction of lifeworlds of individuals and instrumental rationality both refer to parts of a complex field of parameters which in turn refer to both individual and social experience and relate to the model of horizontal and vertical discourse which he seeks to develop. He offers an initial set of contrasts and indicates that many more exist. As mentioned above, his lament is for the lack of a language of description of these forms, which can serve to generate and relate the possibilities for difference.

Bernstein's (1999a) paper serves as important reminder that the theoretical derivation of "scientific and everyday" in the original Vygotskian writing was somewhat provisional. For example, the association of the scientific with the school does not help to distinguish those aspects of formal instruction such as that which obtains in schooling that merely act to add to everyday understanding without fostering the development of scientific concepts. The association also suggests that the development of scientific concepts must take place in the school and not outside it. Bernstein's analysis is suggestive of a more powerful means of conceptualising the forms which Vygotsky announced.

It may be as a consequence of the dualist perspective, which remains so powerful, that the emphasis on the interdependence between the development of scientific and everyday concepts is also not always appreciated. Valsiner (1997) distinguishes dualisms from dualities, arguing that the denial of dualism (inner, outer) in appropriation models leads to a denial of the dualities that are the constituent elements in dialectical or dialogical theory. This echoes the Marxist notion of internal relationship in which two elements are mutually constitutive. Vygotsky argued that the systematic, organised and hierarchical thinking that he associated with scientific concepts becomes gradually embedded in everyday referents and thus achieves a general sense in the contextual richness of everyday thought. Vygotsky thus presented an interconnected model of the relationship between scientific and everyday or spontaneous concepts. Similarly he argued that everyday thought is given structure and order in the context of systematic scientific thought. Vygotsky was keen to point out the relative strengths of both as they both contributed to each other.

My argument is that there is much to be gained through a sustained theoretical engagement with the notion of subject in activity theory and that Holland et al., Hasan and Bernstein provide rich sources of inspiration for such an endeavour. Such theoretical work would, hopefully, provide tools for engaging in the empirical study of the processes of hybridisation that abound in the cultures of our everyday worlds.

These tools would unpack the notions of subject, division of labour, community, tool and rules as they are currently represented in activity theory and permit a form of analysis that allows researchers to undertake the kind of work that Bernstein envisaged.

> It then becomes possible in one framework to derive a typology of educational codes, to show the inter-relationships between organisational and knowledge properties to move from macro- to micro-levels of analysis, to relate the patterns internal to educational institutions to the external social antecedents of such patterns, and to consider questions of maintenance and change. (Bernstein, 1977, p.112)

Bernstein's work has not placed particular emphasis on the study of change (see Bernstein 2000). The introduction of the third generation of activity theory initiated the development of conceptual tools to understand dialogues, multiple perspectives on change within networks of interacting activity systems all of which are underdeveloped in Bernstein. The idea of networks of activity within which contradictions and struggles take place in the definition of the motives and object of the activity calls for an analysis of power and control within and between developing activity systems. The latter is the point at which Bernstein's emphasis on different layers and dimensions of power and control becomes key to the development of the theory. The minimal representation that Fig. 9.1 shows is two of what may be a network of systems exhibiting patterns of contradiction and tension.

Consider the situation in which several professionals meet to discuss a supposedly common issue: for instance, a psychologist, a teacher, a social worker and a mental health worker meet to discuss the education and care of a young person who has been excluded to school. Here we can analyse the historical formation of the professional identities of each actor. They will all have been children, pupils, students, trainees and moved into through professional structures. A historical analysis of the transformations that take place in activity systems could be brought to bear on the formation of dispositions and identities in each of their career trajectories. A situated analysis would need to pursue the ways in which each subject moved (and was able to move) through a short negotiation of possibilities for action as they attempted to understand and work within or impose professional codes. It is here that Bernstein's work on horizontal and vertical structures and pedagogic discourse as an embedded discourse is important. He provides the language of description and the theoretical basis from which to analyse the emergence of "leading" or most powerful activities. Engeström has rightly pointed to the need to analyse contradiction within and between activity systems and Bernstein provides the theoretical tools with which to empirically investigate such phenomena in that he connects the analysis of organisational, discursive and psychological in a coherent language of description.

In response to the challenge of studying new and emergent expert practices, in which, say, different activity systems are brought into different forms of relation with each other, an understanding of discursive hybridity (Sarangi & Roberts 1999) may provide an important opening for the development of an understanding of changes in discursive practice. Research in this field requires a unified theory that can give rise to a coherent and internally consistent methodology rather than a collection of compartmentalised accounts of activity, discourse and social positioning that have disparate and often contradictory assumptions.

The emergence of agentic collaboration between actors is a form of what Engeström (2007, p. 4) has called collaborative intentionality that he argues constitutes a new form of capital and is a central feature of organisations which are successful in developing multi-agency working. The agentic collaboration between the practitioners involved in the sites we studied provided valuable assets for the organisations involved.

> They perform a dual job in that they solve very complex problems and also contribute to the reshaping of the entire way of working in their given fields. They are very cost-efficient in that they do not require the establishment of new positions or new organisational centres. Indeed, these formations tend to reject such attempts. Rejection and deviation from standard procedures and scripted norms are foundational to the success of such amoeba-like formations. Their efficacy and value lie in their distributed agency, their collective intentionality.

In this sense, suggest the notion of collaborative intentionality capital as an emerging form of organisational assets. (Engeström, 2004, p. 28)

In order to make progress in such empirical work there is a need for theoretical and methodological development which allows us to identify and investigate

- the ways in which objects of activity are transformed within the networks of activity systems in which subjects participate;
- the circumstances in which particular discourses are produced;
- the modalities of such forms of cultural production; and
- *the implications of the availability of specific forms of such production for the positioning of subjects in social space.*

References

Bernstein, B. (1977). *Class codes and control volume 3: Towards a theory of educational transmissions* (2nd Rev. Ed.). London: Routledge & Kegan Paul.

Bernstein, B. (1990). *Class, codes and control, volume 4: The structuring of pedagogic discourse.* London: Routledge.

Bernstein, B. (1996). *Pedagogy, symbolic control and identity: Theory, research, critique.* London: Taylor&Francis.

Bernstein, B. (1999a). Official knowledge and pedagogic identities. In F. Christie (Ed.), *Pedagogy and the shaping of consciousness: Linguistic and social processes.* London: Cassell.

Bernstein, B. (1999b). Vertical and horizontal discourse: An essay. *British Journal of Sociology of Education, 20*(2) 157–173.

Bernstein, B. (2000). *Pedagogy, symbolic control and identity: Theory research critique* (Rev. ed.). Oxford: Rowman and Littlefield.

Bourdieu, P. (1977). *Outline of a theory of practice.* Cambridge : Cambridge University Press.

Cole, M. (1996). *Cultural psychology: A once and future discipline.* Cambridge, MA: Harvard University Press.

Cole, M., & Engeström, Y. (1993). A cultural-historical approach to distributed cognition. In G. Salomon (Ed.), *Distributed cognitions: Psychological and educational considerations* (pp. 1–46). New York: Cambridge University Press.

Daniels, H., Brown, S., Edwards, A., Leadbetter, J., Middleton, D., Parsons, S. et al. (2005a). Studying professional learning for inclusion. In Yamazumi, K., Engestrom, Y. & Daniels, H. (Eds). *New Learning Challenges: Going beyond the industrial age system of school and work.* Osaka: Kansai University Press.

Daniels, H., Edwards, A., Martin, D., Leadbetter, P. Warmington, A. Popova, D. et al. (2005b). *Learning in and for Interagency Working ESRC TLRP.*

Department for Education and Skills (2002a). *Spending review: Investment for reform.* London: HMSO.

Department for Education and Skills (2002b). *Safer school partnerships: Guidance.* Issued jointly by Department for Education and Skills, Home Office, Youth Justice Board, Association of Chief Education Officers and Association of Chief Police Officers.

Diamond, J. (2001). Managing change or coping with conflict? Mapping the experience of a local regeneration partnership. *Local Economy, 16*, 272–285.

Engeström, Y. (1999). Innovative learning in work teams: Analysing cycles of knowledge creation in practice. In Y. Engeström, R. Miettinen, and R.L. Punamaki (Eds.), *Perspectives on Activity Theory.* Cambridge: Cambridge University Press.

Engeström, Y. (2004). New forms of learning in co-configuration work. *Journal of Workplace Learning, 16*(1/2), 11–21.

Engeström, Y. (2007). Putting Vygotsky to work. The change labouratory as an application of double stimulation. In H. Daniels, M. Cole & J. V. Wertsch (Eds.), *The Cambridge companion to Vygotsky* (pp. 363–382). Cambridge: Cambridge University Press.

Engeström, Y., & Miettinen, R. (1999). Introduction. In Engstrom, Y., Miettinen & R-L Punamaki (Eds.), *Perspectives on activity theory* (pp. 1–18). Cambridge: Cambridge University Press.

Freeman, M., Miller, C., & Ross, N. (2000). The impact of individual philosophies of teamwork on multi-professional practice. *Journal of Inter-professional Care, 14*(3), 237–247.

Hakkarainen, K., Lonka, K., & Paavola, S. (2004). Networked intelligence: How can human intelligence be augmented through artifacts, communities, and networks? Retrieved June 2005 from http://www.lime.ki.se/uploads/images/517/Hakkarainen_Lonka_Paavola.pdf.

Halliday, M. A. K. (1973). *Relevant models of language, in explorations in the functions of language.* London: Arnold.

Halliday, M. A. K. (1975). *Learning how to mean: Explorations in the development of language.* London: Arnold.

Halliday, M. A. K. (1978). *Language as social semiotic: The social interpretation of language and meaning.* London: Arnold.

Hasan, R. (1992a). Speech genre, semiotic mediation and the development of higher mental functions. *Language Science, 14*(4), 489–528.

Hasan, R. (1992b). Meaning in sociolinguistic theory. In K. Bolton & H. Kwok (Eds.), *Sociolinguistics today: International perspectives.* London: Routledge.

Hasan, R. (1995). On social conditions for semiotic mediation: The genesis of mind in society. In A. R. Saadov (Ed.), *Knowledge and pedagogy: The sociology of Basil Bernstein.* Norwood: Ablex.

Hasan, R. (2001a). Understanding talk: Directions from Bernstein's sociology. *International Journal of Social Research Methodology, 4, 1,* 5–9.

Hasan, R. (2001b). The ontogenesis of decontextualised language: Some achievements of classification and framing. In A. Morais, I. Neves, B. Davies & H. Daniels (Eds.) *Towards a sociology of pedagogy: The contribution of Basil Bernstein to research.* New York: Peter Lang.

Hasan, R. (2002a). Semiotic mediation and mental development in pluralistic societies: Some implications for tomorrow's schooling. In G. Wells & G. Claxton (Eds.). *Learning for life in the 21st century: sociocultural perspectives on the future of education* (pp. 112–26). Malden, MA: Blackwell Publishers.

Hasan, R. (2002b). Ways of meaning, ways of learning: Code as an explanatory concept. *British Journal of Sociology of Education, 23*(4).

Hasan, R., & Cloran, C. (1990). A sociolinguistic study of everyday talk between mothers and children. In M. A. K. Halliday, J. Gibbons & H. Nicholas (Eds). *Learning keeping and using language, Volume 1.* Amsterdam: John Benjamins.

Holland, D., Lachiotte, L., Skinner, D., & Cain, C. (1998). *Identity and agency in cultural worlds.* Cambridge, MA: Harvard University Press.

Hymes, D. (1967). Models of the interaction of language and social setting. In J. Macnamara (Ed). Problems of Bilingualism, *Journal of Social Issues, 23,* 8–28.

Leontiev, A. N. (1978). *Activity, consciousness, and personality.* Englewood Cliffs: Prentice-Hall.

Linehan, C., & McCarthy, J. (2000). Positioning in practice: Understanding participation in the social world. *Journal for the Theory of Social Behaviour, 30,* 435–453.

Morrison, T. (2000). Working together to safeguard children: Challenges and changes for inter-agency co-ordination in child protection. *Journal of Interprofessional Care, 14*(4), 363–373.

Pirkkalainen, J., Kaatrakoski, H. & Engeström, Y. (2005). *Hybrid agency as hybrid practice.* A paper presented at the 1st ISCAR Congress, Seville, Spain.

Sarangi, S. & Roberts, C. (1999). Introduction: Discursive hybridity in medical work. In S. Sarangi & C. Roberts (Eds). *Talk, work and institutional order: Discourse in medical, mediation and management settings.* Berlin: Mouton de Gruyter.

Secker, J., & Hill, K. (2001). Broadening the partnerships: Experiences of working across community agencies. *Journal of Interprofessional Care, 15*, 341–350.

Silverman, D., & B. Torode (1980). The Material word: Some theories of language and its limits. Routledge: London.

Slater, P. (2001). Preventing the abuse of vulnerable adults: Social policy and research. *Journal of Social Policy, 30*(4), 673–684.

Slater, P. (2002). Training for no secrets: A strategic initiative. *Social Work and Education, 21*, 437–448.

Sturge, C. (2001). A multi-agency approach to assessment. *Child Psychology and Psychiatry Review, 6*, 16–23.

Valsiner, J. (1997). Culture and the development of children's action: A theory of human development (2nd ed.). New York: Wiley.

Wertsch, J. V. (1985). *Vygotsky and the social formation of mind.* Cambridge, MA: Harvard University Press.

Wertsch, J. V. (1991). *Voices of the mind: A socio-cultural approach to mediated action.* Cambridge, MA: Harvard University Press.

Chapter 10
Studies in the Theory and Practice
of Professionalism: Ways Forward

Clive Kanes

In Chapter 1 I identified several prominent headline challenges to professionalism. These concerned the nature of professionalism, public trust in professionalism, and implications for education and training. In this final chapter of the book, I want to discuss some possible ways these challenges might be met. My attempt will follow two obviously related paths. In the first (considered in the next section) I want to suggest that an ethical turn could be a fruitful way to forward. Here, discuss an initiative of the Royal College of Physicians of London (RCPL) set out in their recent report, *Doctors in society: Medical professionalism in a changing world* (2005), and bring to this various theoretical thoughts suggesting new directions for practice and investigation. Concerning the second path (in the final section of the chapter), I systematically elicit key themes elaborating professionalism that emerge from contributions made by the previous chapters in this book. I want to show that these analyses can help practitioners, policy makers and professional educators.

Some Recent Developments in the Practice and Theory of Professionalism

The RCPL report mentioned above is written from the perspective of medical practitioners who are becoming growingly uncertain about the nature of professionalism. Given developments in the medical sciences, the escalating costs associated with delivery, growingly complex ethical issues, and so on etc., a sense of urgency, shown in the following extract from the report, has developed.

> Until quite recently the role of doctors in people's lives, in the community and in national life, and the responsibilities that went with professional standing, were well understood. That is no longer the case. Social and political factors, together with the achievement and promise of medical science, have reshaped attitudes and expectations both of the public and of doctors.

C. Kanes (✉)
King's College London, London, UK
e-mail: clive.kanes@kcl.ac.uk

C. Kanes (ed.), *Elaborating Professionalism*, Innovation and Change in Professional Education 5, DOI 10.1007/978-90-481-2605-7_10,
© Springer Science+Business Media B.V. 2010

The relationship between doctors and society, the doctor–patient relationship, and the environments in which doctors undertake their training and their practice, have all changed.
Events that have undermined public trust in medicine, and a questioning of traditional values and behaviour have also greatly influenced the life and work of doctors. They have
challenged characteristics that were once seen as hallmarks of medicine.

Undoubtedly these changes have brought progress, with benefit for patients and for the public good. But there have been insidious (sic) consequences too. There is mounting evidence
that in different ways these consequences can jeopardise the quality of patient care, and the
fulfillment of doctors, whose prime goal is to serve patients well. The trust that patients
have in their doctor is critical to their successful care (RCPL, 2005, v).

Underlying these statements appears to be the belief that new thinking about
medical professionalism requires the empirical elaboration of practice itself. In view
of this, consultations with practitioners and stakeholders were broad – physicians
themselves, professional associations, nursing professionals, patient groups, academics, medical agencies and institutions – and these led to a definition of medical
professionalism worded as follows:

Medical professionalism signifies a set of values, behaviours, and relationships that
underpins the trust the public has in doctors (p. 14).

Importantly – and the report features this – this approach sees the downgrading
in importance of traditional notions of mastery, autonomy, privilege and self-
regulation. Doctoring today, it argues, is a multidisciplinary practice, often involving
teams of boundary-crossing experts, and this makes older concepts of medical professionalism increasingly untenable. Replacing these, new attitudes towards the
exercise of medical knowledge are required, patients' experience of medicine must
improve and public trust in it must grow. As one practitioner put it in testimony,
'it is the interpretation of knowledge, the engagement with new knowledge, the
acknowledgement of uncertainty about knowledge, the sharing of knowledge, not
the holding of knowledge that are the hallmarks of professionalism' (RCPL, 2005, p.
17, emphasis added). What is crucial is how doctors regard themselves, each other,
and the communities they serve. In reviewing the report for *The Lancet* another
practitioner observed the need for practitioners to 'live out in their everyday practices' this new vision of medical professionalism (Braithwaite, 2006, p. 645). The
report, it is claimed, is 'evocative' of the way practitioners must be in themselves
and behave in relation to their work.

Thus the report advocates a double transcendence: a transcendence of public
over private interests, and the transcendence of inter-personal values of care over
knowledge interests owned by practitioners. In achieving these, medical professionalism must be built around a "moral contract" between practitioners and society.
Though the report is less clear about many features of such a contract, what I think
is interesting is the move to view ethical relationships as constitutive of medical
professionalism and away from seeing it merely as a necessary adjunct. Essentially
this displaces a traditional, knowledge-based view of professionalism, which is no
longer seen as either practical or even desirable. Clearly this proposal begs many
questions – though coming from practice itself, it requires careful consideration. In
what follows, I try to tease out what kinds of 'ethical relationships' are consistent
with the thrust of this report.

Ethical Work

Here I want to note three different, but relevant, ways the scholarly literature helps us. In these the central focus is not prescriptive codes of ethical behaviour as such, but the ways practitioners behave in practicing these codes. For instance, in Freidson's later work (2001), we see professionalism depicted as a form of self-transcendence. If professionals are acting in self-interest, then professionalism needs to develop a more conscious countervailing sense of its "soul". Thus, for instance, he writes

> While capital punishment (and lately, the use of torture) by the state is a matter for the public to debate and decide, the use of medical skills to do so is a matter for the profession to decide independently of law and the public. That is, if it has soul (Freidson, 2001, p. 172).

Moreover, if the "soul" checks the interests of practitioners, it also checks managerial and market interests. For Freidson,

> Soul is what is ascribed to human beings that makes them something more than just another kind of animal. Occupations could be said to have soul when they act as something more than just a technical enterprise at the service of the state, employers, and consumers (Freidson, p. 172).

"Soul" thus brings with it an awareness of a way of being and acting ethically. However, Freidson doesn't make clear how 'soul' translates into practice. What they entail. For instance: How does "soul" confer character to a profession? Why, indeed, is 'soul' self-evidently trustworthy? How is it connected with the processes of professional education?

Stepping around some of these issues, there is a second ethical view of professionalism, coming from Young (2006). Drawing on ideas of Basil Bernstein (2000), the sociologist of education, Young takes our attention to the relation of "apartness" in explaining the conditions and thus the nature and importance of professionalism. His key reference here is to Emile Durkheim's sociological view of the "sacred" as a belief, act, person, physical space or object as set apart from everyday ("profane") life. For Bernstein the sacred is characterised by inwardness of orientation, and in the case of professionalism inwardness towards knowledge is deemed especially crucial. For Young, a particular relation with, and commitment to knowledge must come before practitioners' relations with the world. Yet Young's approach is not an argument for professionalism as an esoteric practice. In following Bernstein, he argues that professionalism argues that professionalism needs to be continually re-instantiated as a relation between knowledge and society. In his words,

> It follows therefore, that just as [religious] faith had to be won and re-won, so, likewise, the conditions for professionalism and the production of knowledge – their autonomy, and more deeply, the necessity of putting the 'word' before the 'world' – have to be constantly recreated; this is what professionalism means (Young, 2006, p. 158).

Thus, both Freidson (in his later work) and Young, drawing in varying respects from Weber and Durkheim (respectively), argue that professionalism does, and needs to, recreate its way of being in response to the needs of the day. They seem to do so, however, at the expense of pushing the creative abilities of human agency and responsibility into the background. 'Soul' and 'knowledge' operate through practitioners; what remains unclear is how and on what assumptions this occurs.

A third view of ethics in professionalism arises from Foucault's notion of "acetics", or "practices of the self". For Foucault, the code or prescriptive aspect of ethics entails a study that "would analyse the different systems and rules and values that are operative in a given society or group, the agencies or mechanisms of constraint that enforce them" (Foucault, 1985, p. 28). In contrast, the study of "practices of the self" (he calls these "acetics"), tries to understand how "individuals are urged to constitute themselves as subjects of moral conduct" (p. 29). A "practice of the self" thus amounts to a way a relationship with the self is set up and accomplished. Here it is important to note that his interest is not in "self-awareness" as such, but in self-awareness "[for] self-reflection, self-knowledge, self-examination, for the decipherment of the self by oneself, for the transformations that one seeks to accomplish with oneself as object" (p. 29). No account of ethics, he argues, can focus exclusively on either ethical codes or practices of the self. On the contrary, because "all moral action involves a relationship with reality in which it is carried out, and a relationship with the self" (p. 28), both are always required in ethical considerations. For example, in the report we read that doctor's behaviours must 'protect, restore, and strengthen human well-being and dignity' (RCPL, 2005, p. 22) and do so in their 'day-to-day practice' in a manner that reflects commitment to 'integrity, compassion, altruism, continuous improvement, excellence, [and] working in partnership with members of the wider healthcare team' (p. 15). Thus care is not modeled on the ideal soul, or the sacralising of knowledge, but on the manner in which individuals are constituted as caring selves within practice itself (Englund, 1996).

Writing in a similar vein, Mackey (2007) argues that for occupational therapists, a "reflexive ethical self" in which "occupational therapy identity is based on a relationship of reflexivity through which the construction of identity is made present through working on itself" (p. 99) must be integral to professionalism. In Foucault's terms, reflexivities of these kinds are "practices of self". Mackey maintains that occupational therapists, would

> [exercise] surveillance over and against themselves, through techniques such as reflective diaries, and clinical supervision in which behaviour and performance are examined [and through these] occupational therapists produce a 'truth' about themselves, about what type of occupational therapist they are. When occupational therapists experience themselves as complex and dialogical, they are more open to the influence of the other person, be that service user, colleague, or manager. Creating occupational therapy identity through the reflexive ethical self is about allowing ourselves to be shaped through the eyes and experiences of someone who is an 'other' (p. 99).

Thus, the kind of 'ethical work' (to use Foucault's term) done here is more than 'identity work' as often understood: medical professionalism relates to becoming the subject of one's own ethical behaviours as a practitioner. Focussing on how, subjectively, compliance with ethical codes is achieved in practice may help to underpin professionalism without the need to de-centre practitioners' work – a requirement, as we have seen of Freidson's and Young's accounts.

Boundary-Crossing

In telling this complex story, it seems worthwhile to pick up the theme of boundary-crossing alluded to earlier in my discussion of the RCPL report.

As mentioned in Chapter 1, much theorising about professionalism has focussed on the formation and maintenance of strong boundaries among occupational specialisms. Coming from Weber (1978), Parsons (1954) and Abbott (1981), among others, these have construed professionalism as a rationalising the contrary directions of the legal-rational bureaucracy and the market – Freidson (2001) referred to these as the "logics" of social production. Recent researchers however tend to emphasise the mobility of occupational boundaries and boundary-crossing behaviours of professional practitioners. Two main factors are driving this switch. First, already noted, is the multiplication of disciplinary requirements and advances of specialist knowledge and technologies within occupation. A second factor is the increasingly complex bureaucratic (e.g., regulation and accountability) and market conditions (e.g., intra-professional competition), giving rise to the need to work across professional boundaries. These tendencies have both positive and negative impacts on the nature of professionalism. On the positive side is the increased value of teamwork, particularly where teams consist of numerous kinds of professionals working together. Emphasising this feature, Kenway et al. (2006) have conceptualised the notion of the "technopreneur" referring to the tendency in which field based experts are expected, to become market players. Hargreaves (2000), writing in the field of teaching professionalism, theorises these developments around the concept of 'post-professionalism'. For him, the key issue here is not whether occupations satisfy this or that format for professionalism, but how occupations enact their own understanding of professionalism, and thus achieve quality results within market settings which may involve complex knowledge and complex institutional parameters. On the negative side, Young (2006) (following Bernstein, 2000) argues excessive boundary-crossing leads to the reconstitution of professionalism around capacities seldom before seen by professionals as relevant to the named practice (e.g., marketing, public relations, forming business plans). These tendencies are exacerbated by constant demands for accountability by managerial systems (e.g., cost-benefit accounting, monitoring, competing within quasi-markets internal to organisations and self-reporting) and competitive market participation (e.g., open competition and transparency, pricing and advertising). Some take these as evidence of a growing "de-professionalisation" of professional practice and the convergence of professionalism with other forms of the social organisation of work.

However, it is notable, that even in these negative cases, opportunities to enrich or at least transform professionalism have been found. Indeed, boundary-crossing (often driven by the imperatives of managerialism) is sometimes seen as an opportunity for the renewal of practice – a so-called 'new professionalism' – emphasising lifelong learning, practical research and knowledge sharing (Weert, 2006). Thus, for example, Macdonald (1985) shows how responding to managerial accountabilities, accountancy redefines its own sense of professional competence. Ross (1996) shows how professionalism and managerialism can enrich practice when mediated by "individual [setting-specific] mechanisms, seeking to ensure shared values and norms largely through the exclusion of external diversity" (Ross, pp. 60–61). Some, like Britten (2001), argue that the state of 'confusion and ambiguity' (Stevens, 2002) in the medical professional can be strengthened by jettisoning inefficient and unnecessary practice, under the direction of managerialism. This can help practitioners see what cannot be 'traded-away' from their practice. For Brown and Bhugra (2007,

p. 4), this non-negotiable core is: 'First and foremost [that] we are doctors and the core function of doctoring is to care for our patients and their families' (p. 4). Whilst these practitioners demand 'professionalism be returned to the hands of professionals' some, like Clark (2005), insist that professionals, even in apparently restrictive settings, can make real their professionalism by finding new and specific ways to take responsibility for the quality of their services. In another example, Dewe, Otto and Schnurr (2006) report findings that demonstrate how social workers are able to practice responsibility and initiate substantive improvement in outcomes, even in settings where managerialist control has proved extremely troubling. 'This', they argue, 'is possible because professionalism subsists in the professional's character' (emphasis added). By 'character' here these authors refer to the manner of behaviour of professionals in relation to their occupational duties, a theme that echoes my discussion of professional ethics, above.

Nevertheless boundary-crossing can and does confuse professional designations and roles, and it can weaken a sense of agency, rather than strengthen it. For me, these dangers are particularly strong where de-centring of responsibility has become so extensive as to become diffuse. Viewing professionalism as an ascetic practice, because it foregrounds ethical work as a central project for all practitioners, seems to provide a compass for professionalism that is no longer obtained by either the maintenance of strong occupational boundaries, nor by the Freidson's appeal to the 'soul' of professionalism, nor by Young's knowledge centred focus.

I now want to discuss the contributions of the book as a whole to professional practice and to scholarship on professionalism.

Ways Ahead

What do the works published in this book have to contribute to an elaboration of professionalism? A useful start to answering this question is to examine the key contributions of each chapter organised around the three key headline challenges currently facing professionalism, as set out in Chapter 1. Table 10.1 provides such an analysis. There, looking by author shows how particular works do or could play out across each of the headline challenges; looking by headline challenge gives insights into aspects of debates this book particularly emphasises. This analysis will be of particular interest to practitioners, policy makers and professional educators in all professional fields and help readers build a synoptic view of the contributions.[1] Next, I present a thematic analysis of these contributions in order to bring out a set of common emerging themes. Interesting insights that need to be taken into account when we look deeply at professionalism emerge, and these help satisfy our need to better understand the limits of professionalism and what can and cannot be reasonably be expected of it.

---

[1] Authors of various chapters, of course, will have their own views as to how or if their contributions address these challenges.

Table 10.1 Indications of contributions of chapters to issues around three headline challenges currently facing professionalism

| Chapter author(s) | Headline challenge | | |
	Nature of professionalism	Education and training for professionalism	Public confidence in professionalism
Eva	Eva argues that in complex problem solving, domain-*specific* knowledge, rather than generic thinking processes, is crucial. Thus, to the extent professionalism suggests high problem-solving ability, it follows that professionalism must have an enduring relationship with specificity.	As a higher-order skill, problem-solving ability is more a function of domain-*specific* knowledge than general knowledge – this opens difficult curriculum questions	Eva's findings weaken the idea that knowledge-based models of practice (e.g., Eraut) can work as a starting point for regimes of public accountability
Searle	Searle shows that notions of generic skills do not explain how literacy works in practice. As with Eva, domain-*specific* substantive knowledge, rather than general skills, is decisive. In her work, *specificity* functions as a contextualizing resource in order for framing (i) 'technical competences', and (ii) 'maintaining the social order'. Do these form conditions for working operations in enterprises?	Searle argues that developing specialised skills in literacy is decisive in professional education (and occupational education generally). Because managerialist culture is mediated by its own textual genres, practitioners need to handle these deftly if they are not to be absorbed into the discourses of accountability and management. Because getting work done requires 'maintaining the social order', social skills additional to those of 'technical competence' need to be developed	Enriching the abilities of professionals to build social order increases the capacities of professionalism to enhance social cohesion, and contributes to the standing of professionalism. On the other hand, unduly emphasising technical competence weakens, rather than strengthens, the possibility of high-quality outcomes. This is ironic as an important rationale for managerialist culture is upwards revaluation of technical competence in order to increase the quality outcomes.

Table 10.1 (continued)

| Chapter author(s) | Headline challenge | | |
	Nature of professionalism	Education and training for professionalism	Public confidence in professionalism
Marsick, Watkins and Lovin	Marsick, Watkins and Lovin's findings are consistent with the view that occupational competences do not tend to result as a synthesis of the 'disjunction between anticipated and actual experience'. Instead, competences emerge *holistically* within the context of practice.	By emphasising *holistic* achievements in building workplace competences, curriculums and their pathways need to be framed around rich authentic contexts. Practitioners' stories of workplace experience are often good sites for informal and incidental teaching and learning. Reflection on workplace episodes, facilitated by storytelling, can contribute to quality learning; integrating these into work related protocols could be a powerful way to embed professional education into practice. Sending control of learning to practitioners, however, can contradict the tendencies of excessively managerialist environments.	A greater understanding, valuing and appreciation of the *holistic* nature of occupational competencies help people appreciate them in terms of their character, distinctiveness and *specificity*. Purposefully disseminating exemplary narratives of practice could achieve these ends.

Table 10.1 (continued)

| Chapter author(s) | Headline challenge | | |
	Nature of professionalism	Education and training for professionalism	Public confidence in professionalism
Nembhard and Edmondson	Nembhard and Edmondson's findings are consistent with the hypothesis that quality medical outcomes are positively correlated with inclusive multi-disciplinary medical teamwork. This adds weight to the thesis advanced by the authors of the RCPL (2005) report (discussed earlier in this chapter) which insists that medical professionalism is defined by ethical values embedded in interaction, not by the technical sum of medical competences These findings demonstrate that professionalism can work well in *hybrid* settings.	Because quality improvement in professional teams and inclusive work environments are positively correlated, developing requisite interpersonal capabilities in a purposefully educative context is important This will have methodological implications for educators.	Public confidence in the medical profession is clearly related to both positive health outcomes and to patients' positive experiences of health care. Based on these findings one may conjecture whether extending the bounds of 'psychological safety' to include patients and carers may also offer healthcare dividends. This could amount to purposefully extending the domains of *hybridity* of professional work in order to enhance the scope and quality of professionalism

Table 10.1 (continued)

Chapter author(s)	Headline challenge		
	Nature of professionalism	Education and training for professionalism	Public confidence in professionalism
Morgan	Morgan's findings show that "identity work" in professionalism can, under certain conditions, position a practitioner simultaneously both as autonomous and system compliant. This demonstrates the *plasticity* and responsiveness of professional competences, and thus potentially of professionalism in general. This finding is consistent with a *holistic* view of professionalism	Professional education curriculums need to facilitate the kinds of identity work professionalism currently faces. Interestingly, in Morgan's study, challenges to professional identity are met by the kinds of informal and incidental learning modelled in Marsick, Watkins and Lovin's chapter (see above)	Morgan's study might offer a way to understand Svensson's (2006) empirical finding that clients of professionals have more trust in professionals per se than in the managerialist systems that afford professional services
Brodie	Brodie's findings demonstrate that social, cultural and ethical factors extrinsic to professional work can, in view of the particular qualities of professionalism, shape validity criteria for effective competences intrinsic to its practice. This weakens ideas about the place of generic competences in professionalism, and strengthens our understanding of the *specificity* and *plasticity* of professional work.	Acknowledging that specificity and plasticity can lead to incompatible positions, Brodie's study implicitly raises the question of whether and how professional education can best help professionals understand, and where helpful, maintain these tensions. See my comments on Morgan's chapter above.	Brodie contributes to our understanding of how professionalism can be responsive to client-perceived needs, without loosing a sense of professional authority and legitimacy.

Table 10.1 (continued)

Chapter author(s)	Headline challenge		
	Nature of professionalism	Education and training for professionalism	Public confidence in professionalism
Kemmis	Kemmis provides a framework for understanding how individual work and the demands of the social world are formed reflexively (see Figs. 8.2 and 8.3). This is consistent with the assumption that multifarious resources must work *holistically* within and between practical and theoretical domains	Kemmis provides a very significant argument towards what he construes as the *illimitablity* of practice. Yet professional curriculums often assume exactly the opposite – namely that professional practice, however complex, is frameable within tractable and durable limits. (And that these limits stand as suitable indicators for managerialist intervention.) Kemmis offers a 'practice table', Fig. 8.3, consisting of a rich array of theoretical resources and approaches which could be used as new topics curriculum development and the evaluation of professional education programmes.	Kemmis argues that the prevalent 'technicist view of practice' has 'demeaned practice by its resolute focus on measurable outcome or outputs at the expense' of many alternative needs and agendas that speak to human interests and vitality (see his 'practice table', Fig. 8.3). From this perspective, it does not seem surprising that public confidence in professional practice has suffered.

Table 10.1 (continued)

Chapter author(s)	Headline challenge		
	Nature of professionalism	Education and training for professionalism	Public confidence in professionalism
Daniels	Daniels explores theoretical resources that aim to grapple with inter-agency aspects of professionalism. How are *hybrids* of various professional occupations formed and maintained (see Nembhard & Edmondson's chapter)? It is well known that extrinsic variables can hold inter-agency work together (reporting schedules, managerial mandates, etc) – but he initiates exploration of the inner discursive conditions required in order for coherence to be maintained (see also Searle's chapter). Importantly, this view is consistent with the belief that *hybridity* is not merely a contingent and practical feature of professionalism, but constitutive of it.	Professional education already draws on learning theory inspired by Vygtosky's theory of the zone of proximal development. Daniels' chapter implicitly extends this theory to settings where key players are each (with respect to one field of professionalism or another) either more or less capable peers. This offers insight into reasons underlying the effectiveness of inter-disciplinary teams in Nembhard and Edmondson's chapter (see also the chapters of Marsick et al. and Kemmis). An initial case is made for increased focus on the content and nature of communications discourses needed by professional teams. This draws attention to a field of research critical for the development of curriculums for developing professional education.	In focussing on *hybridisation* Daniels finds ways to amplify diverse professional competences and make their relationships more visible and therefore widely challengeable.

Emerging Themes

By reflecting on the analyses of Table 10.1, I have tried to move towards an overall view of these contributions. For me, the themes that have emerged most strongly can be stated as follows.

Domain specificity: This is shown in privileging the local over the general; the concrete over the abstract; the particular over the general; and the situated over the context free. For instance, Searle and Eva's chapters consider skills that are sometimes, and by some key audiences such as policy makers, taken as paradigmatic examples of generic skills (literacy particularly and problem solving, respectively). However these authors, in common with much contemporary litera-ture, find that specificity is more salient than genericity when trying to understand how practitioners function.

Holism: This is shown by regarding details as only interpretable in the light of the particular kind of context in which the details are placed. For example, Marsick *et al* argue that the significance to learning of informal and incidental settings for developing occupational competences is the bringing together of propositional knowledge and what Eraut (1994) calls process knowledge. In this work, a precon-dition for learning by informal and incidental means is that learners participate in highly purposeful workplace events and scenarios – that is, there must be an holis-tic dimension to their learning. Kemmis's chapter, argues that professional practices bring individual and social worlds together in a reflexive relation – this gives us an understanding of how the kinds of holisms important to professionalism might be constituted.

Plasticity and illimitability: By "plasticity" I am referring to an adaptability of approaches, ideas, ways of doing things and their conformability to con-straints without loss of their core meaning and significance. Connected with this is Kemmis's notion of "illimitability" that emphasises the creative characteris-tic capable of producing plasticity. Important in Kemmis's theoretical chapter is the notion of practice as both reproducing occupational work and producing new forms of that work, in a reflexive response to changing social setting. Both Brodie and Morgan's studies illustrate these. Brodie shows that mathematics teach-ing produces and reproduces mathematical thinking in pupils in ways that are conditional on both the teachers themselves and the larger social context of the classroom. Morgan shows that the behaviours of mathematics teachers, even in highly managerialist settings, can find spaces of freedom sufficient to reassert their autonomous understanding of mathematics curricula and pedagogy. For me, these studies provide empirical evidence of plasticity in professional practices. Kemmis's key point concerning the illimitability of professional practice is also illustrated.

Boundary-crossing and hybridity: By "boundary-crossing, already defined in the last section," I broadly refer to situations in which professional practice crosses professional demarcations. Closely related to this is the concept of "hybridity", by which I mean the synthesising of disparate ideas, practices, outlooks, ways of being, and so on.[2] Eraut (1994, p. 111), notably, makes the important observation that skilled knowledge, though essential for professional accomplishment, can work against plasticity and thus inhibit both boundary-crossing and hybridity. However, considering the large number and variety of decisions professionals routinely need to make (a finding acknowledged by Eraut), this possibility may be overestimated. Indeed, Nembhard and Edmondson show that teamwork, formed on the condition of "psychological safety", can benefit patient outcomes. Daniels takes up the challenge of trying to sort out some of the associated theoretical issues – his working hypothesis (consistent with Searle on literacy and Morgan's on teaching mathematics) is that communicational resources are critical. Morgan shows how certain experienced teachers are able to bring together both managerial and practice-referenced discourses in ways that show themselves complainant to the first, yet responsive to the second.

But now, stepping back both from individual chapters and the themes elicited from them, what does this volume as a whole suggest about headline challenges of professionalism for practitioners and policy makers in particular, and do these themes help address the headline challenges of professionalism? What implications for recent scholarly concerns does this book have?

Toward an Ethical Turn

In closing, I want to recall a remark of Michael Eraut made in his seminal book *Developing Professional Knowledge and Competence* (2004).

> My task is complicated by the primitive state of our methodology for describing and prescribing a profession's knowledge base. Many areas of professional knowledge and judgement have not been codified; and it is increasingly recognised that *experts often cannot explain the nature of their own expertise*. A variety of methods and approaches have been developed by philosophers, psychologist, sociologists and government agencies, each with its own limitations. However, one central difficulty has been the lack of attention given to different kinds of knowledge. The field is underconceptualised (italics added, pp. 102–103).

At face value, this remark seems to suggest that if we come up with a better understanding of the "different kinds of knowledge", one that tacitly presumes the coherence of professional practice, this will help professionals to better explain the "nature of their own expertise". This assumption seems intuitively plausible and, as Eraut suggest, the programmes it underpins would obviously help rationalise systems of professional education curriculums, pedagogies, assessment and certification. It would also help in explaining and advocating the interests of professionalisms to a variety of audiences and competing interest groups. However, does the evidence offered by studies in this book support Eraut's formative assumption?

---

[2] Clearly "boundary-crossing" is required by hybridity, but not the converse; I have treated these together here because of space restrictions.

In thinking about this question, one is struck by the fact that many aspects of the themes elicited in Table 10.1 appear, on the surface at least, to contradict one another. This underscores the difficulty we might have in providing a coherent theoretical representation of professionalism. One example may suffice. As already noted, commitment to specificity, especially when linked to the routinisation of procedures, can have the effect of limiting the scope for holistic thinking by tunnelling vision. Nevertheless, at another level, boundary-crossing and hybridity, plasticity and illimitability seem, paradoxically, to require a grasp of exactly their opposite, domain specificity. Indeed, the studies of Brodie and Morgan are particularly helpful in showing us just how conflictual the nature of professionalism in practice can be. Brodie (focussing on knowledge work) and Morgan (focussing on professional identity) each illuminate tensions within commitments played out within the ambit of professionalism. These, on one hand, are personal commitments to both mathematical knowledge and the 'well-being' of students; further commitments, sourced to the affective and motivational bonds of professional identity of mathematics teachers, are mediated through the instrument of the official curriculum. Thus Brodie and Morgan illustrate how practice shapes behaviours according to a rationality of professionalism that cannot completely be written in advance. Kemmis, emphasising this, refers to the illimitability of professional practice whereby practice ably resists closure. These indications seem to suggest, even if the purely methodological limitations raised by Eraut are resolved, that codifications of knowledge (and thus behaviour and cognition) are insufficient to adequately understand professional behaviours.

Does this mean, however, that we are obliged to think of professionalism as only readable in fragments? I do not think so. To outline my reasons for this view I need to return to my speculation that professionalism be read as an ascetic practice (see the end of the previous section). As such, because the burden of professionalism is carried by ethical work rather than knowledge structures, coherence of professionalism is made to depend on the achievement of an ethical self – one that corresponds to the diverse thematic behaviours of practitioners. Apart from the conceptual convenience of a coherent account of the nature of professionalism – this account suggests the professional education curriculums might usefully orientate their contents towards the ethical enrichment of practice. Professionals need access to specialist knowledge and skills – this is certain – however, as reported above, 'it is the interpretation of knowledge, the engagement with new knowledge, the acknowledgement of uncertainty about knowledge, the sharing of knowledge, not the holding of knowledge that are the hallmarks of professionalism'. For me, each of these lead qualities – interpreting knowledge helpfully, engaging with knowledge openly, acknowledge uncertainty about knowledge frankly and sharing knowledge appropriately – relate to questions about how practitioners behave in their practice against an overriding value of care for their patients. It is the self that corresponds to these behaviours that is the professional, and it is professionalism that commits the self to finding this self. Whether and how we are able to collectively refocus professionalism around an ethical turn such as this is currently uncertain.

References

Bernstein, B. (2000). *Pedagogy, symbolic control and identity: Theory, research, critique* (revised edition). Lanham, ML: Rowman and Littlefield.
Braithwaite, J. (2006). Correspondence. *The Lancet, 367,* 645.
Britten, N. (2001). Prescribing and the defence of clinical autonomy. *Sociology of Health & Illness, 23*(4), 478–496.
Brown, N., & Bhugra, D. (2007). 'New' professionalism or professionalism derailed? *Psychiatric Bulletin 38,* 281–283.
Clark, C. (2005). The deprofessionalism thesis, accountability and professional character. *Social Work and Society, 3,* 182–190.
Dewe, B., Otto, H.-U., & Schnurr, S. (2006). Introduction: New professionalism in social work – a social work and society series. *Social Work and Society, 4*(1), accessed online http://www.socwork.net/2006/1/series/professionalism/introduction, 29/12/2008.
Englund, T. (1996). Are professional teachers a good thing? In I. Goodson & A. Hargreaves (Eds.) *Teachers' Professional Lives.* London : The Falmer.
Eraut, M. (1994). *Developing professional knowledge and competence.* London: The Falmer.
Foucault, M. (1985). *The use of pleasure (the history of sexuality, volume 2).* New York: Pantheon Books
Freidson, E. (2001). *Professionalism: The third logic.* Oxford: Polity.
Hargreaves, A. (2000). Four ages of professionalism and professional learning. *Teachers and Teaching: Theory and Practice, 6*(2), 151–182.
Kenway, J., Bullen, E., Fahey, J., & Robb, S. (2006). *Haunting the knowledge economy.* London: Routledge.
Macdonald, K. (1985). Social closure and occupational registration. *Sociology, 19*(4), 541–556.
Mackey, H. (2007). 'Do not ask me to remain the same': Foucault and the professional identities of occupational therapists. *Australian Occupational Therapy Journal, 54,* 95–102.
Ross, C. (1996). Social closure and the stifling of diversity in professions and management. In R. Fincham (Ed.), *New relationships in the organised professions.* Aldeshot: Avebury.
Royal College of Physcians of London. (2005). *Doctors in society: Medical professionalism in a changing world.*
Stevens, R. (2002). Themes in the history of medical professionalism. *The Mount Sinai Journal of Medicine, 69*(6), 357–363.
Svensson, L. (2006). New professionalism, trust and competence: Some conceptual remarks and empirical data. *Current Sociology, 54,* 579–593.
Weert, T. (2006). Education of the twenty-first century: New professionalism in lifelong learning, knowledge development and knowledge sharing. *Education and Information Technologies.* Dordrecht: Springer
Young, M. (2006). *Bringing knowledge back in: From social constructivism to social realism in the sociology of education.* London and New York: Routledge.

Name Index

Subject Index

Printed in Great Britain
by Amazon

10347416R00129